Work It!

How to Get Ahead, Save Your Ass, and Land a Job in Any Economy

Allison Hemming

A Fireside Book
Published by Simon & Schuster
New York   London   Toronto   Sydney   Singapore

FIRESIDE
Rockefeller Center
1230 Avenue of the Americas
New York, NY 10020

FIRESIDE and colophon are registered trademarks
of Simon & Schuster, Inc.

For information about special discounts for bulk purchases,
please contact Simon & Schuster Special Sales:
1-800-456-6798 or business@simonandschuster.com

Designed by Diane Hobbing of SNAP-HAUS GRAPHICS

Manufactured in the United States of America

10   9   8   7   6   5   4   3   2   1

Library of Congress Cataloging-in-Publication Data
Hemming, Allison.
    Work it! : how to get ahead, save your ass, and land a job in any
economy / Allison Hemming.
        p.   cm.
    "A Fireside book."
    Includes index.
    1. Job hunting.   2. Career changes.   3. Résumés (Employment).
4. Employment interviewing.   I. Title.
HF5382.7 .H45   2003
650.14–dc21   2002035797

ISBN 0-7432-3549-5

To Bart for your incredible strength, wisdom, patience, and most of all, love. Without you this book would be a mere stream of consciousness.

And for my immediate family, Dennis, Carolyn, and Judy. Thank you for being my rock.

CONTENTS

Work It!

During the carefree days of the late 1990s—remember them?—the job market for twenty- and thirty-somethings was flush. Young people could write their own tickets: stock options, outrageous benefits, fat salaries, quirky job titles, and cool working environments were readily available. If you were searching for a job, the 1990s were good times. But the good times couldn't last forever.

When the dot-com bubble burst a few years ago, I threw a party for a bunch of friends of mine who had just been laid off. The party scene had always been a big part of the dot-com world, so with some willful defiance against the employment gods, I called my soiree the Pink Slip Party. It was July 2000, and I had no idea that my little get-together—a "safe haven for dot-com-miserating"—would soon blossom into a major community-networking event. Friends brought their friends, and recruiters even showed up. Soon, hundreds of people were crowding New York City nightclubs, grooving to "I Will Survive," drowning their sorrows in Guinness and Cosmos, but always making valuable connections and discovering that they weren't alone. As the economy continued on its downward spiral, laid-off workers from every industry started showing up and I threw one new Pink Slip Party per month. The idea spread, and by the end of 2000, Pink Slip Parties were popping up all over the country, from Atlanta and Philly to Boston and San Francisco. People even started throwing Pink Slip Parties in London, Berlin, Amsterdam, and Tokyo.

Meanwhile, as the founder of The Hired Guns, an agency that places freelancers into short-term projects, I knew what companies were looking for in new employees. Thus, I was in a unique position to offer career advice to the downsized. As the Pink Slip Party circuit blossomed, though, I had no idea that doling out job-hunting advice would become, quite literally, *my* full-time job. I'm a firm believer in "what goes around comes around," so as people kept asking for help with their job searches, I kept giving it. When I started to get the same queries from job hunters and pink slippers over and over again, however, I realized just how different getting a job is now from when our parents first started out. Landing a job today requires learning the new rules of engagement that govern the current working world. It's easy to develop a false sense of job security when the economy is hot. But if you start feeling smug and complacent, like a milk-fed house cat, your survival will be at risk. You need to keep your job-hunting claws sharp, so that if you get tossed out into the cold, cruel job market, you'll have the skills to compete.

With that in mind, consider *Work It!* your job search scratching post. Whether you're just starting out on your job hunt, are about to go into the biggest interview of your life, or just got laid off, this book was written so that you get the information you need, when you need it. I hate those books that force you to read the whole thing before you can start seeing an improvement in whatever it is that they're trying to get you to do. You should be inspired to implement recommendations on the fly. That's why in *Work It!* every tip within every chapter is written so that you can take immediate action and improve your job hunt. How much more instant gratification could you want? Read it front to back, if you want a total job hunt overhaul. Or skip around to cull the information that's relevant to you, right now. If you only have a few minutes to spare, read it on the bus or take it to the bathroom. *Work It!* is written a lot more like a web site than a career tome. So, pop around and enjoy yourself. Each and every chapter also includes sage advice from career experts as well as epic war stories from job seekers just like you, who share their successes and failures.

If this all sounds like a bit more than you need right now, fear not. The first chapter, "Get Out of Your Own Way," summarizes the major takeaways from the book. Thereafter, each chapter ends with an action plan, "Now Go Work It!," so that you can start making changes to your job-hunting efforts right away.

The first section of the book, "Everything You Know Is Wrong," includes chapters that will challenge you and get you to see things differently so that you can conduct a successful job hunt. The chapters in Part Two, "Back to Basics," provide you with the tactical elements of the job hunt. They're designed to hone your job-hunting skills from resume writing and interviewing to negotiating your eventual job offers. The last section of the book, "Break Open in Case of Emergency!" offers specific advice when you need some job-hunting 911. When your career is at a turning point or crisis, crack these chapters open. You'll get through the tough stuff from figuring out if you're about to get pink-slipped to surviving unemployment without going broke. There's also a special chapter for people just starting their careers.

This book is noticeably devoid of charts, graphs, or those insufferable worksheets. If you want one of *those* career books, head directly to Amazon.com or Barnes and Noble, choose from hundreds of options, and let them collect dust on your bookshelf. (Okay, there is a Six-Month Survival Budget, which you'll need and should use if you get laid off or are still looking for a job. But it's painless, I promise.)

I'm hoping that *Work It!* will debunk a few career myths and radically alter the way you approach job hunting from this moment forward. Filled with in-your-face advice, a needed dose of realism, and anecdotes from the trenches, *Work It!* is not for the wishy-washy. It's meant to be dog-eared and tattered, shared with friends and used and abused. Job hunting is never fun, especially today. But if you adopt the tools and techniques you'll find in these pages, you'll get results.

Now go *Work It!*

Part I:

EVERYTHING YOU KNOW

IS WRONG

1

GET OUT OF YOUR OWN WAY:

Diversify, and Get the Job You Really Want

Economies will rise and fall, but you, my friend, will always need a job. (Unless, of course, you're already rich and successful beyond your wildest dreams, in which case you can close this book now.) Instead of betting the farm on which way the economy's heading, you need to make your job search *independent* of the economy. It's going to be a very long time before we see a job market fueled by as much hubris, hype, and cash as that of the late 1990s. Back then, we could write our own tickets, choose among a variety of glamorous jobs, and reap fat salaries. Those days are long gone.

Somewhere in the midst of the boom years, we lost our grip on (or never learned) time-tested job-hunting strategies. We believed that the Internet would make finding a job (like everything else) easy, cheap, fast, and painless. The result: today, around the country, hiring managers and recruiters are scratching their heads, wondering where the solid candidates have gone. Left in their place are applicants devoid of passion, politeness, and proper business acumen. As painful as it may be to admit, you are probably one of these applicants, at least in some respects. If you are looking for a job right now, are finding it's going badly, and can't figure out why, chances are you are one of the clueless ones.

Face it, that's going to have to change. Job hunting is something you *must* get good at, because you're going to be doing it a lot more often. Data from the U.S. Bureau of Labor Statistics shows that before you retire, you can expect to change jobs at least ten times and switch careers at least three times.* Successful job seekers know that old

* Source: Pew Internet Project Survey, 2002.

school is fast becoming new school. Networking, building relationships, personalizing and tailoring your job search, and focusing on
what you want and where you fit best are skills that will never let you
down. In this book, you can look forward to a hearty helping of
no-holds-barred advice (tough love, if you like) on how you can get
your job search on track and land your next job—no matter which direction the economy is headed.

INERTIA WILL BE YOUR REAL ENEMY

A body at rest tends to stay at rest. It's nearly impossible to land a
job by sitting around in your pajamas surfing the web. Even when
the economy was going gangbusters, people still had to put on
nice clothes and go meet other human beings for interviews. Here's
the bottom line: people don't like job hunting because it's time-
consuming, a little scary, and often involves rejection. The good news
is that if you can live through being single and dating, you can survive and excel at a job hunt. Just don't try to look for the easy way out.
You're not looking for a one-night stand; you want a long, stable relationship.

The most effective jobhunters are the ones that never stop hunting. If you plan on actively managing your career, you need to be out
there *looking* all the time. This isn't to say that you should be *interviewing* 24/7, but you do have to put yourself in the mix so that you're
aware of opportunities and can take advantage of them as they arise.
Start by pressing the flesh and making contact with real live human
beings on a regular basis. You will get back what you put in. This
means that if you approach your job hunt passively, you can expect recruiters and hiring managers to respond passively to you.

For most people, job hunting does suck, but it doesn't have to. It's
impossible to get a new job, one that you really want, unless you're
keeping your "tentacles" out there. Get realistic about how long it will
take to find the job. Don't wait until you're desperate. A good rule of
thumb is to expect the search to last about 4 to 6 months from start

to contract signing. That duration might be shortened if you're approached directly by a headhunter for a specific job or you're getting poached by a direct competitor. Or it could take even longer if you're looking for a highly competitive, unique, or senior position. Also, if you're undergoing a career transition, the process can even approach a year as you reposition yourself for different types of opportunities. Don't wait until you're forced to start your job hunt. If you hold off until you feel pressured to quit, you get laid off, or you graduate without a job lined up, you're waiting too long. If you're out there all the time, you won't fall out of practice when it comes time to do research, to network, to interview, or to follow up. You'll get so comfortable with job hunting that the stress and anxiety that usually go along with it will be greatly reduced. This way, when there's a job you really want to land, you'll be ready to shine.

Being open to other job opportunities even when you're employed doesn't make you a Benedict Arnold. You're just looking out for number one. Keep in mind, you're not required to take the first job that comes your way. In fact, sometimes the best thing to do is stay put and work hard to get promoted internally—the same rules apply to internal and external job hunts.

LOSE THE ENTITLEMENT

Repeat the motto: *I do not have the job until I have the job.* Time and time again, candidates walk into hiring managers' offices demanding and expecting things long before it's appropriate to do so. If this is you, it's time to adjust your attitude. Companies can and will live without you. Even with the perfect work experience and a summa cum laude degree from a top school, a person with a bad attitude at a company is quite simply a bad seed. While you may in fact be the greatest thing since sliced bread, confidence should never be confused with arrogance. Beware of subtle demands that you might hint at in your cover letter, during interviews, or in your follow-up emails. Even simple things like not following directions can rub people the wrong way. That's why you need to have other people check your work before it goes out and why you need to practice before you go into interviews. You've got very little time in front of decision-makers these days, and if you don't put your best foot forward, you will not get anywhere. You're not owed the perfect job; that, my friend, has to be earned.

> I detest self-worship. Don't drone on about why the world can't live without you (hint: they can). Whenever a candidate does this, a red flag pops up, as these folks usually over-inflate their accomplishments and misrepresent their past job responsibilities.
>
> —MARK, CHIEF TECHNOLOGY OFFICER

DIVERSIFY OR DIE

Most people's biggest problem with their job hunt is relying too much on one single strategy, like posting their resumes to online job boards, instead of using the web to augment tried and true, old-school methods of job hunting like networking. It's time to mix it up. Why? Because job hunting *is* tough—and ultra-competitive. Over-dependence on any one technique will severely impair your efforts.

If you're going to have a successful job hunt, you can no longer discount old standbys like resumes, cover letters, and thank-you notes. They are an intrinsic part of job hunting. If you intend to blow them off, or don't plan on treating them as essential, stop reading now (no, really). Think about it this way: if you were going into combat, you'd want to survive multiple confrontations and deal with whatever situation you encounter. You wouldn't want a canteen that leaked water or a rifle that shot blanks. The same holds true for the job hunt. Your war chest should be well stocked with the following basics: a Master Resume from which you can craft individual customized resumes; an array of cover letters and thank-you notes that you can draw upon and personalize; and a database or spreadsheet (or Rolodex) of all your contacts including references, colleagues, business contacts,

Take the Emotion Out of Your Job Search

Don't get caught in the downward spiral of negativity by entering the oh so bitter "they'll sure miss me when I'm gone" job hunt. As humans, we tend to fly off the handle and quit our jobs when we have emotional reactions to work situations that don't go our way. Unfortunately, the grass is not always greener at a new job, and this is where regrets and bad career choices start to happen.

Perhaps you've been passed over for a promotion or maybe your new boss is a total jerk. You need to assess the situation before immediately deciding you want to quit. Is there anything you can do internally, such as position yourself for a transfer? How about taking an honest look at your performance review and seeing if you can do better in the next six months? Fleeing when career disappointment occurs will usually cause you to make irrational decisions, and doing so can be quite dangerous over the long haul. Do you really want to sidetrack your career on an emotional whim?

and companies you want to work for. You also need consistent and easy access to a non-work computer and fax machine (Kinko's will do, but think about investing in your own if you don't have them already), a personal email account that you will use only for your job hunt, a calendar to map out your strategy, and stationery.

Having a well-stocked war chest won't get you the job by itself, but it's a proactive step to getting yourself organized so that you'll find it easier to navigate through the challenges that lie ahead.

WALK A MILE IN THE OTHER PERSON'S SHOES

The one thing that job seekers seem to forget most often is thinking about the needs of the hiring community and the interests of the people helping them along in their job hunt. Before you email, call, interview, or follow up with anyone, take a minute to put yourself in his or her shoes. Ask yourself, What matters to this person? What can I say or do to let them know that I understand their needs? You should do this for everyone from headhunters, recruiters, and hiring managers to your business contacts and the people you plan to use as your references.

On that note, while it's important to have your own agenda and schedule, it is absolutely essential to remember that you are also working under the timetable of your prospective employers. The best companies—and the ones you want to work for—take their time and exercise due diligence when they hire new employees. However much a body is needed, the wrong hire will make an organization worse off than no hire. Industry statistics suggest the cost of even one bad hiring decision can exceed one hundred thousand dollars, taking into account the time spent recruiting, hiring, and training the hiree and the amount of time the job is left undone or done badly by an unqualified applicant.* You need to respect the timetable, without pressuring anyone. Also, remember that the headhunter's reputation is on the line every time a company hires one of their candidates. While you may feel the process is slow moving, there are established procedures and channels that recruiters and clients set up before beginning an engagement.

Most job seekers are obsessed with asking for what they want instead of thinking about what the other person needs. Their utter cluelessness is your big break! If you get behind enemy lines and study what recruiters and hiring managers want, you'll leave your competition in the dust. If you work hard to make the other person's job easier, you'll be more successful, hands down. It really is as easy as that.

I was recently very gung-ho about bringing in one particular candidate for an introductory interview. He had all the right credentials and a great track record. Then I met him. The guy was so pompous

* *Occupational Health & Safety,* April 2002, "Background Screening and Safe Hiring: An Introduction," by Lester S. Rosen.

that I wanted to toss him out of my office in no less than five minutes. The first thing out of his mouth was a question about what we were prepared to give him as an offer because he was deciding between my firm and our direct competitor. I let him know that he might want to go ahead and take the other job because his chances of getting an offer from us were slim: this was his *first* interview, he still had a lot of people to meet, and he was already on my *bad* side.

—THERESA, BRAND MANAGER

NOW GO WORK IT!

Here's the Takeaway:

- Job hunting is 24/7; you need to be looking constantly.

- For best results, diversify your job hunt by combining old-school techniques with new ones.

- Lose the attitude and you'll get a lot further.

- Think about the needs of the people you're interviewing with.

2

The Internet Is
Ruining Your Job Search:

Put Down the Mouse and
Step Away from the Computer

The Internet has radically changed the way you interact with the hiring community. Thousands of new jobs are posted to the web each day. But has the proliferation of all these postings made you more successful at actually *landing* a job? Now that the whole world is online, there's a major catch-22 at work: just as you are learning about more positions in less time than ever before, so is everybody else. Hiring managers now have faster and cheaper access to a greater number of candidates. Instead of competing just with professionals in your city, you're now up against candidates from around the globe. The net result is a much larger number of people applying for each open position, sometimes hundreds per posting. The sheer volume forces recruiters to spend less time with each resume they receive. And that's not all: because the pool of candidates is larger than it used to be, recruiters are raising the bar on minimum requirements. Thus, a job opening that might have been a slam dunk for you a year ago could be a long shot for you now.

Once upon a Time . . .

Long before the Internet came into our lives, there were job seekers and employers. Legend has it that classified advertisements were placed in things called "newspapers." Job seekers would get out and network and meet one another face to face. They'd print out resumes with cover letters on stationery and actually mail them—with a stamp. Sometimes job seekers would go so far as to follow up after the interview, picking up the telephone or sending a thank-you note. Through it all, companies and candidates would find each other, and people would actually get hired. And they lived happily ever after.

Seem like ancient history? Well, here's a news flash: even though many job seekers have forgotten how to employ such basic procedures, these methods still work. One of the best ways to separate yourself from the pack is to integrate old-school job-hunting strategies into your search. In 2001, only five percent of the clients of Drake Beam Morin, a leading provider of career transition services, found new positions through online job searches.* Surprised? There's a valuable lesson here: if you are devoting one hundred percent of your job search to online efforts alone, the odds are really stacked against you. You need to re-engineer your job search to include strategies that give you a better chance of success. It's a heck of a lot easier to sit behind your computer and tell yourself that you're conducting an intensive search. But until you diversify your tactics, your chances of landing a job will remain slim.

This isn't to say that you should eliminate online job boards entirely. Just be sure to couple them with offline tactics that have higher success rates. Create a diversified strategy by allocating a percentage of time to each job search activity. Spend no more than twenty or twenty-five percent of your job search hours working the web, and the other seventy-five to eighty percent networking at industry events, seeking internal referrals, using headhunters, and setting up informational interviews with your contacts. While these "offline" activities don't connect you to as large an audience as the job boards, each offline contact you make has a much higher chance of success than does yet another response to yet another online posting.

It was 3:45 p.m. on a Friday afternoon and I got the dreaded call from my boss: he was assigning me the onerous task of filling a marketing

* DBM: Career Choices and Challenges of People in Transition. 2002 DBM.

post left open by the departure of a colleague. I quickly posted the opening on an online job board and split for the weekend.

When I arrived at work on Monday morning, my inbox contained 316 new messages! And all with the same subject heading, "In response to your posting for a marketing professional." I sat back in my chair and stared at the menacing monitor in front of me. How was I ever going to get through this list? I tried to come up with clever ways to cut the load down. Maybe I would only look at the first twenty responses, or every fourth response. I even thought of restricting the list to respondents whose name I liked (a little less scientific, but I was desperate!). Before I knew it, two hours had passed with not a single email opened, when suddenly my phone rang. "Hello," came a confident voice from the other end, "my name is Javier and a friend of mine mentioned that you might be looking for a marketing professional to join your firm." A smile quickly spread across my face as I responded, "Tell me a little bit about yourself." Two days later Javier was in our office, and a week after that he was hired. He may not have been better than the 316 other candidates sitting in my inbox, but he was the most visible and easily accessible. And as the saying goes, sometimes the easiest answer is the right answer. What did I do with all the responses I got? I respectfully responded that the position had been filled and released them back into cyberspace, where they may have had the luck of landing in the inbox of an applicant seeker with a lot more time on her hands.

—FEDAH, PROJECT MANAGER

STAY FOCUSED

Surfing the web for jobs can waste hours of precious job search time. It's easy to get overwhelmed by the sheer volume of job postings and start applying to anything and everything you see, whether it's right for you or not. Do this and you'll only wind up with the job seeker's variety of "eBay Syndrome," a condition resulting from prolonged web exposure that causes otherwise normal people to lose their ability to distinguish between quality and crap. It may seem logical to think, "I'll never get an offer from just one job posting, so why not up my odds and apply to one hundred?" But you're only kidding yourself. Applying to every posting that pops onto your monitor doesn't increase your chances of finding a job. All it does is waste your time and add to the overall noise level of mismatched jobs and job seekers. Instead, set specific criteria for your search before you hop online, and focus on jobs that match those criteria. Before you log on, establish boundaries and be honest about your own requirements, such as salary range and responsibilities. When you start to look at postings, avoid those for jobs that are too senior or junior. Don't waste your time, or the company's, by responding to postings that are geographically undesirable to you. Pay particular attention to the minimum qualifications for the job; don't apply if you don't meet them. By analyzing each job posting closely rather than gratuitously zapping off a resume for it, you'll fine-tune your expectations without wasting your precious time, or other people's.

If you discover an online posting that isn't right for you but are seriously interested in working at that particular company, don't just apply for the job. Instead, send an email or letter to the hiring manager listed in the posting. In it, introduce yourself and tell them that you saw the job description, and that although you're not a fit for the position, you're very interested in working at their company. Let them know that you would love to be contacted if a position that matches your skills becomes available and be sure to highlight what those skills are. The personnel manager will appreciate that you didn't waste their time by applying for a position for which you're not qualified and you might just get a call down the road.

BIG BOARD BATTLE PLAN

Each day, hundreds of jobs are posted on the Big Boards—Monster. com, HotJobs.com, and CareerBuilder.com. Given the huge number of companies featured and range of positions offered, it's only natural that the first stop on your journey toward finding new employment would be the Big Boards. The larger online job boards have made their sites incredibly easy to navigate and have invested in superior web technology and tools to help you find what you're seeking. They also allow you to check out the supply of jobs in your industry and their salary levels, helping you to determine your market value. The downside of the Big Boards is that because they're so popular, they are also the first stop for thousands of other job seekers (your competition).

This isn't to say that you should avoid using the Big Boards. But you need to be smart about *how* you use them. At the outset of your job hunt, get to know the unique features that each Big Board has to offer. They each do things slightly differently. Sometimes you'll find the same jobs posted on all of the Big Boards, while other times you'll find positions that are unique to each. The range of positions available on the Big Boards is so vast that it pays to devote equal time to all of them.

Here are some tips for optimizing your time on the Big Boards.

✓ SET UP A PERSONAL ACCOUNT. All of the Big Boards allow you to create your own account (i.e., MyHotJobs or My Monster). Once you set up a personal account, the board enables you to save a version of your resume that's quite easy to email. This feature allows you to apply to jobs easily by sending a pre-formatted resume that will look good to a hiring manager.

✓ WATCH YOUR BACK. Don't forget: hiring companies pay fees to the job boards to review the resumes that job seekers have saved there. So be careful if you're looking for work while otherwise employed—you don't want your current boss to spot your resume when they're doing a search for talent. There are blocking and confidentiality tools that can help, but if you know that your current company uses a certain Big Board regularly, you might want to think twice about opting to let the public view your resume.

✓ HANDLE WITH CARE. When you set up your personal job board account, you'll often get a special email address specific to that board. It's essential to choose an email address or "handle" that identifies you in a professional manner and won't confuse the hiring manager. The safest bet is to choose a version of your name such as JamesJSmith@monster.com. Alternatively, you could select an email address that identifies the type of job you're applying for, e.g., graphicdesignmaven@hotjobs.com. If the board requires you to choose a "display name" (the "real" name displayed alongside the email address), be simple and use your own name; this is not the time to get cute. A clear and professional email address will enable a hiring manager to find your resume quickly in their clogged inbox.

When I was in college, all of the members of my Ultimate Frisbee team selected wacky email addresses. I got in the habit of using my Ultimate handle all the time—job hunting included. I had no idea that an alternative name would confuse or alienate hiring managers. Then I changed it, and responses to my cover emails immediately increased.

—MICHAEL, ONLINE PRODUCER

✓ USE ADVANCED SEARCH TOOLS. The Big Boards have sunk millions into thinking up new ways to slice and dice the jobs they list. Instead of searching for jobs by title, consider using some of the search tools the job boards have added to their sites. Try keywords that you think match your background. For example, if you're a web designer, you might type "web design" under the keyword search. In addition, try keying in specific skills you think an employer would want you to have for that position (in the case of a web designer, knowledge of Flash, Photoshop, or Java). You'll be surprised to see completely different yet relevant postings pop up.

✓ LOCATION, LOCATION, LOCATION. If you're looking for work near a particular city, your first inclination might be simply to type the city name into the search. But wait: if you only search this way you might not find out about suitable jobs in the surrounding region.

For example, say you want to work in Boston. If you type simply "Boston, MA" into the search engine, you might miss out on a great job opportunity based in Cambridge, MA, or Newton, MA—two important Beantown suburbs teeming with small, dynamic companies. If you're interested in relocating to an unfamiliar city, it's worth it to invest in a map to figure out what nearby cities you would be willing to work in. To do your search, stay broad and start by searching under the state instead of the city. Don't forget that many major metro areas cross state lines. For example, if your goal is to live in Princeton, New Jersey, you'd be in the range of both the Philadelphia and New York City metropolitan areas. On your search, you would look up a total of three states: Pennsylvania, New York, and New Jersey. Most of the Big Boards are incorporating "search metro area" capabilities into their sites, but since searching is never an exact science, it's still a good idea to try the tips above.

✔ **TIMING IS EVERYTHING.** Sort search results by the most recent date of posting and concentrate on those posted within the last week or two. Postings older than that are quite likely either to be filled or no longer needed; unfortunately, pulling obsolete postings off the boards does not seem to be a top priority for busy recruiters.

✔ **KEEP TRACK OF HIRING AND PERSONNEL MANAGERS.** The real key to a successful job search is building a contact database of real live human beings who can help you in your quest for a new job (see Chapter 4, "Getting Hired with a Little Help from Your Friends"). Job boards are one place to find such contacts. After you respond to a job posting in which you're truly interested, keep track of all contact information for the H.R. representative listed. If possible, find out what other types of jobs that person recruits for. You will find that at large companies in particular, different personnel managers handle different departments. Be diligent about keeping a list of all the people you contact via online job postings, as well as the dates on which you contacted them. Sometimes, companies will list only an anonymous email address like jobs@big-company.com. Other times, however, you'll get lucky and find a direct email address, either for an internal hiring manager or an outside recruiter. Just don't use someone's email address as one more place to dump a generic resume; keep your communications relevant to the recipients' needs.

A friend sent out resumes through an online service for two months without much luck. The problem was, she just zapped without proofing them. One day her email bounced back and she realized that the resume she had been sending for all that time was truncated to the point where it only included her objective statement. No one ever replied to say her resume did not look right (or to set up an interview, for that matter). Lesson: always double-check everything!

–MARK, MANAGEMENT CONSULTANT

TAKE THE ROAD LESS TRAVELED

The Big Boards are great resources, but they're kind of like the freeway in L.A.: they can take you to a lot of places, but there's so much traffic you might get nowhere fast. The smart job seeker, like the clever commuter, learns the uncongested back streets that cut down on travel time. By now you should know which industry you want to work in and what kind of position you want to land. Use these criteria to target lesser-known, industry-specific web resources that are surfed by in-the-know recruiters who have the jobs you want. Here are some tips to help you break from the herd and find a more direct route to your destination:

✔ GET INTO THE INDUSTRY-SPECIFIC SITES. Besides hitting the mainstream Big Boards, diversify your efforts and spend time at industry-specific sites. While the volume of postings will be smaller than on the Big Boards, these sites are likely to have a higher percentage of jobs that match your specific objectives and experi-

Save Time by Using Job Bots

Contributed by Steve Baldwin

A job bot (also known as a "job search agent") is a friendly electronic feature of most major job sites that lets you specify your job criteria, then walk away from your computer with confidence that any positions matching your parameters will drop automatically into your email inbox.

Both Monster.com and HotJobs.com currently offer job bots, which provide a lot of customizable power for scanning job listings without having to perform manual searches. You create an agent by selecting a job location, a job category, and a keyword search term from a web-based form. Name it something distinctive, like "Programmer Jobs in Portland," and save it. You can create several job search agents, edit them, or delete them at will.

Monster.com's job bot lets you specify the type of job (part-time, temporary, or full-time) you're looking for, as well as multiple cities and job categories. You can also specify how often the bot will send you email (daily, weekly, bi-weekly, monthly, or not at all). HotJob's job bot lets you limit your search to direct employers only, staffing firms only, or both. To use job bots on either HotJobs or Monster you must register; fortunately, it's free.

Job bots are so convenient for the recruiting community that forward-thinking Fortune 500 companies are starting to add them to their own web sites. Doing this allows them to call up job seekers' resumes as job opportunities arise. One site that sports such a service is Time Warner's career site, http://tw.tmphosting.com. Watch for more companies to use their own job bots in the future.

Steve, an author and tech producer who was born in New York City, has eleven years of tech biz experience. His best-known projects are Ghost Sites of the Web *and* Netslaves, *a book, web site, and tech community.*

ence. That's because savvy hiring managers know that targeted postings on these niche sites will increase their chances of finding just the right candidate. You'll be amazed at how many industry-specific sites you can find that pertain to very specific aspects of your industry. Not sure where to start or how to find them? Just hop onto your favorite search engine. For example, if you want to work in the health care profession, you might type in generic phrases that describe the industry such as "Health Care" or "Medical" and "Jobs" into the search tool. You'll notice that the industry-specific subsites of the Big Boards, like Monster Healthcare, will pop up first in the search results. Further down, you'll find more industry-specific sites that also match your search. You'll be amazed how incredibly targeted these sites can be. Say you're a nurse. You could search on "nurse" and "jobs" and find Nurse-recruiter.com. Or you could go even deeper: search on "pediatric," "nurse," and "jobs," and you'll find Pediatricnursejobs.com. As mentioned previously, searching is an inexact science, so vary the search terms by using descriptive adjectives and industry terminology to find different results (e.g., "nurse jobs," "nursing jobs," "pediatric nurses," "neonatal nurses"). Each time you change your phrasing slightly, different results will appear. Hint: pay particular attention to the headhunters that advertise on the job sites that best match your background; add them to your contact database and call them directly.

✓ USE TRADE PUBLICATIONS AND WEB SITES. Each industry has its own trade magazines, newsletters, e-newsletters, and web sites. If you are job hunting, you should be voraciously reading the trade magazines that pertain to your targeted industries. These publications break news, deliver commentary on the winners and losers in your industry, and give you the inside skinny on what's going on at companies you might be interviewing with. More important, most trade publications have "help wanted" classifieds, both in print and in their online editions. These classifieds often have job postings from companies that prefer to use highly targeted employment advertising to narrow their searches. Some trade magazines are sold right at newsstands (*Ad Age*), while others require you to sign up for a subscription. Some trade magazines even offer free subscriptions if you work in their featured industry.

✓ JOIN AN INDUSTRY ASSOCIATION. Often, membership in your industry's professional society or trade association will include a subscription to its trade journal, along with other great perks like notifications of industry conferences and trade shows (great networking opportunities, people!). For example, members of the American Society of Civil Engineers (ASCE) receive as part of their membership the monthly *Civil Engineering* magazine and access to special areas of the ASCE web site. While you're on these sites, sign up to get their industry newsletters. This way, topical news and job postings will be delivered right to your inbox on a regular basis. Another great option for tapping into jobs in your sector is to join online discussion groups that are devoted to a specific industry or topic. Work your search engine and see what you come up with.

✓ EXPLORE COMPANY WEB SITES. Before spending money on job boards where recruiters get inundated with responses, many firms will try to find candidates by posting openings on their own web sites. If you already know the firms for which you want to work, check out the "Jobs," "Careers," or "Work for Us" sections of their web sites. First, make sure that a company updates its job pages regularly (many firms don't bother) by visiting the web site once a week. If nothing has changed after a month, it's safe to guess that this isn't a serious recruiting venue for the company. But if posts regularly go up and down, you know that it's an effective recruiting tool. To get an inkling of which departments or subsidiaries might be hiring, check out the company's recent press releases to see if they are expanding into any new businesses or are experiencing huge growth in any particular division. If so, try to develop a contact in those hot areas.

✓ **CHECK OUT CORPORATE ALUMNI WEB SITES.** A new way to connect with employment opportunities is through corporate alumni web sites. Companies have started to realize that some of their best clients are former employees. Not only that, they've found that former employees are excellent at referring quality talent because they're familiar with their alma mater's corporate culture and because they're cheaper to hire than a complete stranger. Companies have started to build their own corporate alumni web sites so that they can create a centralized place where their alumni community can come together and communicate with the firm and with each other. Sites like these offer former employees a bonanza of networking opportunities in the form of co-worker directories, job listings, and events. Corporate alumni web sites are especially great for recruiting, not only for the company hosting the site, but also for former employees who've moved on to different firms or who've started their own companies. To figure out if any of the previous companies you've worked for have a corporate alumni network, hop onto Google or Yahoo! and do a search for the company's name plus the word "alumni." If a company endorses their alumni network outright, they most likely will develop their own site or hire a company to host and build one for them. For example, SelectMinds.com hosts a number of large companies' alumni sites, including that of the consulting firm Ernst & Young, which now boasts more than 100,000 active alumni. During your search, you might stumble onto a grass-roots alumni web site that's been established by a few former employees to keep a former department connected. Or you might find other sites like Corporatealumni.com or Classmates.com that put together unofficial alumni networks. What if you want to tap into a corporate alumni site at a company where you never worked? Ask around. See if any of your friends (or friends of friends) ever worked there. Then ask your friend to join the network and scout the job opportunities listed on the site for you. Or better still get sneaky and ask if you can borrow their user name and password.

Cyber Sleuthing 101

Contributed by Eileen Shulock

Let others pound the online job boards all day long; savvy job searchers know that information is a two-way street. Put the Internet to work for you by signing on for a few free or low-cost information-gathering tools. With a little creativity, these tools—which are typically used by businesses to gather competitive intelligence—will deliver the lowdown on your target companies right to your inbox.

Press Release Services: Get the latest news about a company or industry in the form of electronic press release distribution. You may have to register on the following sites as a "journalist," but hey, you were planning to write about your experiences anyway, right?

PR Newswire: prnewswire.com
Business Wire: businesswire.com
Internet News Bureau: newsbureau.com

Corporate Information: Delve into the inner workings of U.S. publicly held companies at these sites, where you can find the 411 on SEC filings, partners, directors, competitors, and more. Maybe your old college roommate's dad is now a board member at one of your target companies. You never know . . .

Edgar Online: edgar-online.com
Hoover's: hoovers.com
Corporate Information: corporateinformation.com

Spy Bots: Sign on for your very own 007 to crawl the web and deliver any mentions of your targets (people, companies, keywords) right back to your inbox. Be sure to focus your search; like the best secret agents, these spy bots will return a lot of dirt.

TracerLock: tracerlock.com
Agentland: agentland.com

Eileen is President of e-merchandising consultancy Merchant Diva, Managing Editor of Web Digest For Marketers, *and co-author of* Essential Business Tactics for the Net. *An industry leader and champion networker, Eileen is the director of the New York City chapter of Webgrrls International.*

NOW GO WORK IT!

Here's the Takeaway:

- To avoid the pitfalls of the Internet in your job search, diversify your techniques. Integrate the best of what the Internet offers with old-school practices.

- Use the Big Boards (Monster.com and HotJobs.com), but set specific and realistic search criteria that match what you are really looking for. Don't email hundreds of resumes just because you can.

- Industry-specific and corporate alumni sites are a great way to complement your Big Board efforts. They may not have as many job postings overall, but what they have will be more targeted to what you want, and you'll face less competition.

- Trade associations in your target industry can provide great networking opportunities as well as access to publications, web sites, and job postings.

- Always be professional. Don't let the anonymity of job boards and postings lull you into laziness.

- Take information that you glean from your online efforts and carry it over into your offline networking and searching. Keep track of names and contact information, add them to your networking database, and get in touch.

3

STAND OUT FROM THE PACK:

Tattoos Aren't the Only Way to Brand Yourself

You've only got a few fleeting moments to make a lasting impression on a hiring manager. Talk about pressure! How do you make the most of that time and get them not only to remember you, but to *hire* you? It all comes down to marketing yourself. But selling the product known as "you" is much easier said than done.

Imagine yourself walking in to meet with The Big Cheese. By the time you get to the meeting, you need to assume he's barely had a chance to glance at your resume, much less drink his morning coffee. All he knows is that he wants to get the interview over and done with so that he can get on with his day of business. So, as he sits across from you, this is what he's thinking:

"I don't know who you are."
"I don't know what you do."
"I don't know what you stand for."
"I don't know your track record."
"I don't know your reputation."
"Now—why is it that you want me to hire you?"*

Not so easy to sell yourself while dodging bullets, is it? The moral of the story: long before you go into any interview, you have to be prepared with a simple and compelling message, delivered with an unshakeable confidence that will cut through the noise in the hiring manager's head. That message must convey exactly why you will be a

---

* Inspired by McGraw-Hill's classic 1958 "Man-in-Chair Ad," which reinforced the importance of corporate branding.

success in the position and what unique attributes make you the best possible person for the job. If you are ready to convey all this confidently, you'll be as choke-proof as Tiger Woods. And isn't being impressive the whole point?

ESTABLISH YOUR CORPORATE ID

The more you focus on building a consistent message about yourself, the more you will be in control of your "corporate identity." In a job hunt, your corporate identity is the image that will stick with a hiring manager long after the interviews are over. Way before you start the interviewing process, you need to know what key points about yourself you want interviewers to remember. That means defining your corporate identity so clearly that it leaves hiring decision-makers with a definite impression about your personality and capabilities. To make this easy, imagine that you're buying a car. A car must satisfy some basic needs and wants, but it goes further than that. Say you're in the market for a luxury vehicle, and you're considering three makes: Jaguar, BMW, and Volvo. (Hey, we can dream, right?) All three brands are high-end, quality cars, but they're not all alike. What makes these brands different from one another is that each has its own unique corporate identity that will eventually sway you into selecting one brand over another. Jaguar positions itself as the best designed, quintessentially English, and glamorous; BMW is the best engineered, efficiently German, and self-confident; while Volvo is safest, seriously Swedish, and family oriented. You'll base your purchase on which of these corporate identities best fits your needs and desires.

And so it goes with employers. First they'll narrow down the pool of applicants to those who meet the minimum qualifications, then they'll start to home in on those candidates whose definable corporate identities will work best within the firm. When all things are equal among candidates, an established corporate identity—one that's in line with the company's needs—can really bring a hiring manager over to your side.

So before you start interviewing, you had better get in tune with your own corporate identity. Here's a good way to figure out what your "brand" represents to others. Imagine two of your managers or co-workers talking about you in the cafeteria. What would they say about you? About your capabilities and work ethic? What attributes would they assign to you (right or wrong): ambitious, lazy, a creative thinker, back-stabber, diligent, arrogant, innovative, independent, cutthroat? What is it that makes you noticeably different from other people in your department, company, and field? You may think you're perceived as unique—but are you really? If there is a significant difference between you and your peers, is it a positive one?

If you wouldn't change anything about your current image, well, la di da. We can't all be as *perfect* as you. But if you're like most people, either you have no idea how your manager would describe you, or else there's a gap between how you want to be perceived (e.g., a team player) and how you think you're actually perceived (e.g., an insufferable suck-up). If so, you've got some tinkering to do. You must start by asking trusted friends and co-workers to give truthful answers about how you are perceived in the workplace and in social settings. Taking stock of your corporate identity can be humbling, but it also can lead to successful results when trying to position yourself with a prospective employer.

To establish your corporate identity, start by coming up with a short phrase that describes *the one thing that you do best* (i.e., you're a great people manager, problem solver, project manager, etc.). Add to that *the one thing that differentiates you* from all other people who might be applying for the job (i.e., you're well traveled, politically involved, athletic, etc.). And finally, think up an adjective that best describes *the one thing that gives you a unique personality* (i.e., you're witty, analytical, savvy, etc.). You'll end up with a three-part phrase that describes a well-rounded you. That's your own corporate identity. Make it your personal mantra and repeat it in all of your communications with prospective employers. Hiring managers won't remember everything about you, but they will remember a simple message that clearly defines and differentiates you as a candidate. Not only that, they will find it easier to describe you clearly to their higher-ups. For example, "I met a fantastic candidate today; she's a whiz with numbers, speaks three languages, and has a great strategic mind."

Just remember—when marketing yourself, truth in advertising is absolutely essential. If you're unhappy with your old corporate identity, don't just make up new words that don't fit the reality. You need to fix whatever's wrong before you can move forward.

Candidates tend to have similar education levels and work experience, so after a round of interviews, the easiest way to distinguish one person from another is to remember who was the karate instructor, coin collector, sky diver, etc. What people do in their free time also speaks great volumes about who they are and what motivates them. Knowing someone's special interests helps in assessing their cultural fit with the organization and determining if the job offers the type of environment that would make them happy.

—JIM, PORTFOLIO MANAGER

Memorize three things that you want the interviewer to know about you. When the interview is over, tell the interviewer "I'm experienced, capable, and really excited to work here!" Let them know you want the job, so that when the interviewer leaves the room and has to write a report or tell the next interviewer what they thought, inevitably they'll write or say, "Well, she seems experienced, capable, and enthusiastic," as if they came up with that assessment themselves. It works.

—YAEL, TRADER

MAKE YOUR MESSAGE MEMORABLE

Once you know the messages you want to deliver, you're like a politician ready to announce your candidacy. Get up on your soapbox and start letting people know your intentions. But how do you get people to listen and remember what you have to say? After all, decisionmakers are busy people. They have their own deadlines, priorities,

What Makes You Stand Out?

Contributed by Lea Brandenburg

As you've looked at postings on the job boards, have you ever found yourself wondering *"What are they really looking for?"* Do you feel like you need to crack a secret code just to land an interview? Well, unless you're the owner of a well-functioning crystal ball, you've probably found that trying to figure out what companies want instead of focusing on what you have to offer may not be the most effective strategy when conducting a job search.

Accept that you can't be all things to all people. Instead of trying to figure out what "they" want, why not focus your thoughts and energy on identifying and articulating what your strengths, gifts, and talents are? The funny thing about strengths is that they come so easily to us, we take them for granted. Make a list of no fewer than ten of your professional achievements and ten non-work-related, personal accomplishments. Make sure that the things you are the most proud of achieving professionally and personally land on your lists. See if you can identify any recurring themes in your lists; if so, use them in your resume, cover letters, and interviews.

This exercise serves three functions. First, you'll start to feel better about yourself as a human being and as a professional, which is always therapeutic when you are immersed in a seemingly never-ending job search. Second, you'll start to see what is important to you. Third, you'll be able to speak intelligently about your accomplishments in a job interview because you've taken the time to get clear about what you, *and only you,* can bring to a prospective employer.

Lea is a personal and business coach who works with clients to develop effective self-presentation skills and to express themselves with confidence and ease in every situation. To find out more about her and her coaching services, visit creatingstrategies.com.

and crises—all of which are hogging up room in their brains and keeping them from thinking about what a great hire you'd be. There are really only two ways for a message to pierce through all of the noise and take root in a person's cerebral cortex: first, you could get the person to concentrate, really concentrate, on the message to the exclusion of all else (not bloody likely!). Second, you could repeat the message enough times that it gets through their thick skulls! Unfortunately, since you can't count on a hiring manager focusing their undivided attention on you until you get your point across, you need to repeat your message until it resonates.

Don't sit back and expect that a single interview is enough to get someone to want to hire you. Just consider all the distractions and the competition your messages are up against. You need to employ what marketers call a "frequency strategy" in your job hunt.

THE SEVEN-IMPRESSION RULE

Your rule of thumb should be that it will take at least seven interactions (or, as marketers say, "impressions") to get a hiring manager to start remembering you and your messages. That may seem like a whole lot of communicating, but it's not at all excessive. In fact, it's easy to do, because impressions can take many forms: resumes, correspondence (cover letters, thank-you notes, email), phone calls, interviews, recruiters pitching you, and insiders buzzing about you.

Now that you're familiar with some of the options you have at your disposal, you need to develop a strategy to make seven impressions per employer you're targeting. Here's an example of how easy it is to get there:

1. A headhunter who's been briefed on your strengths and corporate identity **calls** the hiring manager to discuss you.

2. You send the hiring manager a **cover letter** and

3. Your **resume**, both of which reiterate your message.

4. The hiring manager conducts a **phone interview** with you to discuss your strengths.

5. You follow up with a quick **thank-you email** . . .

6. Immediately followed by a more **formal thank-you note,** in which you highlight your commitment, your ability to do the job, and what distinguishes you.

7. You're invited in for a **face-to-face interview,** where once again you can discuss and elaborate on your selling points.

You can really start racking up bonus impressions and go well beyond the seven necessary impressions when you meet with multiple people at the firms that you're interviewing with and send follow-up correspondence to each of them. This is how you start building buzz for yourself within the firm, which not only keeps you foremost in the hiring manager's mind, but also makes people eager to meet you. Make sure that your messaging is consistent. Otherwise, you run the risk of confusing people. Don't worry about getting stale and repetitious just because you're becoming comfortable with your message. If you're getting a little bored from delivering what seems like the same old message, calm down: you're doing exactly the right thing. Each recipient, remember, is only exposed to your message a few times. If people are talking about you internally, you want them saying the same things.

T H E   S K I N N Y : Don't be uncomfortable with self-promotion. It's not synonymous with braggadocio, as long as you are sincere in your interest and honest in how you represent your abilities. You must promote yourself in order to remind people why you're the right candidate for the job.

SPECIAL DELIVERY: PACKAGE YOURSELF

Whether you want to admit it or not, part of your corporate identity comes down to the way you present yourself. Because you have limited time in front of a hiring manager, your personal style and how you carry yourself will often establish how you are perceived. Packaging yourself effectively is a subtle way to reinforce your corporate identity. Your so-called "look" speaks for you even when you cannot. Whether you're sitting in a reception area, riding an elevator, or waiting in a glass conference room for your interview to start, all eyes will be on you. Your appearance communicates whether you're creative, intense, polished, detail-oriented, or just a slob. When you're deciding what you should wear for a given interview, think first about your corporate identity. Start by selecting an outfit or two that will support how you want to position yourself. Once you've done that, choose accessories (scarves, ties, cuff links, pens) and other accent pieces that will pull together the look you want to achieve. Always try on the clothes that you anticipate wearing to the interview and then take a look in the mirror. How do you look? Does your attire complement your corporate identity? Be honest with yourself about what items won't work and shove them to the back of your closet. A look that matches the corporate identity that you want to convey will not only impress an employer but it will also help boost your confidence. If you look the part, you will carry off the part.

Our headhunter said she had the greatest candidate for us to meet for the account executive position we were trying to fill. She looked amazing on paper. My publisher talked to her on the phone to schedule the meeting and was even more excited about her from the way she spoke and handled herself on the phone. When the girl came in to see us, though, she was wearing a light-yellow flowered sundress, high-heeled strappy sandals, and a denim jacket. While she interviewed great, showing up to an interview looking like she was on her way to a picnic killed her chances of a second interview.

—SHERIE, MAGAZINE AD SALESPERSON

Try to select one thing in particular about your look that will really stand out and make an impression on the person you're interviewing with. Tom Wolfe, the novelist, seems to always wear a white suit.

Now, you might not want to go *that* extreme—where does he find all those white suits, anyway? But you should pick something that works for you. Perhaps you're into pinstripe suits. Then that should become your trademark—that one consistent thing by which people remember you. Think about it: hiring managers see loads of candidates before they narrow down the field. By giving them a visual cue that complements your corporate identity, you will more easily stay foremost in their minds.

A nasty by-product of a dressed-down workforce is that we rarely get to wear our interviewing clothes. This means that when interviewing time rolls around, you might be forced to *squeeze* into an outfit that no longer fits or—horrors—is completely out of style. At least once a season, do a suit check and make sure that your interview attire still looks good on you. If it doesn't, head to a tailor to determine whether he or she can make alterations. Regarding style, take a few minutes to open a magazine and see what's current without being ultra-trendy. Don't be surprised if you open your closet and find that the clothes in there aren't aligned with the corporate identity you're trying to present. That's a signal to update your wardrobe (i.e., go shopping!).

Finding a job is an investment in your future, so don't be afraid to slap down your credit card and buy some new duds. If you don't trust your own fashion savvy, choose stores that you think match your corporate identity. For example, if you want a confident and conservative look, you might shop at Lord & Taylor, Barneys, or Nordstrom. If you're striving for hip and creative, you might head to Banana Republic, H&M, vintage shops, or a few funky specialty retailers. The goal here is to establish a style of your own that will be compatible with the image you're after.

THE SKINNY: **Select interview clothes that make you feel good.** If you look like you're wearing your dad's stodgy Brooks Brothers suit, it will be obvious to the interviewer that you feel uncomfortable. Or if you choose a skirt that's a bit too short, you might unconsciously tug at it throughout the interview. Whether you want to admit it or not, any fidgeting at all will affect your interview negatively. You need to feel self-confident, not self-conscious.

Once you've found stores that you like, spend some time with the salespeople—*they're the professionals.* Discuss with them the image you want to establish. Tell them about the corporate culture you expect to encounter and the exact impression you're trying to make. Let the salespeople know that you expect to meet with each prospective employer at least three to five times during the interview process, so you need to give the appearance of variety. Your salesperson can help you get the most out of your wardrobe by coordinating all of the pieces you select so that they can be mixed and matched. If you have a suit or an outfit that you already like, wear it (or bring it) on your shopping spree, and ask the salesperson to help you accessorize and integrate the outfit with the rest of the clothing that they are selecting for you. Be sure to specify your budget, or else things might get out of control. It's the look, not the label, that really matters. If you're truly broke, borrow a few accessories from a friend to spruce things up. By developing a wardrobe that reinforces your corporate identity, you'll improve the chances of the interviewer remembering you.

Planning ahead will also remove the stress of figuring out what to wear, which will increase your confidence level. When it comes to interviews, the disheveled look is always out. A well-put-together ensemble bespeaks an organized candidate. Don't wait until the morning of an interview to select your attire. You don't want to whip out your favorite tie only to find that there's a mustard blob on it. Even the most expensive suit will look horrible if it's not freshly dry cleaned and paired with a crisp, ironed shirt. Decide in advance which outfit will make a lasting impression. If something needs to be cleaned and pressed, do it today! Make a habit of sending your stuff to the cleaners as soon as you get back from each interview. If you need to shop, do it at least a week before crunch time, so that you leave time for alterations.

What to Do About the Corporate-Casual Conundrum?

This is a tough problem, but not insurmountable. Hiring managers are expecting that when you meet with them you're putting your best foot forward. Follow the rule that's been repeated over and over again: you're not hired until you're hired. Corporate casual is a perk that companies bestow on their employees . . . and you're not one yet. If you show up at an interview dressed down, it might suggest that you're not treating the opportunity with the respect it deserves. As an applicant, you need to demonstrate to the hiring manager that you take your interview seriously. It rarely hurts to be overdressed. On the other hand, if you're caught underdressed, you will almost certainly be remembered negatively. If you're still concerned about being overdressed, select an ensemble that can be toned down by removing an accessory like a tie or scarf.

The exception to the rule: there are some instances when wearing a suit could hurt you, although they are few and far between. If you think you're interviewing at a company whose uniform is always, always casual, inquire about the appropriate interviewing attire with the recruiter who placed you or with the human resources person who's screening you. Let them know you're just doing your homework and that you want to be prepared (and fit in). They will appreciate your candor and will not look down on you for asking.

Even little things can make a difference: clean out your briefcase and wallet before you go on an interview. You don't want to pull out a card and have a bunch of receipts and crumpled money fall out. Getting a card holder can help.

—BONNIE, CAREER COACH

Clothes don't always make the man (or woman), they are only part of the way you package yourself. If you're slouched or don't maintain eye contact, you might as well be wearing a potato sack. (Mom was right, sitting up straight matters.) How you carry yourself and participate in each interview will make a tremendous difference in completing the package. Your attention to detail demonstrates to those you're interviewing with that you actually care about landing the job.

I recently bumped into a friend of mine in the hallway of the securities firm I worked at just as he was coming out of an interview. As we were talking, I noticed that he had a giant Swoosh on his T-shirt under his crisply pressed white dress shirt. I couldn't resist ribbing him, so I said, "Hey, Jim, nice Nike tee." Jim looked at me in shock and said, "You can't see that, I turned it inside out!" He looked like an idiot and he didn't get the job.

—CHUCK, PORTFOLIO MANAGER

I'm a nail biter. I can't help it. I've been gnawing on my nails for years. I once went on an interview and later found out from the headhunter that my nubby nails were distracting to the hiring manager. While he liked my work, he thought that I might be too nervous or neurotic to work at the firm. At first I was irritated, but then I realized that I don't want to leave that impression with anyone, because that's not who I am. Now, I make it a point to at least file my nails before I go on an interview. They may be short, but at least they're no longer distracting.

—MARCY, CREATIVE DIRECTOR

Get Your Uniform On

Contributed by Stan Williams

When you think of a police officer, an airline pilot, a postal worker, or even a chef, you automatically think of the uniform they wear to work every day, which identifies them with the professions they perform. The police officer wears his trusty blues, the airline pilot his navy blue tunic and military cap, the postal worker her gray pants with the stripe up the leg, and the chef the recognizable puffy headgear. Most likely, if you grew up in the United States, you have a pretty fair assumption of what these uniforms represent.

The president of the United States has a uniform, and you definitely know what he stands for. If George W. Bush got up in front of the world to present his State of the Union address wearing an Adidas sweat suit, you can bet the headlines would be more about what he wore than what he said. A dapper suit and tie is the Bush uniform (unless he's throwing a hoedown for visiting dignitaries; then he wears his folksy Texas getup). On the other hand, if Gwen Stefani, the colorful lead singer of No Doubt, decided one day that she would just wear black and not change her hairstyle every other day, her fans would wonder what was wrong with her. Her creativity and funkiness is *her* uniform. Even the world's top fashion designers, who create radically different collections twice a year, adhere to certain recurring elements in their personal looks. The fashion world would be in shock if they saw Tom Ford, the creative force behind Gucci and Yves Saint Laurent, wearing anything other than black. Black is his uniform.

What do you stand for, and what is your uniform? Are you cool and casual, or funky and off-beat? Whatever your uniform, remember, it focuses the attention on you. It identifies who you are and what you stand for, but it should also fit easily into your chosen career path. To start identifying your personal uniform, think about your future work environment. Is it super-corporate or is it ultra-relaxed? In corporate environments, you don't have much of a choice, since for the most part, it demands some version of a business suit. But in the more casual situations, there are more options. Do you wear jeans? Do you wear khakis? Can you wear short-sleeved shirts? Is it okay to wear a blazer without a tie? If possible, try to check out your prospective new work environment in advance. Take note of what your potential colleagues wear, and try to emulate them on your interview. Always err on the side of being overdressed. It's better to look too serious than to look completely off the wall.

Now on to the more corporate look. It's pretty simple. A suit always commands respect, even if you're going after an entry-level or junior position. The most important part of buying a suit is to make sure it fits properly. Never take a suit off the rack and expect to wear it with good results. Have it altered by a good tailor. (Your tailor can be one of your best image builders.) You might think wearing suits is a total bore, but it doesn't have to be. Even dressing for the most conservative office can allow you ways to differentiate yourself. Let's say you're a guy who's expected to wear a suit and tie every day. Why not invest in a few precisely tailored suits, and splurge on all kinds of ties that coordinate with your suits and shirts? Let people notice you by the array of beautiful ties you wear. (Also learn how to tie the appropriate knots. Salespeople in men's stores can provide this information.) If ties aren't your thing, maybe you could become the cuff link guy. Buy French cuff shirts, make sure they're crisply pressed, and always wear beautiful cuff links.

A woman going into a suity situation should also invest in basic tailored pieces: a jacket that coordinates with either pants or a skirt. Put together a basic suit look, and add several tops that you'll rotate so it doesn't look like you're wearing the same thing every day. Remember that just because you're wearing a suit, you don't have to look plain and drab. Add accessories that make your suit more interesting and identifiable. If you like to wear scarves, become the Scarf Girl. Find them in vintage shops or better stores. If you frequent shops like Hermès or Salvatore Ferragamo, you'll find booklets telling you how to tie them in a variety of ways. Not into scarves? Become the Bag Girl and change your handbag every few days. You don't have to spend a ton of money on bags if that's the accessory you love. Check out consignment shops that sell great designer leather goods, or watch for end-of-season sales. A good handbag that's classic and not too trendy never goes out of style.

Make sure that your uniform follows these fashion fundamentals. Both men and women should make sure your bags, belts, and shoes coordinate. If you are talented at mixing them up, then you know it and everyone else recognizes it. It's sort of like being left- or right-handed. Either you are or you aren't. It's not something you can learn overnight. If you're not sure, stick to the matching rule. No matter what job you're looking to fit into, there's no excuse for sloppiness or bad grooming. Those little things can be a turnoff even if you're dressed to the nines. Do you pluck your eyebrows? If so, make sure it looks like you do. Hold off on extreme makeup. It's too distracting. The same goes for any piercings on the face. If you can remove them before an interview, then do it. You can figure out later how to re-introduce them into your wardrobe once you get the job. Earrings are okay, but if you've got a bunch of holes there, you might want not to fill them all up for the sake of the interview. Overall, hold off on jewelry. Simple rings and watches are fine, but gaudy, trendy, oversized pieces are not. Guys, if you sport a beard, mustache, or sideburns, make sure you've taken the time to snip scraggly hairs. Check out the nose, too. Nose hairs can be a huge distraction to a potential employer. Haircuts, haircuts, haircuts! Need I say more? And as for the fingers, make sure they're clipped and clean for guys, and neat and manicured for the girls. People do look at these things.

Overall, if you're not sure about wearing something in a professional situation, ask for help, but always trust your gut. If you have time to talk to friends or work with a salesperson to show you how to put your clothes together, then do so. But if you're not comfortable with something you're wearing, it will show. It will reduce your confidence level, which detracts from your interview. Personal style is just that—personal. Your uniform has to look right on you. And if you look and feel right for the job you're seeking, you're sure to succeed at making the right first impression.

Stan has been a fashion journalist for almost fifteen years. Currently fashion director at Maxim, *Williams spent nearly ten years at Fairchild Publications in fashion and home editorial positions.*

NOW GO WORK IT!

Here's the Takeaway:

- Brand yourself with a distinctive corporate identity that tells prospective employers what you do best, what makes you different (and better) than every other candidate, and what is unique about your personality.

- Having a distinctive and simple corporate identity makes you memorable.

- Reinforce your identity and make it even more memorable by delivering multiple "impressions" of your message. Employ the "seven-impression rule," delivering a consistent message through your cover letter, resume, interview, follow-up calls, thank-you notes, and all other communications with an employer.

- Stay "on message": don't let your message vary between people at the same company. It may seem monotonous to you, but it's vital not to muddle your identity.

- Package yourself effectively. Find something distinctive and memorable about your personal style and dress that will set you apart. But always look professional.

4

NETWORKING:

Get Hired with a Little Help from Your Friends

Unless you've been living under a rock, you probably already know that networking is the number one way to find jobs. According to TMP Worldwide, one of the world's largest online recruitment firms, networking is a highly effective way to access the hidden job market, through which about eighty percent of people find work today. Knowing that statistic and benefiting from it are two different things, however. When you tell people you're struggling through your job search, they'll tell you straight out that you should network more. Great advice. As if just mentioning the word "networking" will suddenly open the door to success. *Whatever.* It's easier said than done.

Some lucky people can breeze through a party, carefree, shaking hands, slapping backs, and exchanging business cards with incredible ease. And then there's the rest of us: the sweaty-palmed folk who stand back watching in awe as those "networking naturals" get ahead, reap promotions, and land new jobs—jobs that could have been ours. Before you start cursing your genes or your unlucky stars, realize that good networking skills aren't something you're born with. They're something you have to hone. Those killer networkers look like naturals because they *work* at it. They make it look easy because they get out there and practice. They've learned the number one rule of the networking game: it's a full-time job.

YOU HAVE TO KISS A LOT OF TOADS

Networking is ultimately about getting out there and meeting people. If you really want results, then you have to realize that it's a numbers game. Assume that for every twenty people you meet, the odds are that only one of them will ever turn into a solid connection. That may sound like a lousy hit ratio, but it's realistic. It simply means that you need to meet as many people as you can. Once you start increasing the number of contacts you make, your task becomes easier, and your chances of making meaningful connections are greatly enhanced. A successful networker understands that opportunities don't just happen at formal networking events like parties and industry conferences. Networking is about keeping your eyes and ears open all the time—at the photocopier, at Starbucks, or even while waiting for your date to show up. True, opportunities for connecting with people can sometimes just happen, but most of the time you have to *make* them happen. That's one of the toughest things to deal with if you are not yet a "natural," because you really have to take the risk and put yourself out on the line.

Go Talk to Strangers

Networking is not a skill that you switch on and off, but a way of thinking, a light that's always switched on. Getting good at speaking with strangers has to become instinctual. Does that mean you have to turn into one of those pushy, glad-handing, back-slapping, brown-nosing types that nobody can stand? Absolutely not. Great networkers are sincere, confident, likeable people who know instinctively, or have learned, how to engage with other people and make themselves memorable (in a good way!).

How can you do that? Rule number one: have a clue. Before you utter a single word, pay attention to what is going on around you. If a conversation is happening, listen in before you dive in. Don't invade another person's space. Don't get in so close that others feel suffocated by your presence. If someone is furiously typing on their laptop or has their head buried in a pile of papers, they are sending a signal that they don't want to be disturbed (even if you happen to be sharing a cozy armrest with them on an airplane). You need to be aware of personal space and respect it.

And Your Most Unusual Networking Location Is . . .

Dressing room. I ran into Andrea Jung, the CEO of Avon, in the personal shopping dressing room of Bloomingdale's. I had the rare opportunity of a captive audience with a very important woman and I didn't want to blow it. (Then again, it's not like she could run away while wearing only pantyhose!) So, while she was trying on winter outfits for her ski vacation, I introduced myself, told her how much I admired her work, and that I would follow up with her when it was more appropriate (and did).

—**Syl, Online Publisher**

Bathroom. I was an intern at a public relations firm, and the CEO walked in to take a whiz. I was already standing at the urinal, we got to chatting, and by the end of the "meeting," he told me to come to his office and discuss a project he wanted me to work on. Most men will tell you that conversation at the urinal is verboten, but I gladly made an exception in this situation.

—**Michael, Publicist**

Airplane. Not unusual, but a score! I was coming back from an interview in New York during grad school; I got bumped to first class. An older gentleman across the aisle asked if I was a lawyer (I guess my shuffling through all those school papers made me look important). It turns out that he had just accepted a job in New York. He ended up getting me an interview there, which led me to relocate for a new job. It pays to talk back on planes.

—**Amanda, Advertising Executive**

A One-Night Stand. You never know how someone you meet will affect your life professionally. I was a left-coaster on vacation in Mykonos, Greece, and met a "special someone" from New York City. We had a wild week and kept in touch, becoming email buddies thereafter. When I moved to the City four years later, he was the best contact in the world to have. He lined up tons of interviews for me. You never know where your best connections will come from!

—Sandra, In-store Manager for major fashion brand

A conga line!

—Ed, Sales Manager

The Street. I was dressed as a 1920s newsboy handing out financial newspapers as part of a guerrilla marketing campaign. A woman stopped and asked me what the promotion was all about. Turns out she was head of marketing for another weekly paper and was looking for a copywriter. I interviewed the next week. I was offered the position but ended up taking another job, from a lead that I got by bumping into an old friend at the supermarket.

—Aaron, Writer/Comedian

Community Garden. I made a fabulous contact once while composting over a worm bin.

—Maureen, Graphic Designer

The Bar Car. My prime networking turf is the commuter train. I make it a point to commute home in the bar car, not because I want to drink, but because the more outgoing, extroverted people gravitate there. The whole atmosphere—close quarters, a common experience, no TV or radio—is conducive to conversation. Not to mention that it also gives you the immediate opportunity to exchange gifts with new contacts with the simple declarative: "I got the next round."

—Dave, Account Executive

Next, be confident and poised. Interactions can happen in a fleeting moment, so visual cues are vital. Be sure to make solid eye contact with the other person—there's no better way to build trust and demonstrate confidence. And smile! Not some fake, toothy, motivational-speaker sort of grin, but a warm and friendly smile that will set people at ease. If you're approaching someone and want to start a conversation, pick a solid opener like, "The speaker made a really good point about such-and-such," or, if you're nervous, simply introduce yourself by saying "Hi" and giving your name. You're there to network, so make sure that the topics you bring up are related to the discussion at hand or are at the very least interesting. You don't want to be remembered as the guy with a bizarre addiction to the Weather Channel or the gal that couldn't shut up about her car getting towed. Check your ego and your personal eccentricities at the door, because you've got people to entertain.

A networking event or career fair, where time is short, is the perfect time to dive into a quick sales pitch about yourself (remember the corporate identity stuff from Chapter 3). A more relaxed setting or a chance meeting is not the time for the hard sell. You don't want to give your new acquaintance that "deer-in-the-headlights" sensation. Instead, have a natural, friendly conversation. Get to know a little something about the other person, then say your piece when it fits naturally into the flow. Chances are, the other person will provide the perfect opening for you: "So, what do you do?"

Avoid being a blabbermouth. Even though you have an agenda, you don't want to be known as the guy or gal who monopolized the conversation. It's better to be remembered as the person who paid attention, listened, and contributed meaningfully. People just love to talk about themselves, so let them. Find out what makes them tick. And when it's your turn to speak, keep your side of the conversation short. Try to ask more questions than you are asked. Pose open-ended questions and don't be afraid to probe. The more the other person talks, the more you'll find out about how you can work together in the future.

After you make a good connection with someone new, dash off a quick email continuing your dialogue or send an article relevant to your conversation. Just don't get carried away by the miracle of technology—nothing is worse than sending a promising new contact a form email that you have obviously blasted to every person you met at last night's cocktail party. Not only is it annoying (it's *spam,* people!), but it speaks poorly of your social skills and your ability to follow up effectively in business situations. If you truly want to build a relationship with a new contact, you need to do it the old-fashioned way: carefully and with individual attention. Invite people to get together again and give them a reason to want to meet with you.

Follow-up is vital. When you meet new contacts, they may not respond right away, simply because they are busy and have their own agenda (especially if the contact is a heavy hitter—they just *might* have other things on their mind besides li'l ol' you). Make contact via a phone call, email, or (most impressively) a handwritten note. Then give it a little time to simmer. Some people will take a few days to respond, others longer. If someone isn't responding, vary your channels of contact: some people like a quick phone call, others respond best to email. Always keep your tone positive and professional, and don't turn into a stalker. Sending twenty emails or leaving a pile of phone messages makes you come across as desperate . . . or dangerous. As frustrating as it is to feel like you're being ignored, don't get peevish or nasty. Maybe the person is simply not able to help you and is not comfortable telling you straight up, or maybe you just didn't click. You may just have to move on. If you cross paths with that person again, I'm sure you'd rather have them smack their forehead and say, "Oh, my God, I'm so sorry I never called you," than have them whip out the pepper spray and scream for the cops.

I didn't always have the "networking gene," but I did always have the "helping gene." Helping people was the way I was brought up and it's always been part of my personality. My life is a case in point: I have done innumerable favors for people in business. Consequently, when it was my turn to look for a new job and ask for help, I got over a hundred referrals! I spoke to each of these referrals and they, in turn, gave me additional referrals. I had to create a fifty-three-page chart to keep track of everyone. I ended up having an incredible forty-two interviews and/or meetings in thirty-six days! Because I was still working at the time, I met people for breakfast, lunch, afternoon coffee, after-work meetings, and I had several meetings each weekend day. I was exhausted, but ended up with a job offer that changed the course of my life.

—DANIELLE, ATTORNEY

WHAT GOES AROUND COMES AROUND

The best networkers are people whose enthusiasm for meeting other people and learning about them is driven by genuine interest, not a hard-nosed agenda of maximizing the short-term return on every encounter. They know that every exchange is a two-way street. When you first meet someone, think about how you can help them make connections from your existing network. When you're through thinking of ways you can help the other person, do something about it—not because of the potential payoff, but just because you can. You're taking the first step to establish a connection, rather than waiting for someone to do something for you. We're not talking about anything expensive or labor-intensive. We're talking about making a phone call: you could put someone you met at the airport in touch with a client, or you could make an out-of-towner a reservation at your favorite restaurant. Just be sure to follow through on any offers you make, and do it quickly. Even if something doesn't pan out, they'll know you tried. When people see your dedication and generosity, they'll start doing some of your networking for you: "Hey, I know this terrific woman who really helped me out. She'd be perfect for your company. . . ."

On the flip side, whenever a contact goes out of their way to help you, show your gratitude. Send a thank-you note (handwritten is best), or a small gift. Then be on the lookout for ways to return the favor. Don't get tied up in keeping score. You may not get perfect reciprocation for every good turn, but you'll earn a deserved reputation as a stand-up, trustworthy, always-there-when-you-need-him/her kind of person.

Every time you make a connection for someone, you're making a deposit into the "Good Will Bank and Trust." And that deposit will pay interest over time. Building a network means establishing relationships wherein each party trusts and looks out for the others. Your task is to create an ever-expanding web of these relationships, in which each additional link is another person who's looking out for you. If you approach networking from a selfish, "gimme" perspective, you will probably get some leads and maybe an interview. But if you never look out for the other guy, your network will never grow and thrive. As you get better and better at building the relationships that make for a strong contact base, networking will no longer be just something you have to do—it will become part of you. You'll enjoy it so much, you won't be able to stop.

> Don't be a user. People weren't created just to do what you want them to. Remember that relationships need to develop over the long haul, and that these relationships are the stuff of life.
>
> —SARA, EXECUTIVE DIRECTOR OF A NON-PROFIT

Develop Your Network

Contributed by Karen Page

Career experts have long known that most available positions go unadvertised. Here's a perfect case in point: my friend Margaret called me looking for recommendations for someone to take over her fabulous job when she resigns this summer. Her position won't ever make it to a headhunter's desk or an alumni career newsletter, let alone a newspaper's classifieds section. Instead, the placement process had begun, and would doubtless end, with networking. Becoming a better networker can enhance your life in many ways, including giving you access to new people, information, and opportunities.

Here's a baker's dozen of my best tips on networking:

1. **Know what you want and what you have to offer.** Even while you're looking for a job, you've still got plenty to offer, including your education, experience, and contacts. Don't just ask for favors; instead, share what you have with others. Successful networking is, first and foremost, reciprocal.

2. **Always put your best foot forward.** Be respected, *then* be liked. A close friend referred a job-seeking colleague to me who spoke of her current job so disparagingly that I didn't feel comfortable referring her in turn to my contacts. A referral depends on someone else's willingness to say, "Okay—you can use my brand." Be sure to earn that right first.

3. **Practice basic etiquette.** Say "please," "thank you," and "you're welcome." As you were taught long ago, they really are magic words.

4. **Follow up on new contacts.** Drop notes to new acquaintances, mentioning how much you enjoyed meeting them, thanking them for their help, forwarding an article, inviting them to an event, etc.

5. **Be easy to reach.** It will make it that much easier for people to find you and to recommend you to others. So offer others your card. Set up a web site. Include a signature on your email that tells people who you are and what you do.

6. **Establish your network before you need it.** Enough said.

7. **Be open.** I met a friend who went on to become my consulting partner when she was standing in line in front of me at a take-out lunch spot, and I complimented her on her dress.

8. **Be fearless.** Just ask! After stumbling upon a book I found completely captivating, I decided to make it the topic of a monthly dinner. When I noticed that the authors lived in New York, out of the blue I invited them to join us. They did, and have since become great friends and contacts.

9. **Keep in touch.** Make it a point to write occasional notes—sharing information, offering congratulations, offering birthday greetings, etc.

Ever since running my own birthday cake delivery business in college, I've tried to keep track of the birthdays of people I meet so I'm able to keep in touch at least once a year.

10. **Get to know others.** Between my journalism schooling and political campaign advance work, I've been trained to research people before I meet with them. These days, it's so easy to do an Internet search on someone you'll be meeting. Aside from research, the best thing you can do is *listen* to someone when they talk, and pay attention to what's important to them.

11. **Know and use basic psychology.** Put people at ease, and meet them on their turf. Recognize that not everybody is wired the way you are. So, it helps to adapt yourself to the other person's communication style. For example, introverts tend to value their privacy and may prefer communicating via email, while extroverts may value a "live" connection, either face-to-face or by phone. While "feelers" might be swayed by a passionate pitch, "thinkers" need to know the facts and the logical arguments behind whatever you're proposing.

12. **Trust the law of karma—and "add value" at every opportunity.** When a friend forgot to tell me that she'd given my number to two guys visiting New York, I good-naturedly met up with them anyway—and ended up falling in love with and marrying one of them!

13. **Help others develop their own networks.** If you know of people with common interests, link them up. If you make it a point to connect your contacts, it will make your network more dynamic and enhance your own reputation as a power networker.

Karen is a New York City—based, award-winning author and runs her own specialized coaching practice, working with high achievers to reach their next level of career or business success. She also chairs the Harvard Business School Network of Women Alumnae. Her email is: KarenAPage@aol.com.

GET SIX DEGREES OF YOU

If Kevin Bacon can do it, why not you? Networking is about getting in touch with someone, who knows someone, who . . . well, you get the picture. The process of finding people who know people needs to happen both when you're helping someone and when you're asking for favors. Sometimes the easiest way to get started is to write down everyone you know on a sheet of paper. This ritual seems like something you did in the fifth grade, but it really is quite helpful. Start by writing down close friends and family members. Then add their parents, spouses, sisters, brothers, and cousins. Do the same with colleagues, acquaintances, college pals, and workout partners. Once you've written down everyone that comes to mind, think of this group as your "inner circle." Next, write down where each person works (and where they used to work) and put that information into your database of contacts. Study your list carefully, and ask yourself whether any of those people can help you get closer to the job you want. Chances are great that someone can, and by getting in contact with people who know people, you're truly starting to get six degrees of you. Email or call everyone in the inner circle, tell them what you're up to and what you're interested in doing, and then ask them if they know someone who might be able to help in your quest to find a new job. Taking the first step is key. Thereafter it gets easier, because at least a handful of the people you contact will get back to you. Then you're off and rolling. As your inner circle begins to introduce you to new people, keep track of each "degree of separation." People will feel more comfortable and willing to help if they know you were their colleague's first roommate after college or worked at a summer camp with a friend of a friend in high school. And it's a great network-strengthener to keep people abreast on how their referrals were helpful to you.

Be aware that not every person you enlist will be in a position to help you get a job then and there. This process is like the ancient water torture . . . painfully slow. What these contacts might be able to do is provide you with direction and, ideally, additional contacts that you then can work to your advantage. Ask for referrals without being presumptuous. The more inspired and inquisitive you are, the more interested they'll be in helping you. Be careful how you ask for referrals. "Hey, I need a job, I was hoping you can find me one" is not a message you want to send. Being direct is fine; there's no advantage in sounding wishy-washy about what you want. But you shouldn't force a contact into a corner. It will make them feel uncomfortable, and make you look desperate. That's why if you come across as crass and in-your-face, all you'll get is a chilly "Can I get back to you?"

Always follow up, but don't be annoying about it. If your contacts want to help, they will. If they don't, move on. And most important, if one of your contacts puts you in contact with someone or gives you a number to call, don't dawdle. Follow up immediately! If you don't, you'll look bad and so will your connection. The person who refers you to someone else is putting his or her own reputation on the line. Don't make them regret helping you. The referral process is a delicate house of cards that can come tumbling down if you don't do the right thing at every juncture. This is especially true as you weave more contacts into your world. Tracking who referred whom is indispensable in avoiding screw-ups and embarrassments, which is why you need to remain extremely organized.

THE SKINNY: **Get permission first.** Say you get a business card from a contact that works at a company you really want to work for. What harm is there in using their name in a cover letter to the HR department? A lot! Never drop a person's name in a networking situation or as any kind of reference until you get their explicit permission. To create a solid contact base, you need to cultivate advocates, not enemies.

A college buddy of mine got laid off from a sports marketing company. It just so happened that I had a contact at a sports entertainment company. I let him know that I would be willing to put a call in on his behalf. He was psyched for the favor. I lobbed in the call, and my contact proceeded to call his boss and they both agreed to meet with my friend. In fact, they needed a person with his background, so the timing was perfect. I called my buddy, and let him know that he should call my contact directly to set up the interview and take it from there. Two weeks later, I get an email from my contact at the sports entertainment company, asking what ever happened to the friend I had recommended. I immediately called my buddy, who admitted that he had dropped the ball and had never followed up. I let him know that I had gone out on a limb for him and was disappointed at his lack of response. I asked, "Why wouldn't you call when I set something up for you?" All he could say was that he forgot. It was pathetic. This guy didn't think that what he did put me in an odd position with my contacts. This mishap has made me gun-shy about referring anyone.

—SCOTT, EVENT MANAGER

Too many people network as if they have to be best friends with every contact they meet. I try to use a friend of a friend to get ahead. I have found that acquaintances, people I only know in passing, have been far more helpful than the people I know very well. The closer connections tend to have major agendas, while remote connections have fresher leads and are less invested in my move.

—JOSH, BOND SALESMAN

REACH OUT AND TOUCH SOME BODIES

Now that you've built your inner circle, it's time to start building new contacts. But where do you go? Again, everywhere and anywhere! Your only limitation is yourself at this point. Here are some places to get started.

✓ USE YOUR REFERENCES! Most people tap into their references at the end of their interviewing process, right before they get offered a job. What a mistake! Your references can be a bonanza of excellent connections because they already like and respect you (or else they wouldn't be references in the first place). They can also vouch for your work ethic. This means they'll be more likely to go out on a limb for you, whether it be making a call on your behalf or keeping their eyes peeled for interesting opportunities. It's always a smart idea to keep your references "active" and aware of you at all times.

✓ GET TO KNOW AN INSIDER. The single best way to get hired by a company is through contacts with existing employees. In 2001 WetFeet, a career resource site, surveyed twenty-two U.S. employers that hire hundreds of people each year. They found that nearly two-thirds of respondents identified employee referral programs as their largest source of new hires. That shouldn't be surprising. When a company finds a new hire via an employee referral, they get out of paying headhunter fees, which can be as much as thirty-five percent of the hiree's annual salary. At the same time, they get a more dependable stream of high-caliber applicants, because employees will not put their own reputations at risk by referring marginal candidates. Finally, employees have an intimate understanding of the firm's needs and corporate culture, so they are unlikely to refer someone who would not be a good fit.

To take advantage of employee referrals, you need to find a company insider, someone who can be your "mole" and find out what's going on at the companies where you want to work. This means you should spend time in places where you can network with these people. Do you know somebody who works at a target company? Can you attend an event where the company will be represented and where you're likely to bump into the right people? Figure out where the company watering hole is and plant yourself there at happy hour. Your mission is to get to know people who work at the firm, or who know of people who work there.

Once you identify an insider, you need to demonstrate to them that you're worthy of candidacy at their company and that you won't embarrass them if they recommend you. Everything starts with their confidence in you. If you get them to believe that you can add value to the firm while making them look good to their own higher-ups, then you've got no problem. Hopefully by this point they'll be so impressed that it won't be hard to convince them to make an effort to help you.

At larger firms in particular, the human resources department will have a policy of trying to fill positions internally before they open them up to outside candidates. Sometimes these positions are posted only within the confines of the HR department or in some common area like the coffee room, which might require your insider to make a special trip on your behalf. Nowadays, your insider might be able to find the positions featured on the company intranet site. Some larger companies even send out weekly e-newsletters that highlight job openings. Have your insider inquire about the positions that are listed: ask if they are for internal transfers only, or if they might be placed via an employee referral. The most important thing is that your mole can give you a jump-start on knowing which departments are hiring, so you can get on their radar screen in case they don't find the right person internally. Have your insider pay attention to any personnel changes that are happening in departments you want to work in. Look for opportunities when people quit, get transferred, promoted, or fired. Track these changes closely, particularly in the areas that fit your skills. Also, look for departments that are understaffed or in upheaval. Depending on the seniority of your insider, they might be able to go directly to the business unit manager to discuss upcoming openings. A quick email or conversation might uncover some priceless information. If the position goes into the employee referral program, jump on it quickly. Timing is everything. The great thing about landing a job via an insider through an employee referral program is that both you and the insider benefit. You get a job, and they get a referral bonus.

Nine Tips for Effective Email Networking

Contributed by Eileen Shulock

Email networking, once the haven of the shy, the sullen, and the agoraphobic, has emerged as an efficient and productive career-building tactic, for those who do it well. When trying to reach time-constrained contacts, it can even be more effective than face-to-face communication. Strangely, however, many job seekers unintentionally reveal far more in their emails than they intend to: bad attitudes, personality defects, and deficiencies in their career histories. Don't let this happen to you. Follow these tips for professional, psychosis-free email networking.

1. **Establish your connection.** Your reason for contact should be right up front, in the subject line and in the first sentence of the body of the email. Often, the contact has come about as the result of a referral, which is very powerful. Include the words "Referral from Mary Smith" in the subject line of your email, and begin the body with "Your cousin Mary Smith suggested that I contact you about . . ." If you are following up on a face-to-face conversation or introduction, you need to give the person a little refresher. A sentence indicating where you met, under what circumstances, and the subject of any conversation will help the recipient recall who you are.

2. **Have a goal in mind.** Whether you are emailing someone "blind" or following up on an introduction or meeting, it is important to have a clear goal for your email in mind. What do you want? A meeting? A referral? A lunch date? Be as specific as possible. "I'd love to take you out to lunch to pick your brain about pharmaceuticals marketing. How about next Tuesday?" is so much more manageable than the pathetic, anxiety-ridden, unfocused "Here is my resume, if there are any jobs in the universe that you think I might be good for, please let me know."

It's also less threatening—you're much more likely to get a positive reception if your stated objective is information, rather than a job.

3. **Write in clear, grammatical sentences.** Now is not the time to reveal your inner e.e. cummings . . . in random thoughts . . . that might or might not be important. Organize your thoughts, and then articulate them in complete sentences. Save the informal style for people who know you.

4. **Keep it short and sweet.** Just because an email gives you virtually unlimited writing space doesn't give you license to ramble. Respect your recipient's time. Expecting him or her to invest more than five minutes in your message is just like cornering a contact at a cocktail party and launching into a monologue—except that via email, your recipient can simply hit "Delete."

5. **Offer something in return.** Beware of being perceived as a "mind suck" who simply wants information and connections. What can you offer in return? Why should someone help you? Position yourself as an ally, not a charity case, by suggesting ways that you can help your recipient. If you don't know how you could be of help to your target, ask.

6. **Don't overstep your bounds.** Don't let the anonymity of email tempt you to unleash your repressed, demanding ego. You will most likely meet your recipient face-to-face eventually. If you would not feel comfortable asking for something in person, don't do it by email, either.

7. **Be persistent.** Everyone gets lots of email. Yours might have been overlooked, or set aside and forgotten, or deleted accidentally. If you don't receive an answer to your request, do try again—politely.

8. **Follow up.** You've made the initial connection. You may have even achieved your goal. Now what? Follow up. Don't turn into the networking equivalent of the one-night stand. Keep the connection going by sending articles of interest, event invitations, or helpful information to your new contact.

9. **Include your contact information with every email exchange.** If you have started an exchange with your recipient, that's great. But don't assume that the details you included on your first email—such as your full name and phone number—have been lovingly stored for future reference. Remember to use your sig file on every mail! *(See pages 121–23 for more about sig files.)*

Eileen is President of Merchant Diva, an e-merchandising consultancy; Managing Editor of Web Digest for Marketers; *and co-author of* Essential Business Tactics for the Net. *She is the director of the New York City chapter of Webgrrls International, and co-founder of Silicon Alley Cares.*

WORK THE INDUSTRY EVENTS

Industry associations are fantastic sources for new contacts. There are literally thousands of industry associations, big and small, specialized and general. The bigger ones even have Special Interest Groups that allow you to focus on those areas that most interest you. Attending trade shows and meetings and getting involved in industry activities and events are other great ways to expand your cadre of contacts. Not only do you gain networking perks by joining associations, but you often get access to "members only" newsletters and proprietary job listings. Your current company may even underwrite your membership fee because it makes good business sense for you to be out keeping up with industry trends. (Little do they know your true motives!)

Clubs, whether work-oriented or recreational, are also good sources of contacts. You can join them online or off. And the great thing about them is that you've already got something in common with the other people in the organization: a love of something. This makes breaking down barriers much easier.

College alumni chapters are fantastic places to generate contacts, too. But don't stop with the booze cruises; they may be a
blast, but you'll get a lot more networking mileage from a presentation by that prestigious alum who's now a Fortune 500 CEO. For
alumni organizations, investing in the career development of former
students is the gift that keeps on giving. Alumni love to hire other
alumni, strengthening bonds between alums and making the
school look good. And if you're just getting started on a job search,
alumni functions are a great place to build up your networking
chops, because everyone in the room has a common heritage (not to
mention the best ice-breaker of them all: "So, what year did you
graduate?").

That said, there are only twenty-four hours in a day and with so
much out there, you need to be choosy about the organizations you
join. Some clubs are worthy of the membership fee, while others will
gladly take your money but offer little in return. If you're thinking
about joining a new organization, ask around and get people's opinions. Are the organization's events good? What are the members and
events like? It's a good idea to get a friend or a sponsor who belongs to
the association to bring you along to attend a meeting or an event before you join. And here's the most important advice of all: once you
join a club, don't take a back seat. Get involved. Get out in front and
make an impact.

> Some associations do a bang-up job of booking high-level members
> and speakers. Others are one giant mutual admiration society for
> folks who want to feel important about what they do. I would rec-
> ommend speaking to a member whom you trust about the value of
> their association. Or attend at least one meeting or function before
> making a commitment. I look at the list to make sure all of the high-
> ranking folks I need to meet will be there. If it's just a bunch of ven-
> dors or a dog-and-pony event where a company's just spending a
> bunch of cash to show off, I don't go.
>
> —Scott, Merchandising Manager

I want to chime in with a networking secret that has worked for me—start your own networking group! Inviting speakers to my events has been a great way to meet prominent people in the industry. People are always interested in sharing their knowledge and experience with others. And at the events themselves, attendees always approach me at the end to chat. I rarely find myself standing alone wondering whom to speak to next. But even in those infrequent instances, it's psychologically easier for me as the "host" to wander over to someone and start a conversation, even just to thank them for coming to the event and to ask what they got out of it. If you can't start a networking group, then join a committee of an existing one, particularly a committee in charge of programming.

—LIZ, MARKETING CONSULTANT

If you are going to join the board of an organization, don't do it in name only. If you commit, you should really give it your all. That means following through and finishing what you start. Being on the board of an organization helped me from many perspectives. I learned to juggle my day-to-day job responsibilities with my outside-industry organizational responsibilities. I broadened my networking base. I learned to work within budgets. I learned to get creative on the membership subcommittee to secure more members.

—LISA, ACCOUNT EXECUTIVE

ON-THE-JOB NETWORKING

So, you're gainfully employed. You like your company; you just hate your boss. Maybe the secret is to leave your department and not your firm. Problem is, you may be the best-kept secret in the place (and your evil boss, the selfish bastard, wants to keep it that way). In such a situation, it's up to you to make a name for yourself. What do you have to lose? Volunteer to work on intra-company initiatives (especially high profile ones), where you'll be able to mix it up with co-workers from other departments and get noticed. You need to develop your sixth sense for networking opportunities inside your company. It starts by opening your eyes and ears. Once you do, you'll soon begin meeting people who can help you in your intra-firm job search.

Another great way to network is to get on a fund-raising committee for a charity that's important to the company. Pick a cause that you're particularly interested in. In addition to scoring a few brownie points, you might be surprised to see how rewarding it is to work on an important fund-raiser. Company athletic teams and other extracurricular clubs are also a great opportunity to meet people outside your department in a fun, relaxed setting. Even if you don't play, you can attend games and cheer your colleagues on, then invite yourself out for the socializing afterward (where all the real networking is done). Not only do you get to hang out with your co-workers and managers, but you also get a chance to mingle with people from the teams representing the other companies in your industry. Bigger companies have a great variety of other options, like fielding runners for Corporate Challenge races or running their own meetings of Weight Watchers (hey, even senior managers enjoy a few too many Snickers now and then). The key is to participate.

I was an intern in the accounting department at a trading firm during my summer vacations from Notre Dame. After I graduated, I was planning on going back to MBA school, which meant that I needed another internship. It was 1991, and the U.S. economy was in a recession. The trading company, my old standby, had decided not to have an intern program that summer, so I was out of luck. I sent out dozens of resumes and cover letters, none of which got a response.

I didn't know what to do. A few of my old friends at the trading company called me to see if I still wanted to play on their softball team, where I had been the starting third baseman for the past couple of summers. At my first game back, the head of the sales department, who was pitching for the team at the time, came up to me and said, "Hey, Dan. It's great to see you are back interning with us. Are you still going to be working in the accounting department?" I told him that the intern program had been canceled. He said, "I'll call you to-morrow." We played the game, and I went home, forgetting his words and not expecting what would happen next.

The next morning, my mother came into my room to wake me up at 8:15, saying that there was someone from my old company on the phone. In disbelief, and a little groggy, I picked up the phone. It was the sales manager, who said, "Hey Dan. When can you come up to the office?" I said, "Anytime." "Great, come by around noon. I have a bunch of things for you to do." He had called the HR person who had killed the intern program and told her that he was going to hire me as his intern. I worked there that summer and the next, and was given a job offer as a sales trader on the desk after I got my MBA! I broke into sales and trading on Wall Street, all because I could make the throw from third to first (and because my mom woke me up)!

—DAN, EQUITIES TRADER

THE COCKTAIL CULTURE: KNOW THE RULES

Whether it's an industry function, a family gathering, or a boss's wedding, many events have the all-important cocktail party connected with them. The cocktail hour is when much of the best networking gets done. If you're on the job hunt, don't think of the cocktail party as just a party. Think of it as an opportunity to meet people who might be able to help you later on in your search. With the following tips, you'll be well on your way to kicking butt on the cocktail party circuit.

If you do something dumb at a cocktail party, it never hurts to be disarming. I've dropped countless hors d'oeuvres on myself while talking to CEOs and the one-liner that always works is, "You didn't see that, right?"

—KENT, FINANCIAL PLANNER

I was out in a bar. The girl sitting next to me overheard my conversation with my friend and discovered where I worked. She interrupted

Cause a Stir, Don't Get Shaken

Contributed by Anthony Giglio

Liquor is the social lubricant of our times. Don't ruin the perfect opportunity to schmooze with a key contact or your boss just because you don't know the ins and outs of cocktail party etiquette. Follow these rules and you'll stay in the game:

Your cocktail is a prop. *That means don't suck them back like they are going out of style. If you're in a crowded room drinking a cocktail from a glass with a stem (like wine or a martini), put your pinky under the flat part of the glass as support. That way you won't pour your drink on your neighbor.*

Never have more than two. *Unless you're out with a group that you know extremely well, this rule holds for every occasion where networking is the dish of the night. Always pay attention to how many drinks you're consuming. Never get drunk.*

Be a copycat. *If you're looking to speak with one person in particular at the cocktail party, do a little reconnaissance before you meet and greet. See what they are drinking and then order the same before you approach. When in doubt, skip the beer and choose wine—it's always a safe bet.*

Don't eat too much. *You may be inclined to grab a tasty hors d'oeuvre as the waitress floats by. If you do, you guarantee that you will be asked a question at the very moment your mouth is glued shut by a piping hot stuffed mushroom. Instead of getting caught gorging yourself on baby wieners, try to eat a snack before you arrive. Or stand by the kitchen and snag a few appies unobserved before you roll into the crowd.*

Go, go, go. *Get in, get out, get on with it—especially with the guest of honor or host. Always acknowledge their time constraints with "I know you're very* *busy, but if I could just ask you one thing . . ."* Then say it and let them go! They have a party to run.

Get dressed. Ladies: never wear sneakers with a suit at a cocktail party. Gentlemen: if you're unsure of the dress code, err on the side of caution and wear a tie. If you're inclined to loosen your tie, just remove it. A loose tie never makes you look relaxed, it just makes you look drunk and disheveled.

Anthony is an award-winning journalist who took his first sip of wine at the age of seven ("from a gallon of Carlo Rossi Burgundy"). He's a trained sommelier who writes about wine and cocktails for a living. His articles have appeared in Esquire, Details, Redbook, Mademoiselle, Marie Claire, Food Arts, Time Out New York, and Boston Magazine.

and insisted that she buy me a drink. She then proceeded to pitch me on how desperate she was to break into my industry and how incredibly talented she was. The trouble was, not only was she persistent, she was incredibly *drunk*. She kept interrupting my conversation with ideas that were sloppily, slurringly delivered. When I tried ignoring her, she became belligerent about how rude I was. (All she wanted was "a little advice.") The next morning she had the gall to email me her resume. I didn't respond.

—KIM, DIRECTOR OF MARKETING

✓ **DO YOUR HOMEWORK.** A few days before the big event, do your homework on who will be attending. These days you can do a Google search on just about anyone, and something interesting will pop up. Strategize some stunning conversational openers to use on the people you'll meet at the event. Maybe it turns out that you and an invitee both went to college in Ohio, or that you both are avid mountain bikers—who knows? No matter what, you're guaranteed to have a more interesting and fruitful conversation if you're armed with some intelligence.

✓ **DON'T DRESS LIKE YOU JUST ROLLED OUT OF BED.** Look presentable. If you look good, people will remember you. If you feel good, you'll be more confident. The two are inextricably linked. Don't forget to brush your teeth or pop a mint before you arrive at the event. Don't make your bad breath the main thing people remember about you.

✓ **THE EARLY BIRD EATS *ALL* THE WORMS.** Always be on time or even *early* for a cocktail party. That's when the real networking gets done. When you get to a function early for the first time you might feel a little weird, but so will the other three people who got there early. The advantage is that it will force you to start talking, with less hurry and less competition. A half hour into any cocktail party, the room will be abuzz and people will be huddled in groups that are hard to break into gracefully, so think twice about arriving "fashionably late."

✓ **ESCAPE THE MAGNETIC FORCEFIELD.** Are you the type who goes to a function and ends up talking to your co-workers all night? Unless you're kissing up to your boss for a promotion, this is a bad habit to get into. Sure, it's easier to hang back and chat up your pals, but it's not helping you to build your contact base. Get outside your comfort zone. Use this opportunity to meet new people, get to know employees from other departments, or even charm your boss's boss. If you're the type who finds it difficult to engage new people, practice starting up conversations in social situations with people that you already know. If you're shy, seek out intimate networking settings where you'll feel less intimidated than you would working a gigantic room. And remember that practice makes perfect. The next time you find yourself in a situation that is ripe for networking, make it a goal to interact with at least one or two new business or social contacts. Don't just sit there—work it!

✔ **DON'T DO THE BUM'S RUSH.** A lot of people think that they're successful at networking if they get a ton of business cards in one evening. All these people are doing is dive-bombing new contacts, dropping ten-second elevator pitches, and hoarding cards—they're not being effective, because the people they meet will never remember them in the morning. Make certain that when you interact with others it makes a difference—or don't do it. Your goal is to have them be receptive to you the next time you contact them. By getting out there and making the effort, you'll not only amass more meaningful connections, but you'll also see your confidence increase. Soon you'll be ready to try new things and add new skills to your repertoire, which will push you further out of your comfort zone.

✔ **DON'T BE CAPTAIN INTERRUPTER.** Ever been in the midst of a stimulating conversation when some interloper jumps in and takes over with a completely inappropriate declaration? (Have *you* ever been that interloper?) At cocktail parties and events, people are apt to engage in long conversations with one another. Don't assume that if you are lurking nearby, you can just jump right in and interrupt. First, wait your turn. Pay attention to body language: if the person you want to speak with is avoiding eye contact or isn't giving you any indication that they're about to finish up with the other person and come and talk to you, move along to a new person. If you hover, you give off stalker vibes. If you miss the opportunity to network with someone, such as a key event speaker, follow up with them after the event via email or ask the person who organized the activity for a more formal introduction. When you follow up, let them know that you noticed they were busy at the event but that you still wanted to touch base with them on whatever subject you're interested in discussing. You might even find that you have a better interaction, because this person might have more time for you outside of a party setting.

✓ **DON'T PUT SOMEONE IN "THE CONFERENCE ROOM."** A networking occasion is a chance to mix and mingle. People arrive at functions at different times with different agendas. Don't back someone into a corner and make him or her feel obliged to spend the next two hours hearing about your career woes. Spend a few minutes chatting and then bow out. If time and situations allow, you both can circle back once you've both had a chance to work the room.

✓ **KNOW WHEN *NOT* TO TALK SHOP.** Uh oh: you're at an industry function where you expected to meet a lot of great contacts, and you find that people are talking about everything except business. Not so surprising, is it? Sometimes people want to relax and get off the topic of business. Don't get irritated; join in. Being a good networker doesn't mean you always have to talk biz. It means paying attention to the ebb and flow of the conversation. You can make just as great a connection talking about kids or sports as you can talking about business plans.

I'm at an industry cocktail party, when a casual-looking young man wearing, um, much-loved, "Chuck Taylor" Converse hi-top sneakers duct-taped together approaches me. (Rule #1: Don't dress like a pre-pubescent at a networking night.) Without introducing himself he says, "Yeah, I've been catching bits and pieces of your conversations with some other people here, and you give great advice. How about answering a couple of additional questions for me?" (Rule #2: Lines like this are fine. It shows that you are focused enough to find time to listen to me, that you absorb what is being said, and you aren't in my face asking questions during other people's time. It's also a nice setup to a potential conversation.) I smile and reply, "Of course." I then extend my hand for a handshake. That throws the fellow off guard, and as he backs away from me, he whispers his name and musters a limp handshake. (Rule #3: Learn basic introductions. I don't care if you have to practice in the mirror. And don't give me a dead-fish handshake just because I'm a woman.) As I ask about his interests, goals, and previous employment, he pulls a crumpled copy of his resume from the pocket of his cargo pants. (Rules #4 and 5: You can figure them out.) As we move through the usual basics, he breaks into a nervous sweat and begins edging into my personal space. When I ask him a specific (and easy) question about a project he worked on, he starts doing this weird little hop thing. Picture jumping jacks, arms flailing wildly. His whole baggy wardrobe defies the law of gravity. I look around in horror to see if anyone is watching (no one is). I must look like a deer in headlights because he stops on a dime and asks me a question. I mutter something along the lines of "Oh, I just heard someone call my name. Have fun tonight!" and make a break for it.

—TARA, ACCOUNT DIRECTOR

THE TRUTH ABOUT HEADHUNTERS

So you've been pounding the pavement for a while now, networking your brains out, but things just don't seem to be happening. Hmmm . . . maybe it's time to call a headhunter. After all, they're professional job finders, right? You plumb the dark recesses of your Rolodex and make a few calls to headhunters you haven't spoken to in a while. And—surprise, surprise—you hear nothing back. Animosity starts to fester in your cold, anguished heart. You whine: "Headhunters, they're useless . . . They never return my calls . . . Clearly they don't understand the tremendous value I can bring to the table!" Soon, an unparalleled loathing starts to develop. You're now certain that headhunters are keeping the prime jobs out of your reach! Paranoia sets in. Who do these people think they are anyway? *It's all the headhunter's fault!*

People! You're doing it again: looking at the world entirely through your own eyes. Remember what we've talked about—you've got to put yourself in the other guy's shoes if you're going to get anywhere. If you're like most job hunters, you probably think a headhunter's calling in life is to find you a job. Wrong! Think for a second: they're not

Don't Leave Home Without Them (Your Business Cards)

Picture this: you're at a cocktail party, and you meet a fantastic new business contact. At the conclusion of your conversation, your new business associate gives you his card. You, most impressively, scribble your contact information on the back of a soggy bar napkin or a book of matches. *Smooth move.* Get out of the pee-wee league and get yourself a business card. In today's transient work culture, a personal business card complete with your contact information, telephone number, and email address is something you need for the rest of your career (even if you just graduated college). Keep the information on your card up to date and make sure that it reflects your corporate identity.

While going high-end is always an option, getting a personal business card doesn't have to cost a fortune. For under thirty dollars you can choose from one of hundreds of preformatted styles at Staples or Office Depot—and they can be ready in under a week. If you're really broke, you can buy blank business cards at many office supply companies, design them in Microsoft Word, and then run them through your printer at home. Finally, there are a variety of sites on the web that will print a limited supply of business cards for free. The hitch: you pay the shipping and get their logo slapped on the back of the card.

Whenever you leave the house, always bring more business cards than you think you need. You always hear people complaining about how they ran out of them, not that they brought too many. Then, when you get the opportunity, hand them out two at a time. It's sort of like sending out a group email. Hopefully, your new contact will keep the first card (like an email), and then will forward the second card out to a new relevant business contact on your behalf. If the second card gets passed along, you win.

called "jobhunters," they're called "headhunters." They're hired and paid by companies that are looking for heads—like yours!

The only role of a headhunter (or "executive recruiter," as they invariably prefer to be called) is to find qualified candidates for their clients, the folks paying the bills. When a headhunter places a candidate, the headhunter earns a commission, generally ranging from fifteen to thirty-five percent of the candidate's first-year compensation. Sounds like big bucks, no whammies, no? But remember: the headhunter doesn't see dime number one if they don't fill the position. And in most searches, the headhunter doesn't have an exclusive on the position—they'll be up against other recruiting firms as well as their own clients' internal hiring efforts.

Yes, it's a dog-eat-dog world for the headhunter, and time is money—big money. Experienced recruiters can look at a job description from a client and sense almost instinctively what kind of resumes the client will want to see. They are not going to waste an instant of the client's time, or their own. They'll scan your resume in about ten seconds and decide whether you have a snowball's chance in hell. That's right: the headhunter is not going to employ extrasensory perception to look beyond your piece of paper and sense the wonderfulness of the inner you. If the job's not a fit for your work history, *you're* history.

This may be enough to send you shrieking back to the cozy comfort of cyberspace, where at least you can get ignored in the privacy of your own home. But the truth is that headhunters do, in fact, connect candidates with great jobs—executive recruiters or search firms actually place between ten to fifteen percent of all new hires, according to John Lewison, a director of human resources and past Executive Director of the New York State Society for Human Resource Management. So now that you know something about how the executive recruiting industry works, you're in a much better position to strategize how to work the system to your advantage.

You know the old saying "One hand washes the other"? You get headhunters to help you by helping them. Blasting out unsolicited resumes to a bunch of recruiters might benefit them *if* they just happen to have a search under way that's a perfect fit. But if there's not an immediate fit, you're unlikely to get any feedback. Maybe they'll keep you in mind, maybe they'll forget about you, but either way, they won't tell you where you stand. Why? Because unsolicited resumes like yours are a dime a dozen; they put you at the bottom of the food chain. You need to move up from bottom-feeder status to a level where headhunters know you as an individual and begin to look out for you.

To rise up the pecking order of headhunter-dom, you need to cultivate relationships with recruiters. This takes time and effort, but the dividends are tremendous. A good recruiter will introduce you to positions that you might not find out about on your own. Recruiters can give you "insider" information about the position and the company. They can coach you on improving your resume and enhancing your interviewing skills so that you have a better shot at landing a job. Best of all, they can help you negotiate with the client after you land an offer (the bigger your salary, the bigger their fee, right?).

Quality recruiters can size up a candidate in seconds. Pad your background, or try to bluff your way through a job description, and I'll know immediately.

—JASON, EXECUTIVE RECRUITER

Persistence is a good trait; don't let it become a bad one. If you've left someone a message and you call back a couple of hours later with the first words being "I left you a couple of messages, did you receive them?" or "You never seem to be at your desk," chances are you are going to put the recruiter off.

—PAOLO, EXECUTIVE RECRUITER

It's best to have about three headhunters, one from a large agency and two from boutique agencies, all working in your industry and discipline. If you have too many headhunters out there, your resume will start to look like wallpaper. So choose wisely and plan on spending time getting to know one another and building trust. Last, whenever you start a new position, always touch base with your trio of headhunters and let them know where you landed—that is, if they didn't already help you get the job.

—KELLY, EXECUTIVE RECRUITER SPECIALIZING IN SALES AND TRADING

So how do you develop a mutually beneficial relationship with a head-hunter? First, start figuring out which headhunters you want to work with. Many recruiting firms specialize in a certain industry or a cluster of a few industries. Others focus on particular functions, like information technology, sales, or finance. Some work only with very senior managers or entry-level candidates. You need to research which recruiters will be most useful by asking colleagues in your field. When broaching the subject with your co-workers, of course, you're gathering all this info for a college buddy (wink, wink, nudge, nudge). Ask clients and vendors which recruiters they've used in the past.

It also pays to be out and about. Headhunters can often be found prospecting for clients and "heads" at industry functions—introduce yourself. The web is also a robust resource for finding headhunters. Do searches on the Big Boards that specify "Staffing Firms only" or "Recruiting Firms only." Read the fine print of the Help Wanted pages of your local paper to identify recruiting firms in your area and field. After a short time spent studying these sources, you'll start to see which recruiters tend to have the jobs that you want. Once you've established a hearty recruiter list, start contacting them. *Warning:* prepare to deal with rejection. During the contact period, you may find that you don't even get return phone calls or emails back from the headhunters that you contact. The headhunters you're approaching may not be recruiting someone with your talents right now. Instead of feeling insulted, consider that they don't want to waste their time—or yours! Finding a suitable headhunter is far more Darwinian than Machiavellian. There aren't any ulterior motives at work. It's simply survival of the fittest.

The best time to establish recruiter relationships is when you're gainfully employed. (What's true in love is true in employment: you're never so attractive as when you're unavailable!) The best thing you can do for yourself is to pick up the phone when a headhunter calls, even if you're thrilled with your current job. Things change! Chat with headhunters and get an understanding of the marketplace. Always be cordial and appreciative; you may not be so happy in your job the next time they call you about a position. Taking a call doesn't mean you're committing treason; you're simply establishing a dialogue, no strings attached. If you're not interested in the position they're talking about, offer to keep your eyes and ears open for them. Let the recruiters know about acquaintances and colleagues that are in the market. If you help them make a nice fat commission, you're golden.

Once you click with a headhunter, you'll most likely be invited to do an informational interview. Treat this as a vital part of the relationship-building process. Your little "meet and greet" is a chance for the headhunter not only to learn more about your needs, aspirations, and capabilities, but also to apply the "smell test": do you present yourself well? Do you dress the part? Do you employ basic hygienic practices? During the interview, you should come across as confident but not an egomaniac. Every communication, every meeting, every phone call, every email will re-shuffle the deck either for you or against you. So pay attention to what you're doing. All the basics still apply: send a thank-you note, follow up, and stay informed.

Headhunters have a mandate from their clients to find the best candidates for the position. If a recruiter becomes confident in your abilities and psyched about you as a candidate, they'll spend more time pitching you to their client. The most important thing that you can do is convince the headhunter that you have what it takes.

Once a headhunter becomes one of your fans, take advantage of that. Work with them to sharpen your interviewing skills. Pick their brains about which companies are hiring. Because headhunters have a strong understanding of their client's needs, they may be able to answer questions about corporate culture and strategize with you about how best to make inroads with the people who will eventually interview you. The more you approach the job seeker-headhunter relationship as a partnership, the more you'll get out of it and the greater the trust you'll build.

It's impossible to develop mutually beneficial partnerships with more than a few recruiters, so don't spread yourself too thinly. If you use too many, you may find your headhunters running into each other when they pitch you to the same client. This happens all the time and makes you look a little shady. To get to a short list of three or four headhunters that you'll partner closely with, you'll most likely need to contact about sixty headhunters. That gives you a response rate of about five percent. Sure, it takes a lot of elbow grease to make the initial contact, but you're working toward a payoff that can last throughout your career. Once you've identified a few headhunters who cover your industry and whose style you like, start building a relationship with them.

Pssst . . . follow instructions. When a headhunter asks you to re-word or update something on your resume, do it. Most likely they know something about the client that you don't. They're not trying to load you up with extra work; they are trying to help you get the job. If you blow off their suggestions, expect the same treatment in return. Ouch.

Once you agree to work through a headhunter, keep in mind that they will coordinate all interviews and meetings with the hiring company. Always keep your headhunter well informed of any client contact during the interview process. For example, let the headhunter know when a client calls you directly and blind copy them on emails you send to the client. An informed headhunter is the best head-hunter.

And for goodness sakes, *never, never, never* "end run" your head-hunters. The absolute worst thing you can do is go around your head-hunter's back and contact the client directly. The headhunter's whole job is to act as the go-between. If they have even the slightest suspicion that they are getting cut out of the process (and maybe their pay-check) you will make them very, very angry. You might think you look like a real go-getter, but you actually look like a real idiot. The client and the headhunter have an established procedure and you need to follow it.

A headhunter can float your resume, pitch you over the phone, and send follow-up emails, but ultimately the client makes the decision on whom they interview and whom they hire. This also means that sometimes a headhunter has to deliver bad news. Maybe the client didn't select you to be interviewed. Or maybe another candidate was

The Headhunter Hit List

To get the most out of working with a headhunter, you've got to play by their rules or you're done for. Here's how:

- **Remember that they are not there to help you find yourself.** If you're in the middle of a career crisis, get a coach or a counselor or even a shrink, but definitely not a headhunter. Sending mixed signals about what you want to be when you grow up will most certainly get you a "don't call us, we'll call you" response.
- **Stay focused.** A recruiter does not want to hear that you are a jack-of-all-trades. (Did you know that that's only half of the old saying? The entire phrase is, "Jack of all trades, Master of none.") All the recruiter needs to know is that you have the right personality and can actually do the work required of the job. You won't get the call if you look like a cook with fifty spoons in the pot.
- **If you're a square peg, move on.** If you're going to use a headhunter, make sure that you fit into their niche. They have no time for candidates who kind of, sort of, maybe fit.
- **Be assertive—not annoying.** A headhunter has to work at their client's pace, not yours. So don't be a nudge. It will happen when it happens and not a minute sooner.
- **Always debrief.** Following up is always good protocol. Make a call to your headhunter after every interview and give them the play-by-play. If you debrief them, they might be able to gain insight for you when they touch base with the client.

selected. It's not your headhunter's fault that you didn't get to the next level, so don't take your disappointment out on them. By no means should a little bad news end your relationship with the headhunter. If you're professional about handling the situation, they won't hesitate to pick up the phone and call you the next time they get a position that fits your background.

> I had the perfect candidate lined up for a position at a mutual fund. All I had to do was give the client the green light and set up the interview. Before I ever got the chance, this candidate went ahead and contacted my client directly, without telling me. I was pissed. My client later complained about how he felt put on the spot by this hyper-aggressive candidate. I called the candidate and, without trepidation, I informed him that he was being deleted permanently from my database!
>
> —DAVE, HEADHUNTER

> The hardest thing about doing my job is rejecting people. For better or worse, many decisions at the hiring-manager level are based on chemistry. It's no more fun rejecting a candidate than it is rejecting a suitor after the fourth date—especially after a super expensive dinner at a fancy restaurant.
>
> —NANCY, HEADHUNTER

NOW GO WORK IT!

Here's the Takeaway:

- Networking is a numbers game. Whether you're a natural or not, you need to work at it all the time in order for it to pay off.

- Have a clue. Be confident, respect other people's time, and follow up effectively.

- Networking is a two-way street. Don't always be a taker. Look for every chance to be a giver as well.

- Networking is all about the "six degrees": the person who knows someone who knows someone who knows . . . Start figuring out where your connections are by creating a master list of people you know, starting with your inner circle of family and friends, and find out whom they know.

- Build your network by seeking out opportunities to connect with people, such as industry events, clubs, alumni organizations, and activities within your present company.

- Maximize your networking potential (and gain valuable experience) by taking leadership roles within the organizations you join.

- Headhunters are the ultimate networkers. Understand how they operate, build mutually beneficial relationships with a few good ones over time, and they'll be one of your most valuable resources.

Part II:

BACK TO BASICS

5

Lose the McResume:

Five-Star Resumes for a Fast-Food World

I'll take a number five, with cheese! If creating a resume were as easy as selecting a Value Meal at Mickey D's, we'd all be rich and success-ful. Unfortunately, if your resume reads like a fast-food menu (high in calories and low in nutrients), no one is going to supersize your pay-check. Face it: the sole purpose of a resume is to get you an interview. It's that first impression that will get you in the door. Most people, however, just dust off their old resume, paste in their most recent work experience, and zap it out. Any more work than that is . . . too much work. And then they wonder why they don't get called in for an interview.

After your resume enters a company, it takes on a life of its own. It will be reviewed, compared against other resumes, and passed around, all without your being present to defend it. That means it needs to be not only an accurate dossier of your work history, but also a document that will position you for the company and the opportu-nity. If you're not getting the interviews you feel you deserve, con-sider that it may be that piece of paper, and not your background, that is holding you back. It's a tall order to transform a flat sheet of paper into an enticing story for a prospective employer, but that's exactly what you'll learn to do in this chapter. Get ready for a resume makeover. It will leave prospective employers energized about meet-ing you, instead of giving them indigestion.

BUILD A MASTER RESUME

In order to make the greatest possible impact on potential employers, you need to create a different resume for each job to which you apply. Giving up the one-size-fits-all approach may sound like a nightmare, but it'll be smooth sailing if you start with a "Master Resume." Think of your Master Resume as your very own professional memoir, a place to archive and document all of your work experiences. It should include all the information from which you will eventually create many customized resumes (more on that later). It should describe in detail all of your jobs and responsibilities, key projects, success stories, promotions, and major achievements, both professional and personal.

Don't get bogged down with the look and feel of your Master Resume. It's meant to be a continuous work in progress, for your eyes only. That means that it should be comprehensive: the more information the better (unlike the polished resume you would send to a hiring manager, which should contain only a carefully selected subset of your Master Resume). If you've never built a Master Resume before, it will be easiest to start with your most recent work experience, since that will be freshest in your mind. From there, work backward and try to capture all of your work experiences in detail. Be sure to include the following:

- Job descriptions from all your former employers
  - Specific duties
  - Start and end dates for positions and projects

- Special project highlights
  - *Your* contributions to these projects
  - Project results (both quantitative and qualitative)
  - Impressive statistics (e.g., percentage increases in sales, total cost savings)
  - Challenges that were unique to the effort
  - Skills attained

- Promotions and raises
  - Copies of performance reviews
  - Compensation increases (total values and percentage increases)

- Managers and co-workers for each position and project
  - Work, home, and mobile phone numbers
  - Work and personal email addresses

- Education and training
  - Degrees and achievements
  - On-the-job training
  - Special and related skills (certifications, software proficiency, etc.)

- Personal achievements
  - Charity work, fund-raising
  - Special awards
  - Athletics/hobbies

Once you've gathered all the initial information for your Master Resume, update it on a regular basis. Whether you're job hunting or not, it's important to revise it each time you complete a project or achievement so you don't forget essential details. You should also make entries each quarter and after your annual review. Each time you finish a project get contact information from the managers and clients you worked with. Think about it: someday you might need these honchos as a reference. (Just remember to keep in touch with these folks at least bi-annually, so that they don't forget about you.)

Even if you're not actively looking for a job, your Master Resume will serve you well at review time or when you're up for a raise or promotion. Unlike your slacker co-workers, you'll be able to build your case for a raise or a dynamite performance review by assembling a checklist of all your accomplishments for the past year. Now, that's ammo worth stocking.

THE SKINNY: Be your own champion. Instead of looking for a new job at a new company, why not find one at your current company? The best way to gun for a promotion is to let your boss know about your achievements as they happen. At a lot of companies, decisions can be made long before you have your annual review with the big cheese. Managers can only digest so much information at a time. If you hold off on tooting your own horn until the exact moment you're due for a promotion, you might get passed over.

As a management consultant interested in moving into the fashion industry (and willing to take a salary cut), I was fairly confident that fashion firms would jump at the chance to hire me. Boy was I wrong. I applied to numerous fashion positions for which I felt overqualified. Nevertheless, I never got callbacks from any of them.

Only after a friend suggested that I scale down my resume, omitting information that made me look too smart for the position, did I get interviews and offers for entry-level jobs in fashion.

Lesson learned: a hiring manager may get suspicious if you seem over qualified and too impressive for an entry-level position.

–BOAZ, BUSINESS MANAGER

. . . NOW CUSTOMIZE

Now that your Master Resume is complete, it's time to cook up a Customized Resume. Think of yourself as the head chef. Your Master Resume will serve as your "cookbook," a reference manual that will allow you to create savory resumes that will whet the appetites of prospective employers. When you set out to craft a Customized Resume, it's as if you're preparing a special entrée for each job you want to land.

Before you start "cooking," think long and hard about what work experiences will most likely leave prospective employers licking their chops and hungry to meet with you. Compare the employer's job description to your own work experience. Highlight aspects of your track record that best meet the hiring manager's needs. Refer to your Master Resume often and select experiences and accomplishments that are most relevant to the position you're seeking. Don't make a hiring manager guess whether or not you're qualified for the job they're offering. Prove that you meet the requirements using specific examples from your past experience, and you will significantly increase your chances of standing out as a candidate worthy of an interview. While it may initially seem like a lot of extra work, a Customized Resume will really pay off, because it makes the hiring manager's job easier.

> I work at an investment bank where lots of deals get done. And when I interview someone, I dig deep to figure out what they did or did not do. When it comes to work history, the best rule of thumb is to speak confidently about everything on your resume. If you're going to put something on your resume, even from five years ago, you better refresh yourself before you walk into an interview with me. If you can't remember what you did, or your participation on a project or deal was so minor that it's not relevant—get it off your resume. You may think that padding your resume will impress me; trust me—it won't. Once the stammering starts, that's the gotcha moment, and then you don't have a chance in hell of getting hired.
>
> —SANDY, INVESTMENT BANKER

RESUME MAKEOVER: BIGGER ISN'T BETTER

Most job seekers tend to load up their resume with too much information, causing recruiters to roll their eyes in despair. Just because you *can* "supersize" your resume doesn't mean you *should.* It's time to trade in your high-fat, low-nutrient resume for a slimmer, sexier one that will leave prospective employers salivating for more. Hiring managers want to read about your capabilities and achievements, but only as they relate to the job at hand. So be selective about the details you include and stick to what's most relevant and impressive, nothing more. Cover in most detail the work you've performed most re-cently or that is most pertinent to the job that you're trying to land. Bottom line: if you leave the reader wanting more, they'll have to in-terview you!

Make sure that your writing style is consistent throughout your re-sume. Most people are in the bad habit of inserting their most recent job into their resume and sending it out without re-reading the entire resume and seeing how the new material flows with their previous work experience. Ideally, you want each and every assignment listed on your resume to reflect your uniqueness as a candidate. The best way to do this is to lead off each job description and bullet point with action-oriented verbs. Use present tense verbs to describe your posi-tion at your current employer (i.e., "lead," "oversee," "run," "strate-gize," "implement") and past tense verbs for your former employers ("led," "oversaw," "ran," "strategized," "implemented"). An added ben-efit: when you start with a verb, you will cut out irrelevant text at the beginning of each sentence.

HR people are plain, simple people; write your resume in plain, sim-ple English. Keep away from the thesaurus. Fancy words that you think make you sound smart will only make the reader feel like you are trying to baffle them with your yet-to-be-proven brilliance. Industry jargon, in particular, comes across on a resume as inane and pompous (two traits you really don't want to convey). Your attempt to sound im-pressive may backfire if an HR person can't figure out what you do.

Limit your customized resume to one page for each decade you've worked professionally. Any more than that, and they'll think you suf-fer from delusions of grandeur or the inability to edit yourself. Where can you trim? Cut down on your descriptions of your earliest posi-tions, and don't list aspects of your job that won't be relevant to the hiring manager. A one-pager demonstrates your ability to prioritize and maintain focus in the workplace—a highly commendable trait.

A one-page resume doesn't give you license to cram as much copy as you possibly can onto that page. As you're cutting text, you also need to make room throughout your resume for precious white space so that your resume isn't a beast to read. Recruiters have been known to throw resumes in the trash just because they're too text-heavy. To get a range of ideas, spend time reviewing the resumes of friends and colleagues. If you have a friend who's a graphic designer, bribe him or her to lay out your resume for you.

You should establish a consistent look and feel for your resume. For example, if you're going to use boldface for your company's name, then you need to use boldface for the company name of each firm where you've worked. Or, if you're going to italicize the start and end dates for each position, you need to do this for every position you've held. Also, once you've chosen a font, stick with it. Bold it, italicize it, but don't stray from it. Use it not only on your resume, but also on your cover letter and any thank-you notes you send as follow-up correspondence. These rules may seem nitpicky, but consistency is noticed by recruiters and hiring managers alike.

White Space Rules!

Here are a few basic rules for adding white space to your resume:

- Margins should be set at one inch on all sides. Do not go below three-quarters of an inch.
- Justify the alignment so that the text on the right doesn't look jagged.
- Use double space between each company you've worked at and one and a half spaces between each position you've held at a particular company.
- Point size should be readable. The ideal size is 11 to 12 point. Never go smaller than 9 point.
- Sans serif fonts like Arial and Geneva are more condensed and will help you squeeze an extra line or two into your resume.
- Don't bother listing "References furnished upon request"—it's a given if you get that far along on an interview.
- Still not enough white space? Keep cutting, and cutting, and cutting . . .

THE SKINNY: Don't get lost in the shuffle. If you absolutely have to use more than one page for your resume, number each page. This will help a hiring manager keep track of all your information, especially if page one gets orphaned from page two.

THE SKINNY: Try the parental litmus test. Before you send your customized resume out into the cruel world, present it to your folks and have them read it. If after reading it they understand what you do, you're safe. If they have no clue (beyond their usual cluelessness), then it's back to the drawing board to lose the industry lingo and simplify the wording.

> People often throw around management buzz words to make themselves sound current with popular trends. When pressed, I usually find out that they only know the buzzwords themselves, nothing about the subject matter. It turns me from thinking very positively about them to wondering what else on the resume is meaningless.
>
> —DAVE, GENERAL MANAGER AND CHEMICAL ENGINEER

KEYWORDS ARE KEY

Don't make your Customized Resume a scavenger hunt. Recruiters don't have time to play along. Gone are the days of recruiters sifting through thousands of faxes and hand-filing them away for the future. They can now use keyword searches to zip through thousands of resumes at warp speed and pull out only those that have the exact requirements they're looking for. Take note: if your Customized Resume doesn't contain the right keywords, it will never be read. To improve your chances of getting your resume reviewed for a particular job, try to anticipate the keywords the employer might use and include them in your customized resume. For example, if a job requires proficiency in a certain software program and you have it, list it under your related skills. Or say a job is based in New York; a recruiter might do a search of New York resumes first. If you live in California but wouldn't mind moving to New York, write, "Willing to relocate to New York" in your objective statement. This way your resume will get picked up by the keyword search.

If you really want to lead the reader's eye to the important stuff, make keywords, phrases, or titles stand out. You can try bold or italic type, enlarged fonts, or a different, yet complementary font. Ultimately, you want a hiring manager to be able to do a quick scan of your resume, top to bottom, and have an immediate understanding of what you can do for him or her.

> My resume is a quick read: bullet points of my major achievements and responsibilities at each firm where I've worked. Behind each bullet, however, is a full five- to seven-minute story of my success and development. (I save those stories for the interview.)
>
> —DAVID, PHARMACEUTICAL SALESPERSON

BUILD A TEMPLATE

A Customized Resume doesn't have to be a chore to build, especially if you make things easy on yourself by creating a template of basic information that won't change from one customized resume to the next. Save the template as its own file on your computer, and use it as the starting point for each Customized Resume going forward. The template you set up should include the following:

- Personal contact information

- Employer names, locations, brief company descriptions, dates worked, your titles

- Education, graduation dates, degrees, honors

- Related skills, software proficiency, etc.

Since your resume can lie dormant in a recruiter's database for years, make sure that your personal contact information will stand the test of time. Never use your current work telephone number or email address on your resume. Only use your home or cell phone number and an email address that can be set up for the sole purpose of job hunting. Ideally, this information will stay current for at least the next two to three years.

Always list the company name in full and the location where you worked. If you work at a subsidiary of a larger, well-known company, put the subsidiary name first, followed by the parent company's name in parentheses. Even if you work (or worked) at a Fortune 500 company, don't assume that a hiring manager will be familiar with what that company does. To remove ambiguity, include a brief company description of each company where you've worked—even if you think it's overkill. The description should immediately follow the company name. Here are a few examples:

- Dewey Ballantine, Law Firm

- Cap Gemini, Management Consulting Firm

- Sephora, Cosmetics Retailer

On a resume, chronology counts. It's always best to list your most recent position at the top of your resume followed by each previous position. This demonstrates how your career has progressed over time. Functional resumes, which go in and out of vogue, force hiring managers to spend extra time figuring out where you worked when. They can make it look like you're trying to hide something, even if you're not. Generally, your education should go at the bottom of your resume, unless you're pursuing an academic or policy career (or you went to Harvard Business School).

Tricks like only listing the calendar year during which you worked at a company or omitting the months from your start and end dates will instantly make recruiters suspicious. It's better to be honest and forthright in your description. Many resume scanners look for full dates in employment history like January 2003 or 1/2003 instead of January 03 or 1/03. So be careful.

Quirky job titles like Minister of Fun, irritatingly popular during the late 1990s, might be harmful to your job hunt now. When a hiring manager does a keyword search, they're not going to enter a funky title like "Head Bean Counter" into their search engine—they're going to use the common, industry-standard ones, like "Chief Financial Officer" or "CFO" or "Finance Director" or "Controller." An unusual title may confuse a hiring manager about what your job was (or is) in the real world. If you feel you must use your New-Agey title, put a more business-like equivalent next to it in parentheses. For example: "Chief Talent Maven (Director of Recruiting)."

An unusual phenomenon happened during the most recent economic boom: suddenly twentysomethings who were normally forced into entry-level-job hell were promoted into decision-making positions and given hefty titles to go along with the job. If you fall into this category, you might now be experiencing reverse age discrimination as you go out to look for new jobs with your inflated titles. Keep in mind that many of the people making the hiring decisions are from—imagine menacing Darth Vader voice-over—"the old school." This is the crowd that had to walk twenty miles to work in the freezing rain and slowly climb the corporate ladder. Quite simply, they'll look at a twenty-four-year-old with a Director title as a young whippersnapper who's never truly paid their dues. This isn't your fault, but alas, you have to live in this world. To survive this reverse discrimination, search for jobs that match the experience that you've earned and the amount of time that you've worked, not the job title you've held. Also consider "deflating" your title on the resume to one that is more in line with your age and experience. For example, if you were the director of marketing at your small startup, you might want to use a title like "Marketing Manager" on your resume.

Now for the Secret Weapon

Once you've finished building the template, you can now start pluck-ing information from your Master Resume and assembling a Cus-tomized Resume that presents you as the ultimate candidate. Don't get lazy and start mechanically cutting and pasting. If you really want to get invited to an interview, you must be willing to tailor your resume to each specific opportunity that you're being considered for. That may mean re-writing and editing job descriptions that will draw attention to your most relevant experience. The information that should change regularly from one resume to the next will be objective statements, job descriptions, and related skills and interests.

If you're going to the trouble of creating a Customized Resume, spend the extra time to create a targeted objective statement, too. It's a good way to indicate to the recipient, right off the bat, that you've done your homework and have tailored yourself to meet their needs. A rambling objective statement will be the kiss of death. Keep yours short and to the point: one to two lines at most. And make sure it has, well, an objective. Your objective statement shouldn't be about what a company can do for you. Use it to summarize what you can do for them.

For example, if you live in Chicago and are applying for a position in San Francisco, make your intentions clear in your objective state-ment (and also when you write your cover letter). This demonstrates that you are ready, willing, and able to relocate. Also, never rant: keep your personal philosophy about what corporate cultures should be like out of your objective statement.

Objective statements can be irritating, particularly dumb ones like, "I want to learn, grow, develop, etc." People need to understand that a resume should tell me about what you can do for me, not what I can do for you.

—Ellen, In-House Corporate Recruiter

You're not a pre-packaged value meal! Job seekers regularly make the crucial mistake of not re-tooling their previous job descriptions for the jobs to which they're currently applying. To a hiring manager, this is the most important part of a resume. Now is the time to make use of all information you archived on your Master Resume and use it to your fullest advantage. Review each job description and figure out what aspects of your previous work history will make you a stand-out candidate for *this* job.

Your updated job descriptions should be clear and concise, not bloated. Put down enough information to get you invited to the interview, where you can share all the background details. While you need to make your job descriptions sound enticing, exaggerated ones will come back to haunt you. (Ever heard of a reference check?)

Instead of making your job descriptions read like a laundry list, highlight projects you've handled and your contributions to those projects. Include facts, figures, and percentages that demonstrate results and achievements. For example, if you saved your last firm $100,000 because of a project you implemented, or if you increased sales by twenty-five percent during your tenure, include these numbers—they'll catch recruiters' eyes.

When a company lists a particular skill that is a requirement to land the job, and you have that skill, list it! Recruiters, while quite talented, have not perfected the art of mind-reading. Don't wait until the interview to share important information—you may never get there! Include proficiency in any basic software packages, special training that you've received, and other skills that might make you an even more useful candidate, such as knowledge of foreign languages.

Interviewers love to see dynamic and interesting things on a candidate's resume, and the Interests section can be a great place to make yourself truly memorable. Your outside interests can help a hiring manager determine if you'll be a good overall fit at the company. Don't be afraid to dedicate precious white space to a non-work-experience entry on your resume—this could be the very material that wins you the job! The more creative you get about telling the story of who you are, the more memorable you'll be to everyone with whom you interview. Just be careful about seeming too eccentric. Pick interests that you think hiring managers will consider achievement-oriented, not bizarre.

Take a look at two different ways a person might document their personal interests.

Personal Interests: Biking, Travel, and Volunteerism

Versus:

Personal Interests:

Volunteerism Advocate: In 1995, started new Habitat for Humanity chapter on an Indian reservation in New Mexico; still coordinate yearly retreat to reservation.

Avid Biker: Traveled to Paris in Summer 1999, biked Tour de France route solo.

Maybe It's Time to Join Job Hoppers Anonymous

Chronic job-hopping can raise serious "red flags" about company loyalty and work ethic. Whether you quit, were fired, or were laid off, it's a real issue that you may have to contend with the next time you interview. If you've held several short-term positions in a row, rethink how you might list them on your resume. Perhaps you could list them as "consulting" assignments (but only if someone on the inside will vouch for your work). If you worked on a great project, then list what you achieved during the experience. If you left a company after only a couple of months, you may not want to list it on your resume at all.

Hiring managers want to determine whether you will be a strong and committed player. To compensate, you should try to emphasize your loyalty quotient in other ways, such as by showing a track record of active charitable or community service work.

Be Three-Dimensional

I've interviewed people just because of what they write down for their personal interests. The most memorable interests that I've seen include firewalker, trapeze artist, and my personal favorite, "Will play pickup basketball with anyone, anytime, anywhere."

—Quint, Portfolio Manager

My biggest issues are with people who include excessive info about themselves on their resume, like religious beliefs, sexual orientation, or how many pet lizards they have.

—Zak, Director of Sales

It's always helpful to put something eye-grabbing on your resume. I busted on my friend for writing "Discovery Channel" under an "Interests" sub-heading. However, that nugget actually landed him his job because his future boss said, "I love the Discovery Channel." Personally, I include my brief internship at Rolling Stone on my resume even though it was a million years ago and has little to do with anything I do, because every time I interview the first thing they ask is "What was Rolling Stone like?" Tidbits like that sure beat boring highlights like "Can type 55 words/minute," "Hobbies: reading," and "Experienced with Microsoft Word."

—Kenneth, Reporter

I once received a resume that at the very end had the disturbing line "Saved a human life" added to it. The candidate was an acquaintance of my associate, but I still refused to even interview him. Some people might find it intriguing, but I found it unsettling and it turned me off. I would question the integrity and character of someone who wanted to market an event such as that to an employer.

—Anna Patricia, Hiring Manager

T H E   S K I N N Y : School's out . . . forever! You loved attending your alma mater (those *were* the glory days). By the time you land your second job out of college, you'd better hope you have some new achievements to put on your resume. Sorry pal, it may be time to delete those collegiate roles like "Rush Chair, Delta Delta Delta."

> After the name, the first thing I read on someone's resume is the objective. If it's dull and/or pointless, I'm done reading.
>
> —JESSICA, LEGAL RECRUITER

T H E   S K I N N Y : **When to use a web-based resume.** Here's something that may come as a surprise: most hiring managers and HR people hate it when applicants send an email with a hyperlink to their web-based resume. It's especially bad if your email doesn't even contain a cover letter, merely "Hey, I'm the guy/gal you want, everything you need to know is on www.smarmygit.com." But even if you write a nice cover letter/email and list a hyperlink to your resume, you may still rub some people the wrong way. Why? (1) It looks showoffy. If you're an HTML whiz, put that fact on your resume. (2) You should be customizing your resume for each position you apply for, not showing everybody the same generic C.V. (3) What if your recipient wants to read his email offline?

You should only refer a recruiter to your web site if it's worth the trip; say, to show them your portfolio of web site pages or graphic designs, or to direct them to lengthy case studies you've written or articles you're quoted in. If all you're offering is a garden-variety resume, they'll be much happier to get an ordinary email attachment.

RUN IT THROUGH THE WRINGER

Once you've completed your Customized Resume, you're ready to do your first review. As you look over your work, be sure to ask yourself the following: Have I accurately described each work experience? Have I proven that I meet the minimum requirements of the position? Can I confidently respond if I'm pressed to give more information? If the answer to each of these questions is yes, you're ready to put the finishing touches on your Customized Resume and get it out the door. If you think you can do better, it's back to the drawing board for additional tweaking until you get it right.

Before you share your resume with employers, invite some close buds, who will be brutally honest, over to a resume pow-wow (you supply the beer). Before they start to tear it apart (not literally), ask them to try the "One-Minute Scan Test"—take an initial sixty-second peek at it. Once the minute is up, ask them a few pointed questions about what they learned about you and your work experience. Your goal is to see how much they were able to glean. Really listen to what they have to say, and if your key points aren't sticking in their heads, you need to re-work your resume. The experience will be cathartic, highly fruitful, and quite humbling. If your friends deliver a harsh critique, don't get defensive. Instead, look at it as an opportunity to correct a problem that needs fixing. In the end, you'll end up with a much better resume than the one you started with.

You may have the perfect qualifications, but your chances of landing a job will evaporate if your resume is riddled with typos and spelling errors. To recruiters, this indicates a lack of attention to detail. Always do a spell check after every revision, but remember that spell checkers are not foolproof. Also, look for layout problems like offset margins or spacing issues. If you're a poor speller, sweet-talk a friend or colleague who has a penchant for prose into reviewing it for you. If no one's around to do a copyedit for you, try reading your resume backward from the bottom up. (This forces you to look at each word and reduces your tendency to skim-read.) Spell-check every cover email before you hit the Send button.

If you work on your resume or other job search documents at work during your lunch hour, be anal about saving them on disks, instead of your hard drive. Remember, your work computer is the property of your company, so your privacy is not assured, and some companies will can you immediately if they catch you preparing to jump ship. Besides, if you get terminated unexpectedly, you don't want to lose access to the valuable documents and databases you need to find a new job. No one is to be trusted except you!

> I wrote "baking" instead of "banking" once. That slippery little sucker of an "n" that both the spell checker and I missed made the objective on my resume read something like "Looking for a challenging position in the baking industry, to utilize my excellent quantitative skills and financial background, blah, blah, blah . . ." which baffled the headhunter somewhat.
>
> —JADE, RESEARCH ANALYST

> My very first interview was for this big financial editing job at a bank. I even had to get someone to pull strings to get me the interview. So, I sit down with the senior editor, and she just starts circling and circling all these spelling and grammatical errors on my resume. After a few minutes, she said, "It was nice to meet you. I don't think being an editor is the job for you." And the interview was over.
>
> —MARNI, FASHION MERCHANDISER

GET ON THE A-TEAM

When a hiring manager receives your resume they need to size it up quickly and decide which pile it will land on. The "A" pile is for standout candidates: "Let's do a phone or face-to-face interview with this person as soon as possible." The "B" pile puts you in limbo: "Not bad, but let's see if we get enough better resumes before we interview this one." The "C" pile puts you directly in the circular file: "Send this one to the trash." Harsh? Yes. Realistic? Absolutely. Before you email, fax, or mail, consider how the person on the receiving end will react to the information you choose and the way you present it on your resume.

Every time you send out your resume, ask yourself, "Am I doing everything in my power to ensure that my resume lands in the A pile?" If you can confidently say Yes, you're one step ahead of most everyone else applying for the job and that much closer to getting invited to an interview. So don't get discouraged if you don't immediately get positive results; this is a process of trial and error, and the peculiar predilections of hiring managers ultimately rule. Just remember that different people look for different things in a resume, and even if you wrote the best damn resume possible for the job, it still might end up in someone's C pile.

Bear in mind also that the first go-through of building these tools will be rough. But it'll get easier once your Master Resume gets filled out and you get more comfortable creating Customized ones. Just re-

Top 10 Resume Pet Peeves

1. Spelling errors and typos
2. Long, multi-page resumes
3. Disorganized information
4. Unexplained chronological gaps
5. Employment end-dates that are missing
6. Buzzwords and industry jargon
7. Poor presentation/layout
8. Misrepresentation of responsibilities
9. Pointless (and endless) objectives
10. Resumes written in the third person

member that all this work will be worth it when you land the job of your dreams.

NOW GO WORK IT!

Here's the Takeaway:

- Your resume is what gets you in the door for most job openings. Nothing kills your chances faster than a generic resume that doesn't speak directly to the needs of each position you pursue. That means every resume must be customized for the opportunity.

- To begin customizing your resumes for each job you go after, start with a Master Resume—a full-blown list of every job, skill, accomplishment, and attribute, arranged in chronological order.

- The Customized Resume is a selection of relevant items from your Master Resume, chosen, crafted, and tailored to make you look like the perfect candidate for whatever job you are seeking.

- The Master Resume and each Customized Resume should follow certain rules of style: use action verbs, avoid jargon, keep it readable.

- Make an effort to limit your resume to one page for each decade of work experience. Don't pad; excessive length does not impress.

- Quirky dot-com era job titles are out. Go old school, and use titles that tell a prospective employer what you were really doing.

- Get friends, family members, etc., to eyeball your resume and offer critiques. It's too important a document to depend solely on your own judgment.

- Proofread thoroughly. Most hiring managers are unforgiving of typos and grammatical errors on a resume.

6

THE LOST ART OF CORRESPONDENCE:

You Are What You Write

It's fast, cheap and oh, so easy: email is fast becoming the leading cause of dysfunctional correspondence in the United States. No longer do people write, call, or fax—everyone emails their brains out. According to the International Data Corporation, a research firm based in Framingham, MA, the typical businessperson handles an average of seventy emails a day. All this lackluster emailing can cause the law of diminishing returns to kick in, making you complacent and ultimately preventing you from writing strong and persuasive job-related correspondence. So if job offers aren't pouring in for you, maybe it's time to evaluate whether your lousy correspondence habits have anything to do with it.

Be warned: a badly written email can make even the most qualified candidate look unprofessional, and thus unhireable. But there's a silver lining: given how widespread these bad habits are, most of the applicants you'll compete against will write horrible cover letters and thank-you notes (that is, if they even write them at all). Hiring managers love to hear from these lazy-ass applicants because they're incredibly easy to eliminate. What does this mean for you? Opportunity!

In this chapter, you'll learn to fix bad habits and start writing stand-out correspondence that would make even Miss Manners proud. You'll learn how to use prose to distinguish yourself as a leading candidate. And you'll no longer think of sending follow-up letters as a hassle, but rather as a way to leave other candidates crying for their mommies.

THE COVER LETTER: THAT'S YOU IN A NUTSHELL

The first piece of correspondence a prospective employer or head-hunter sees will be your cover letter. If it sucks, the chances of getting your resume read will be somewhere between slim and none. And you can say "sayonara" to that job opportunity.

Remember your corporate identity (go directly to Chapter 3)? Think of the cover letter as the recruiter's first look at who you are and what you can deliver. First, you have to make your pitch: why you're the best person for the job and why you'll be a great success if hired. Second, you have to back up those claims by presenting relevant experiences and attributes that prove you meet the key qualifications and are ready to hit the ground running. Third, you have to entice the recruiter to take action and call you in for an interview. That's a lot for one simple letter to accomplish, and that's why writing cover letters is just about the most difficult job-hunting task to do effectively. Luckily, there's a ten-point formula to help you create whiz-bang cover letters every time.

THE 10 COMMANDMENTS OF COVER LETTERS

1. **KEEP IT SHORT AND SWEET.** Make sure that your cover letter is succinct and easy to read. Say what you need to say without embellishing, and keep it well under one page in length. Chances are that if it's boring for you to write, it'll be a chore to read. However, don't take this advice too far: "Attached is my resume for your review" ain't a cover letter, Jack.

2. **TAILOR IT.** Just as a McResume screams "This applicant is a loser," a form letter disguised as a "unique" cover letter won't fool an HR pro. Get with the program and take the time to tailor your cover letters. Lose the "Dear Human Resources Director" salutation along with its ever-so-lame siblings "To whom

it may concern" and "Dear Sir or Madam," and make the effort to find out the hiring manager's name. (Get the correct spelling while you're at it.) Your recipient may be screening applicants for multiple posts, so mention the title of the position you're going for in the first paragraph. Just because a friend or networking acquaintance has referred you, don't try to pass off "Per Jim, attached is my resume for your review" as a cover letter. Craft a proper letter, prefaced with a full explanation of who you are and who referred you.

3. BE CREATIVE. Resumes tend to follow a formula, whereas cover letters allow you to get truly creative in selling yourself and your skills. Tell your story, let your personality show through. Prove that you're an effective written communicator. Work really hard on your opening sentence to be sure it makes an impact. If it reads like an objective statement, you're sunk.

4. BE ENTHUSIASTIC. No hiring manager wants to waste time on someone who is lukewarm about an opportunity. Your cover letter—and every piece of correspondence thereafter—must reinforce that you are truly excited by the position being offered, the company, and the industry. Without getting too verbose, demonstrate that you have some knowledge of the company and of trends in the industry and relate that knowledge to your interest in the job.

5. ASK NOT WHAT THE COMPANY CAN DO FOR YOU . . . Too many cover letters ramble on and on about what the job seeker is looking for in a company: "This position is a perfect fit for *me* because *I'm* looking for a fun and creative work environment where *I* will be able to interact with stimulating colleagues in a dynamic industry." To be brutally honest, your happiness and self-actualization are not the top priorities of the hiring manager. To him or her, the most important thing is that *you* are a perfect fit for the position, not the other way around—that you

will be successful and will make your boss, your division, and the company as a whole successful. That means that right up front, starting in the first sentence, you need to start convincing the reader that you'll be an immediate asset to their company and that you have a vision for how you will succeed. Make no mistake: this is the most important commandment of all.

6. THOU SHALT NOT COMMAND. If it's bad to overemphasize what the company can do to satisfy your professional, emotional, or spiritual needs, it's atrocious to cross the line from needs to *expectations.* But believe it or not, many cover letters actually lay out how much authority *I expect,* how soon *I expect* to be promoted, how much money *I expect* to make, when *I expect* my first raise. If the hiring manager's first impression of you is that you are arrogant and presumptuous, count on that being the last impression, too. Save the expectations until they decide they love you and must have you, then negotiate, diplomatically, for what you want.

7. COMPLEMENT YOUR RESUME. Your cover letter and resume travel together, so they need to work together. The cover letter flows, it has pizzazz, it hits the high points, it makes the pitch. The resume is more formal, the concrete evidence that substantiates your extravagant claims. Be sure that the career highlights you mention in your cover letter, such as major projects and accomplishments, are clearly supported by the details on your resume, but don't make your cover letter a dry laundry list that duplicates every point on your resume.

8. BE SUPER-SPECIFIC. It's hard enough to get through the job screening process; don't *give* them reasons to ding you before they even get to your resume. Position yourself as an expert with a specific skill set, not as a jack-of-all-trades. They're looking for a person to fill a burning need, and you have to make sure they see you as that person. Resist the urge to write

"I'm interested in *any* position you have available at your company," even if you'd sell your soul to work there. This is likely to come across as "I'm not sure what I want, but I was hoping you could figure it out for me."

9. BE REACHABLE. Cover letters and resumes often get separated. Make sure your contact information (home phone number, cell phone number, and email address) is on both your cover letter and resume.

10. FOLLOW DIRECTIONS. Before sending your cover letter out, pause and take a moment to review the directions listed in the job posting. Make sure that you're sending everything exactly the way the hiring manager requested. If a hiring manager requests "no attachments," they mean it. (Maybe they got burned by a virus once and swore "never again." Who knows?) Remember that your recipient is probably getting hundreds of resumes; if you don't follow instructions to the letter, they won't hesitate to bin you. If you can't follow the rules when you submit a cover letter, how will you be at following them as an employee?

Command of the English language is the lifeblood of public relations. Typos on cover letters are glaring and grating! I can't tell you how many I've received that start with: "I'd really like to get into pubic relations . . ." I'll bet!

—JEANNE, PR EXECUTIVE

SEND OUT THOSE THANK-YOU NOTES

Some people may tell you that thank-you notes are unnecessary or out of style; others will say that dashing off a quick follow-up email will suffice. They're wrong.

A thank-you note is more than a chance to be polite and thank the interviewer for their time. It's an opening to re-confirm your strengths as they pertain to the job for which you are currently interviewing. Look at thank-you notes as an opportunity to start building your fan base. For one thing, it will put you in a privileged minority: that of folks with class. That alone will get company insiders buzzing about you.

The thank-you note is not a place to talk about your needs. In it, you want to talk about your interest in the company and why you are the one candidate who can make a difference. The "One-Two Punch Technique" is a great approach to thank-you-note writing. One: the day after the interview, send a thank-you email or handwritten note to the interviewer. It should be quick and polite, and it should touch on how much you enjoyed the interview. Be sure that you specifically thank the interviewer for their time. Here's part two: mention that you'll be sending a second letter that will further highlight your specific experience and how it relates to the items you discussed during the interview. This letter is much more important than the email, so take the time to formulate a well-thought-out response. The next day, as promised, send a more formal thank-you letter. Print it out on your personal stationery. Send it via the good old U.S. Mail (yes, we're talking snail mail, with envelope and stamp). A nice alternative to sending a short email immediately after the interview is to drop a quick handwritten note in the mail to the interviewer. Hand-penned cards are so unusual that recruiters have been known to tack them up on their bulletin boards or display them as desk trophies for weeks at a time. This is a great way to stay omnipresent in the interviewer's mind when they're making their decision.

Look at the One-Two Punch Technique as an opportunity to get your name in front of the hiring manager two different times right after your interview. This can really make a difference, especially since most of your competitors won't bother with even a single thank-you note. You might think that sending one thank-you email should be enough, but it's not. Think about how much attention you give to incoming emails on a given day. If you're swamped, you'll hardly glance at them. On the other hand, when you get a personalized letter, you will generally stop what you're doing and read it. Hint: this approach should also be applied as a follow-up to phone interviews. Time is time, whether it's in person or on the phone, and you should respect it and show your gratitude.

Once you get rolling and are on an interview rotation, meeting with lots of folks at the company, be sure to send formal thank-you notes to each and every person who interviews you. You can bet that all the folks you interviewed with will be comparing notes on you, and this is quite a nice touch to help set yourself apart. Additionally, you should send a quick thank-you to anyone who helped get you the interview, whether it's a company insider or a networking associate. Let them know whom else you've met at the firm so that they can begin championing your cause and following up on your behalf.

Even if you think an interview went poorly, it's still a good idea to send a thank-you note. It could get you that special consideration that you just might need! By following up and sending thank-you notes to the right people, you'll gain a much-needed edge over your competition.

THE SKINNY: On Stationery. If you're going to send your cover letter, resume, and thank-you notes through the mail, put some thought to the paper stock that you choose. Heavyweight paper looks classier and stands the test of time better than the cheap laser printer kind. For more conservative positions, you can't go wrong by selecting shades of white, ivory, or cream. If you're in a creative profession, you can go a bit bolder with your color selection. Remember to purchase matching letterhead and envelopes at the same time so that your look and feel stays consistent throughout the interview process. When buying stationery, purchase about four times as many sheets of letterhead as envelopes, as you'll be sending cover letters along with your resume. You might also want to buy smaller matching notecards and envelopes as well for those handwritten thank-you notes. And you can never go wrong with monogrammed stationery, it's timeless. Never use your current employer's letterhead for your job-hunting correspondence. It's tacky and inappropri-

Tele-hunting: Don't Be Afraid to Pick Up the Phone

Contributed by Adrian Miller

Sending out loads of emails won't get you the job, but picking up the phone just might. Often, the key to success is being flexible and open-minded about trying something new.

- **Don't do the bulk of your calling during prime business hours.** A call placed at eight a.m. or six p.m. will often be answered by a decision-maker—at a time when he or she has more time to talk.
- **Don't underestimate the value of leaving voice mail messages at night.** These will be the very first messages that your potential employer will hear in the morning, so you're more likely to get a return call.
- **Periodically tape-record a random sampling of your cold calls.** Listen to the tape and assess your tone and voice. How did you sound? Would you want to speak with a person who sounds like you? What about your words? Were you clear? Did you sell your benefits? Taping gives you the opportunity to correct your presentation.
- **Pace yourself.** Making search calls can be a real grind. Allocate a specific amount of time each day and keep to the schedule. It is always easy to put something ahead of the "tele-hunting" activity, but make an appointment with yourself and don't break it.
- **Maintain a good sense of humor.** Make the employer smile, and you're halfway there!
- **Follow-up and follow-through are keys to success.** In gardening, if you don't water the seeds, the garden will languish. And so it is with job hunting: if you don't remain in contact, you will never break through.

Remember: there's no magic bullet. Looking for a job takes time, and if your pipeline of potential employers isn't filled with prospects in various stages of being worked, then you are in for disappointment.

Adrian is founder of AMDM, a sales training and new business development consultancy that delivers high-impact, results-driven training programs designed to address real-world selling challenges.

ate: you're not writing as a representative of your employer but as an individual job seeker, so use personal stationery.

> My company has a creative and casual atmosphere. While hiring for a recent job opening, I received a ton of responses. I ended up hiring a woman who sent her cover letter and resume in a purple envelope. It got me to open her cover letter and left me with the feeling that she was casual without being a slacker; unique but not too eccentric.
>
> —WARD, SYSTEMS ANALYST

GET YOUR EMAIL EXPOSED!

These days, corresponding via email at some point is inevitable, whether you're trying to land a job at a stodgy law firm or a high-tech startup. But you have to be wary of its many pitfalls.

If a hiring manager doesn't know you yet, be careful! Many people are extremely paranoid about getting viruses from email addresses that are foreign to them. Instead of sending attachments, cut and paste the text of your cover letter, followed by your resume, into the body of your email message. That way there's no attachment involved in the opening decision, so your potential employer has one less reason to delete your email. Once you've pasted your cover letter and resume into the body of your email, try sending a draft to yourself to see what it looks like on the receiving end. You most likely will have to tweak it a few times before it's right. If that virus-phobic hiring manager is impressed by your text resume despite the bare-bones formatting, he or she will probably ask you to send your resume as a nicely laid-out attachment in Word, now that you're no longer a stranger!

So let's talk about attachments for a minute. From time to time, a hiring manager will request a resume attachment. Before you just attach that file, think ahead. When a company is hiring, it is very likely that your cover letter and resume will be forwarded throughout a firm to all those involved in the hiring decision, so you want to ensure that your attachments will be readable by the largest possible number of people. Create your attachments in a widely used program like Microsoft Word. (For those of you prone to refer to a certain Redmond, Washington-based outfit as the "Evil Empire," just remember that your job hunt is not the time to make a political statement by using some obscure open-source app that nobody else has.) If you produce attachments in less-popular programs (e.g., Acrobat, Illustrator, Quark, or Powerpoint), you risk narrowing your audience. You don't want to inconvenience a hiring manager by making them fiddle with an unfamiliar application. If you're in a creative field like graphic design, it's a good idea to send two versions of your resume, one created in Word and one produced in a program that lets you show off your creative chops.

Before you send that attachment, check your settings. Nothing is more annoying to a hiring manager than when your resume opens up in Word and it's set to view at eighty-five percent of full size (it looks tiny on the screen) or has margins set improperly so that the text goes right off the screen or becomes a pain to print. Don't make a recruiter have to change a bunch of settings because you don't know what you are doing. Before you attach a Word document to an email, open it one last time. Make sure that the zoom is set to a hundred percent and that the margins are set correctly. If it doesn't look right, fix it. (If you want to be really sure, attach the file to an email and send it to yourself, then open it up and eyeball it.)

Software incompatibilities, firewalls, and other platform-to-platform issues could also prevent your attachments from being read. Whenever you send an email with an attachment, always follow up with the recipient in order to confirm that they were able to open it. You might also find that some recipients may have trouble opening attachments because they are running an earlier version of the same software program. If you're an Apple evangelist, be sure to add the suffix ".doc" to your files so that recipients who have PCs can open your attachment.

If you're like most job seekers, you save your cover letter and resume on your computer as Coverletter.doc and Resume.doc. That

Seven Steps for Sending a Better Job-Related Email

The downside to sending text-based cover letters and resumes in the body of an email is that they can look terrible, which is why people generally don't like sending them in the first place. The upside is that if you follow a few easy rules, they actually get read more often than when you send an attachment. At this stage of the game, it's the information that matters most, not the fancy graphics. Here's how to ensure that your email correspondence gets read:

1. Send your email in Plain Text format. You get more snazzy, word-processor-like capabilities in an HTML-format email, but you also run the risk of reaching a recipient whose mail program can't support it.

2. Create your cover letter in an email window that takes up less than half the width of your computer screen; this causes the text to "wrap" automatically and minimizes the chances that your paragraphs will break in weird places.

3. Hit the <enter> key only at the end of a paragraph or at the end of a section. This means that a new line will begin and the text will not wrap.

4. To accentuate section headings like WORK EXPERIENCE or EDUCATION, use all capital letters. Without the option of using bold or italics, it's your only hope to get text to stand out.

5. Use characters to help break text into readable sections. For example, the star (*) can be used for bullet points, and the hyphen (-) or equals sign (=) can be used to separate text.

6. If you decide to include a web site, always type the full web address starting with http://. By doing this, you're ensuring that the web site will be hyperlinked directly from the body of your email. For example, you should list the address as: http://www.mysite.com instead of www.mysite.com.

7. Always send a copy to yourself before you email anything out.

Each email program varies from provider to provider and computer to computer. If you have an email account with AOL as well as with a more standard Internet service provider (ISP) like Earthlink, try sending your text-based cover letter and resume to yourself at all of your various addresses to see what the recipient will see.

makes perfect sense until you think about it from the hiring manager's perspective. (Remember the section "Walk a Mile in the Other Person's Shoes" in Chapter 1?) Hiring managers get copious quantities of cover letters and resumes all named exactly the same indistinguishable way. It's not in your best interest to have a hiring manager have to rename and save your attachments. A good protocol to follow is to name your attachments so that they include your first and last name plus the word "resume," such as JaneDoeResume.doc, or at least your first initial and last name: JDoeResume.doc. By doing this, you're ensuring that the recipient can find your documents quickly and easily.

GETTING OVER EMAIL ANGST

Think before you zap! Don't let good manners disappear behind the veil of a computer screen and a keyboard. Once you've established a rapport with a recruiter via email, you don't want to let yourself fall into your email comfort zone and get sloppy. Hiring managers are easily put off by correspondence that comes across as curt, informal, or inappropriately direct. Don't let email slang, such as "Why don't U review my resume and we can IM about it later. K. THANX," slip into your correspondence. One word: inappropriate. It's easy to fall prey to this, especially when a recruiter or hiring manager is getting chummy with you online. Their one priority is to find the best candidate for the job, and by getting you to let your guard down, they'll discover clues that will let them see what kind of employee you'll really make. You want to be perceived as someone who has the ability to put pen to paper for memos, presentations, and other professional communications, not as someone whose judgment and maturity are questionable.

That's why when it comes to email correspondence, you need always to maintain a level of formality that suits a business relationship. If you come across as too informal, the hiring manager might get the feeling that you'll do the same thing in your dealings with co-workers or clients. Email text should be written in the same proper grammatical form that you would use for a business letter. Make a conscious effort to use complete sentences and don't respond by writing a few flip fragments or rambling run-ons, two common bad habits in "email speak." Don't use all lowercase letters—you'll look lazy. Also, avoid using all uppercase letters, as this will make you seem excessively urgent and possibly paranoid. (Many people interpret all capitals as "screaming.") Finally, before sending any important email, always create a draft of your email and be sure to spell-check, print, and review it before you send it.

If you receive an email from a recruiter asking for more information about your background or to elaborate on specific work experience, *take a deep breath,* and collect your thoughts. The person on the receiving end doesn't know that you've been checking your inbox all day long, waiting with anticipation to get an email from them. While you'll be tempted to fire back an email right away, doing so can cause more harm than good. If you hurry to zap something out, you may not get in all the information you need to make a solid impression, or you may not deliver a convincing argument. Instead, draft a well-thought-out, articulate response and then . . . *step away from the computer.*

Come back fifteen minutes later and put a fresh eye on your draft. Make sure that you've responded to all of the hiring manager's questions in one email. Try the snail mail test: before zapping your email back, print it out and re-read it. Does it read like a formal business letter or thank-you note? Have you clearly answered all of the hiring manager's queries? Are you selling yourself to the best of your abilities? If you've answered yes to all of the above, then you're doing great. Ask yourself one last question before you sign off on your note: will the hiring manager need to re-read his or her original email to understand your responses? If so, then you need to revise your draft in such a way that your response can stand on its own. Rephrase so that the original questions are contained within your responses: "In answer to your question about my project management skills . . ."

Thereafter, look upon every email communication as a further opportunity to sell yourself. Make sure your responses highlight a desirable attribute or skill that you have. Let's use an example of a hiring manager who wants you to elaborate on your people management skills. You could quickly zap off an email that says: "Yes, I do have experience managing people. I have re-attached my resume. When you open it you'll see that it lists several jobs where I have managed people. Please let me know if you need anything further."

On a first read-through, the above response sounds fine—that is, until you start to dissect it. Why? It's clear that the candidate has missed out on an opportunity to pitch herself and has merely directed the hiring manager to refer back to the resume (which they have already read) if they need more info. What the hiring manager really wants is a more elaborate explanation of her relevant work experience that they may have already seen on this candidate's resume. A better approach can be seen in the following response: "Yes, I do have experience managing people. In 2002, at Acme, I was a project manager. In that role, I ran a high-profile project where I was responsible for overseeing five employees from three different divisions. At year-end, I was promoted and now have two direct reports. I am responsible for their performance and will be giving their mid-year reviews shortly. While this experience is also detailed on my resume, I would love to come in and meet with you at a convenient time to discuss my personal management style, which is very team-centric. I will call you tomorrow to follow up." The second response works better because the candidate uses it as an opportunity to sell her skills. Additionally, the candidate used the moment to bring up the potential of a face-to-face interview; always a good move.

Each email you send should build on the previous ones to get the powers-that-be to remember you. By maintaining consistent and persuasive email correspondence with firm insiders during the hiring process, you will begin to cement new relationships. Once you get influential people into your camp, they can help build a case within the firm for hiring you.

PERSONALIZED SUBJECT LINES OPEN EMAILS

When your email pops up as a new item in a recruiter's inbox, the only information they are likely to see is your email address, your "display name" or "from name" (which spells out your real-life name), and the subject line of your email. Since the recruiter doesn't know you yet, the first two items are not going to get your email opened. That makes your subject line critically important.

Remember the "Tailor it" commandment for cover letters? It's amazing how many candidates write generic subject lines like "My Resume for Your Review" or even leave their subject line completely blank. The subject line that you choose will determine whether or not your cover letter gets read. Think of it as your *only* chance to send in a five-word pitch or mini-advertisement to the hiring manager. Subject lines need to be brief, but captivating. To illustrate this, think about the descriptive cover lines on best-selling magazines like *Maxim* ("Double Your Salary Now," "Naked Twister") or *Shape* ("Flatten Your Abs with One New Move"). Good cover lines suck readers in and entice them to read by promising to deliver on a need. That's your objective too; your subject line is the "bait" that tempts them to bite.

Even when the recruiter is familiar with your name, you should continue to use a subject line strategy for each and every email you send. Most people just leave the "RE: the same old topic" as an email flurry continues back and forth. This is a mistake. Always create a new subject line that pertains to the content of your email. As you continue to send more correspondence, it will make it easier for a hiring manager to go back and find an important email that you sent.

A wee digression: before you embark on a job hunt in which you'll be sending emails, take note of the email address you'll be using. You shouldn't use your work address, because your privacy can't be guaranteed (regardless of what your company policies may say, they're allowed to read your mail). But what about your personal address? If it's a scary sounding hacker-handle-type moniker, or something cute, funny, or faintly suggestive, don't use it. You're corresponding with future employers, not Match.com dates. Again, set up an account with an email address that's straightforward and professional sounding, along the lines of firstnamelastname@mailprovider.com. Also, consider the impression your domain name (i.e., the part after the @) might convey; if your domain is communismlives.com, that might be a turn-off to many prospective employers. Again, this is not the time to make political statements or to flaunt your eccentricities.

. . . And Now a Word on Spam

Before you jump on the email bandwagon, make sure that your correspondence doesn't turn into spam (a.k.a. junk email). Zapping out cover letters and resumes to hundreds of job postings won't get you any closer to landing a position. Sure, an email blast may be the fastest route to reaching a lot of recruiters, but it won't be very effective. Recruiters know that spam blasts are unlikely to contain any information that will help them fill a position, so they delete them immediately. "How do they know it's spam?" you may ask. Oh, the telltale signs:

- No specific company name, address, or date

- "Dear Recruiter" salutation

- To: field says "Undisclosed Recipients" or is blank (this happens when you blind cc: your addressees)

- To: field contains multiple addressees at multiple companies (this is a big no-no; people get extremely paranoid when their email address is visible to strangers)

- You screw up while changing the names from the last time you used this form letter/email, and wind up telling a guy from General Motors that you are really excited about the opportunity to work at Ford.

Even emails sent selectively to individual addressees can go astray if you're careless in such procedures as selecting recipients from your email program's address book. Be extremely careful, and double- and triple-check the recipient list before hitting Send.

Most people view spam, like junk mail, as invasive, and they delete it immediately. Hiring managers are no exception. These days, a recruiter might receive hundreds of resumes for a single posting. Your correspondence will stand out if it is informative and personalized. Whatever you do, before sending a cover letter and resume by email give it a good read, and be honest with yourself about how it would feel to be on the receiving end. Baby, if it looks like spam and reads like spam . . . it *is* spam!

THE SKINNY: **Access insider information.** If you want to send an unsolicited email and you know the spelling of the recipient's name but are not sure of their email address, try this little trick. Call the company's receptionist and tell them that you're having trouble sending "so and so" an email. Pretend you need to confirm the format of company email addresses—firstname.lastname? firstname_lastname? or what?

Make Your E-Mail Signature File *Work* for You!

Contributed by Alexandria K. Brown

Whenever you send a cover letter or a thank-you note, always take advantage of a very simple yet effective marketing tool: the email signature file. Also known as the "sig" file, it's the few lines of contact information inserted at the bottom of an email message. People who don't use sig files defend their position by saying "All the people I'm networking with already have my contact info." If this is you, stop! Think about how many emails you actually send each day. Adding a sig file gives you the chance to sneak in your own subtle messages about your own job hunt. Here's what good sig files do:

Keep your contact info at recruiters' fingertips. Hiring managers love it when you make information easy to find. Sure, your contacts have your phone number somewhere, but they'll really appreciate it when they have it right in front of them, on the bottom of your email, when they're looking for it. Also, if people want to put your info into their contact management software (Outlook, ACT, Palm, etc.), they can simply copy and paste it right from your sig file.

Tell strangers what you do. When you email recruiters who aren't familiar with what you do, your sig file can act as a subtle sales pitch. Think of your sig file as a little messenger who speaks to everyone you send an email to. What do you want this messenger to say? Something about the position you're looking for? Something to establish your business persona? You need to tell people succinctly what they need to know via your sig file.

Travel well. Emails get forwarded all the time. You never know where yours might end up, and one of the recipients may be very interested in your experience or have a position available that fits your background.

Are consistent. If you're interviewing with a number of people at one company, set up one sig file template and use it throughout the interviewing process at that firm. This way anyone who's a part of the hiring process won't get mixed messages. Of course, you can change the promotional message if you're going for a position at an entirely different firm.

Are fewer than six lines long. More than that will overwhelm the reader. Besides, it will look silly if your sig files are longer than your email messages! Keep your offer or announcement to one or two sentences only. Avoid random literary quotes or philosophical musings, cute illustrations made up of keyboard characters ;-), or your weekend phone number at your summer home. Here's a good example:

Jane Smith, Network Administrator
"Take a Byte Out of Network Headaches"
ph: 800-321-0000 fax: 212-321-0001 jane@smithly.com
Visit http://www.smithly.com and see my 5 Tips for keeping small and large networks functional and headache free

Notice that Jane opted not to give her mailing address here, in order to use the space for her tagline and an invitation to receive her five tips. It's all up to you. Decide what bits of info are most valuable to keep, and use the rest of the space for a unique message or promotion!

Here are several items you should consider listing in your sig file. Important: do not attempt to insert them all! Choose what's most important for you to get hired or to make a connection:

- your name and title
- your email address (sometimes people can't get it directly or quickly from your actual email)
- your tagline, or a short phrase that describes who you are or what you're looking to do
- your mailing address
- your phone, cell phone, and/or pager numbers
- your fax number

- your company name
- your Web URL (be sure to include the "http://" prefix to ensure it will translate as a hyperlink on most email programs)

You should also consider putting promotional info in your sig file, especially if you want to draw traffic to your web site. For example, you could include:

- an offer to do something in exchange for an interview
- an offer for a free consultation
- a personal announcement about an award you've won or an accomplishment you've made
- a link to an article you wrote

Alexandria, "The E-zine Queen," is the author of the award-winning manual "Boost Business with Your Own E-zine." Learn more now and sign up for her FREE tips at ezinequeen.com.

NOW GO WORK IT!

Here's the Takeaway:

- Job-search-related correspondence must impress at every turn. Drop the email-induced laziness and informality.

- Cover letters are usually your first opportunity to establish your corporate identity. Lazy, one-sentence covers pretty much guarantee that your resume will not even get read. Expressive ones that convey your personality and enthusiasm, on the other hand, get potential employers excited about you.

- Thank-you notes, especially ones that are *not* emailed, are rare these days, but always proper, always appreciated, and certain to get you noticed.

- The One-Two Punch for thank-you notes (a quick note or email immediately after an interview or other contact, followed by a more formal, mailed letter that combines a message of thanks and a restatement of your corporate identity and qualifications) reinforces your message and impresses the hell out of people.

- Email is a great tool, no two ways about it. Just use it well. Write your emails as if writing a formal business letter.

- When replying to an emailed request for additional information, don't just hit the Reply button for a hair-trigger response. Take the time to think about your answer, craft a careful message, and make the subject line informative (not RE: interview).

- When attaching documents such as resumes to an email, give the attachment a name that will be useful to the recipient (hint: resume.doc is not helpful to a recruiter receiving hundreds of resumes).

- Emails and attachments exemplify Murphy's Law (if something *can* go wrong, it will). Proofread everything carefully. Be incredibly anal about formatting. Email it to yourself and make sure that it will look right on the receiving end.

- Always tailor, never spam.

7

GET PRIMED:

Training Tips for Peak Interview Performance

You've penetrated the first line of defense: your cover letter and resume have impressed all the right people so far, and you have been invited to an interview. It's make-or-break now: time to blow away all the other candidates who made the cut, until there is only one person left standing—you! Before you go out and try to knock 'em dead, keep in mind that interviewing isn't exactly like riding a bike. You will be rusty. Not only that, between the last time you interviewed and now, you hopefully have added a number of new skills to your work experience. Discussing your newfound abilities can be quite challenging the first time out. The trick to "giving good interview" is not about wowing the hiring manager when you walk in the door. It's about planning ahead, knowing your material, solidifying your discussion flow, and practicing in advance. Yes, you heard right, practicing. You need to train, pace yourself, and visualize the entire session from beginning to end so you can smoke your competition.

DO SOME RECONNAISSANCE

Before a general sends his troops into combat, he learns everything he can about his enemy, studying their every move. You too need to gather as much information as possible about the companies you're interviewing with so that you can anticipate questions and prepare responses. It's always impressive to an interviewer when a candidate has done their homework. Information is everywhere these days, so tap into it. Simply reading an annual report and a job description won't give you nearly enough material about a company—you need to sink your teeth into the whole firm: their performance, strategy, competitors, and people. Before you go in:

✔ **IMMERSE YOURSELF IN THE COMPANY WEB SITE.** You want to check out the company's entire site. Seek out the "Press" or "Media" section in particular. Because these areas are targeted to journalists, it's usually what the company wants the world to know about them. While you're there, spend a fair amount of time studying the recent company press releases, in which they might talk about new hires, product launches, quarterly announcements, and other important company news. Also, check out any articles that are linked to the web site. They are usually great for figuring out what's happening in the industry.

✔ **DO A WEB SEARCH.** Go online and Google or do a Yahoo! search: you won't believe the amount of stuff you can find out about the company and its officers. Read employees' individual web pages and lurk around on egroups that dish the dirt on the industry or the company.

✔ **GET MORE JUICE.** Hoovers.com is a great business information web site that can get you an unbelievable amount of info on the companies you're interviewing with. Want to dig deeper? It may be worth it to buy an all-you-can-eat single-day subscription to Lexisnexis.com where you can do searches on their news, financial, public records, and legal databases. You can pay by the week, day, or item or article. Search by company name, competitor name, future boss's name, etc. If you dig deep enough, you may be able to teach the people you're interviewing with a thing or two about their own company.

✔ **GET INTO THE NITTY-GRITTY.** Don't get ho-hummed by the SEC filings, listings, and annual reports. Here's where you can find out the good stuff about a company and really come across as impressive and knowledgeable. Get it all at <u>FreeEdgar.com</u>. Want to know about a firm's corporate culture or what it's like to work there? Become a prisoner of <u>Vault.com</u>, <u>http://Company.Monster.com</u>, <u>Wetfeet.com</u>, or the company research tool on <u>Businessweek.com</u>.

✓ **TALK TO HR OR YOUR HEADHUNTER.** A critical piece of information you need to get is whether you're replacing a person who left the firm or filling a new position. If you are replacing someone, try to get some insight as to why the person left the company (did they quit or get fired?). What did the person you're replacing do well? What could they have done a better job at? If the position is being added to a department, there are other things to consider, like understanding specific expectations for this new role. In either case, when a position is in transition and has yet to be filled, departments can often be stretched to capacity. If this is the case, you need to reiterate that you won't need to have your hand held, but that you will come in and hit the ground running.

I deal mostly with MBA candidates whose biggest problem is over-selling themselves and acting on an interview as if they have nothing to learn. The best candidates are sincere and humble. While you may be extremely smart, you also need to respect people for what they can teach you. Before you sit down to an interview, learn about the firm and the position and have a general understanding of the responsibilities expected of you. This way you can map out how your experience and background speaks to the position.

–KATHY, IN-HOUSE RECRUITER

LEARN HOW TO GIVE A GOOD INTERVIEW

The ability to take a hiring manager through your resume with incredible ease is merely the price of entry into the interview. You must be able to shape a detailed story around each work experience, if requested. Be prepared to give concrete examples that demonstrate such universally desirable talents as creative idea generation, problem-solving, and people management. In particular, employers are looking for transferrable skills that you can bring from your old job to a new one, like written and oral communication skills. Work hard throughout the interview to draw parallels between your work experience and the requirements of the position. Ultimately, you need to get an interviewer to see you as *the* ideal candidate for the position. Of course, staying on track is a whole other story. It's amazing how many candidates "um" and "ah" through no-brainer questions like "So, what do you do in your free time?" Instead of barfing out a stream of consciousness, you need to have articulate responses at the ready, which means anticipating the questions that will be posed. Preparing for an interview is a self-fulfilling prophecy: the more comfortable you feel with the material, the more self-confident you will appear and the better you will perform.

List all the questions you think you'll be asked. Start by listing broad questions that are common to almost every interview. To that, add questions that will be unique to the company you're going to meet. If you need help generating these questions, make a phone call to your recruiter or to the person that helped you get the job lead. Here are fifteen automatics to get you going:

1. What made you decide to get into this field?

2. Why do you want to work at our company?

3. Take me through your resume or through your responsibilities in your last position.

4. What was your favorite project?

5. Let's talk about your extracurriculars—what do you like to do in your free time?

6. What or who has inspired you?

7. Tell me about a situation that challenged you to the utmost?

8. What or who has had the biggest impact on your professional career?

9. What is one thing you'd like to accomplish, no matter how crazy?

10. What can you bring to our company?

11. Walk me through a day in your current/most recent job.

12. How are you at troubleshooting? Can you give an example?

13. How do you handle difficult people, whether bosses or subordinates?

14. How are you with multi-tasking?

15. What would you eventually like to do/where do you see yourself in five years?

Once you've drawn up your list of anticipated questions, print them out, and—*step away from the computer.* Go sit somewhere where you can think and insert your answers into the document. Expressing your responses in written form stops you from rambling, and ensures that you put together cohesive thoughts. As you're writing down your answers, keep in mind that you don't want to deliver one-word or single-phrase responses. You want to respond by giving strong examples that play up your work experience and attributes that are most important for landing the job you're after. When you're done, go back to your computer and type your answers into your document. You'll be amazed at how much editing you will have to do; this probably means that had you been in a live interview, you would have stumbled over your delivery. Work on getting your responses tight, really tight.

After you're done typing them in, read them *out loud* (get ready for fingernails on a chalkboard, people). When you hear yourself saying the words, you'll be able to edit them so that they sound smoother and more natural. For each answer, your goal is to be able to deliver a succinct soundbite, no longer than one or two minutes long. Longer than that, and you're likely to lose your train of thought, or worse, make your interviewer lose focus. Mental telepathy does not work on an interview—your answers need to reflect exactly what you want the interviewer to know about you. If you want to get a point across, come right out and say it. If you forget to mention critical details about your background that could help you get hired, it is no one's fault but your own.

PREPARATION IS KEY

Interviewing is a lot closer to public speaking than you may realize. To come across as polished, you need to practice as much as possible. Always let the interviewer know that you want the job, you can do the job, and you're the best person for the job. Interviewers can sense performance anxiety, which is why they start digging when you start stammering. You might be the right person for the job, but something you do or say could prevent you from getting it. In fact, you might not even be consciously aware of what you're doing. Things to ask yourself include:

✓ **ARE YOU TOO SUCCINCT?** You may think that you got your point across, but did you? Pay attention to the interviewer; does it look like they're waiting for more information?

✓ **ARE YOU TOO VERBOSE?** After you've made your point, do you embellish or restate without adding anything essential?

✓ **ARE YOU WAITING YOUR TURN?** Don't jump on people's questions. Wait until they complete the thought, then pause and think through what you're going to say. It tells the interviewer that you're processing what they are saying.

✓ **DO YOU HAVE ANY BIZARRE QUIRKS?** Are you a nose-scratcher? Pen-chewer? Change-jingler? Or a toe-tapper? These things can distract an interviewer from your message.

✓ **UM, LIKE, UH, CAN YOU SPIT IT OUT?** Dude, like, are you adding a lot of um, ya know, words to your delivery that don't make you seem as smart as you are?

✓ **DO YOU HAVE POOR BODY LANGUAGE?** Do you slouch? Cross your arms? Fail to maintain eye contact?

✓ **DO YOU SOUND LIKE A POLITICIAN?** You don't want to sound like you're delivering the State of the Union address when you're talking about your work experience. Be articulate but natural. Never sound pompous. (Rehearsing on your own, or better yet with a trusted friend, will help you achieve the right tone.)

Before you agree to your first official interview, find an interview buddy to practice with you. You might want to pick someone who is in the midst of his or her own job search. This way, you can both take on the roles of interviewee and interviewer. Pick a pal who's going to be brutally honest. Your goal is to improve, not become charter members of a mutual admiration society. Often, when one moves from a written description to an oral description, key details are rushed or omitted due to nervousness. Have your buddy make sure that you're communicating the need-to-know information to the interviewer. If you're a bit rusty at interviewing, plan on videotaping yourself. Set up a typical interview environment: high desk, uncomfortable chair, oppressive lighting. This way you'll be able to witness *all* of your nasty habits, from nail biting to folding your arms to shrugging your shoulders. Through repetition and continued videotaping, you should be

MEET THE STUMPS

In every interview, there comes a time when the interviewer will wryly curl his or her lip, raise an eyebrow, and deliver the mother of all left-field questions. You can writhe in your chair, sweat uncomfortably, and stammer through a lame response, or you can confidently answer the question. The reason a hiring manager asks these off-the-wall questions is to gain insight as to how you'll fit in with the rest of the team. "I interview mathematical geniuses for an investment bank, and since I can't really evaluate applicants for their technical expertise, I ask a bizarre question like, 'When you land on those really cheap purple properties in a game of Monopoly, do you buy them or pass them up? If you do buy them, would you build hotels on them?' " says Nancy Levine, an executive recruiter with the Pacific Firm. "There is no right or wrong answer for this question, so I sit back and watch how candidates respond to the weirdness of the question. Will they get flustered or respond in a playful and fun-loving way? If the candidate becomes bewildered by the question or tries to answer it seriously, he or she isn't the right one. The candidates who show some humor and a sense of irony at the apparent absurdity of the question tend to get the job. Tricky, huh?"

So how do you deal with a real doozy of a question? The answer is to be prepared. Practice answering a few "stumpers" so that you won't go into shock when you get hit with one in a real interview. Here are a few beauties from the hiring community for you to cut your teeth on:

Q: If you could interview one person, past, present, future, celebrity, or unknown . . . who would it be?

—Irene, Headhunter

Q: Tell me a story about you and your life. It could be from when you were two, or from last week, but it cannot be work related. The story should be about something that you want me to know about you. (And then I hum some Jeopardy music.)

—Debra, Market Researcher

> *Q: Why are manhole covers round?*
>
> **—Pat, Chief Technology Officer**
>
> *Q: If you were on a baseball team, which position would you play?*
>
> **—Dana, Headhunter**

able to minimize some of your individual quirks and start to see a marked improvement in your interview style.

> I always ask people why they want to work at my company. Invariably, seventy percent of candidates say, "I want to work with people." No kidding! Everybody works with people. If you didn't want to work with people, I'd be worried. Please come up with something original.
>
> —DEBRA, MANAGEMENT CONSULTANT

> I had pegged one particular person to be the lead candidate after an amazing phone interview. He came in to meet with me impeccably dressed and very well prepared, with his portfolio fully updated with his latest work. The interview was moving along fine when all of a sudden, he crossed his leg, took off his shoe, and started picking at his toes. (I'm happy to say he was wearing socks.) It was incredibly distracting to me as an interviewer and I'm quite certain he wasn't even aware he was doing it. Perhaps it was nerves, or something else. When I lined up the three candidates—all of whom had equally impressive backgrounds—I had to eliminate Mr. Toe Picker.
>
> —JANELLE, HEADHUNTER

How to Start Your Own Interview Club

Contributed by John Murphy and Martin Vonderheiden

Practically everyone has had a bad interview experience and wishes they could have practiced more. But where can you practice and get constructive feedback? That's what we asked ourselves one night after a tough day of pounding the pavement. Over a few beers at a local pub, we hatched an idea to start an interview club that would help fine-tune our verbal job-hunting skills and those of members we could enlist. Our club meets regularly to practice our interviewing skills, focusing on three major areas: The Personal Pitch, Networking, and The Practice Interview.

1. **The Personal Pitch.** Think of this as your thirty- to sixty-second commercial. It includes what you are doing (or want to do), what your skills or accomplishments are, and what position you are looking for. We encourage people to plan their pitches ahead of time. Think about whom you'll be talking to before you go into your pitch. This way you'll learn how to tweak your pitch on the fly to fit any situation.

2. **Networking.** We practice introductions and what to say to a new networking contact, how to ask a colleague or a friend for a contact name or introduction, how to make small talk at an industry function, and how to ask questions without becoming an interrogator.

3. **The Practice Interview.** Improving one-on-one interviewing skills is the focus of our meetings. To get people warmed up, we toss out random, impromptu questions, giving members the chance to answer both typical ones and off-the-wall ones. We ask a volunteer to keep track of time and warn people if their response goes over one minute and thirty seconds. Another volunteer watches for grammar and verbal distractions (umms and ahhs, etc.). Next, we break the group up into smaller role-playing groups and have one person volunteer to be

a hiring manager and another play the interviewee. We try to tailor the questions to that person's goal and the other members provide instant written and verbal feedback.

Need to hone your interview skills? Start your own interview club—it's a great way to network as well as sharpen your skills—or just try these techniques at home with a friend or two.

John and Martin are co-founders of The Interview Club. John has worked in advertising and marketing for ten years and has delivered presentations in boardrooms and auditoriums. Martin was a consultant for an SAP subsidiary and delivered seminars to over 1,400 professionals. Visit them at: theinterviewclub.com.

CAN YOU PLAY IN THE SANDBOX?

If you're the most qualified person for the position, shouldn't you get the job? Not always. Put yourself in a manager's shoes for a second. Whom would you pick: a candidate with ideal work experience who has dubious interpersonal skills, or a candidate with slightly less experience who has a good attitude and an exemplary ability to work in teams? The latter will win out every time. The right work experience will get you in the door and probably put you in the finalist category, but most managers will agree that landing an employee with fantastic qualifications is not worth destabilizing a well-oiled department. Because it's so important to a manager that all his or her team members work together productively, the people with whom you interview will be looking for insight into the "inner you." Organizational fit, enthusiasm for doing the job, and other wild-card attributes will have a lot to do with whether or not you get an offer.

When you ask a hiring manager why they chose one candidate over

Prepare for Success

Contributed by Lea Brandenburg

Every performer and athlete recognizes the value of rehearsing. Can you imagine Tiger Woods simply showing up at a golf tournament without practicing ahead of time? How many practice swings has he taken to build on his innate talents and gifts? It's rumored that even Jerry Seinfeld, the comedian whose sitcom was known for being about "nothing," practiced 450 times in one year when he was developing his standup routine and comedic voice. Even if you aren't planning on winning a PGA trophy or getting your own television sitcom, you too can utilize rehearsal techniques to create successful outcomes for yourself. Here are a few methods you can use to rehearse for new opportunities, challenging situations, important meetings, interviews, or stressful circumstances.

Give yourself permission to explore. One of the biggest benefits of rehearsing prior to an event is that you have the opportunity to experiment with what works and what doesn't. During the rehearsal phase, don't force yourself to do it "right" or be "perfect." Give yourself the opportunity to make mistakes.

Become aware of your thinking. Take a moment to try this experiment: don't think about pink elephants. Really, don't think about pink elephants. What happens? Chances are, you just thought of pink elephants. If you want to succeed in a situation, think about how you want it to be—specifically. Thinking about what you don't want to happen increases the odds that it will happen, because you haven't rehearsed how you want the situation to play out.

Take your thinking one step further. If you don't want to appear insecure in a business situation, ask yourself: what would self-confidence look like? How do you want to be perceived in this particular situation? How can your body and voice convey confidence and security? In what way might you specifically communicate confidence through behavior? See yourself accomplishing your goal. Feel it, see it, believe it. Make your desired outcome tangible in your own mind by mentally rehearsing the behavior and then physically practicing it.

Play out your worst-case scenario. What if you blow your interview? What if the interviewer asks you a question you don't want to be asked? To prepare for a worst-case scenario, use this sentence structure: If _____ (fill in the blank with your fear/concern) happens, then I will _____. For example: If a recruiter asks me about my recent layoff, I will _____. By giving yourself the opportunity to play through the worst-case scenario, you shift your worry into anticipation and can prepare yourself with alternate plans of action. Rehearsal gives you the chance to challenge your fears and work through them before they have the opportunity to inhibit your performance.

Daydream. As you prepare for difficult situations, tense interactions, or new opportunities, don't lose track of what's important to you. Daydreaming helps you connect to your heart's desire and discover what you really want.

Replay a past win. We've each experienced victories in our personal and professional lives. When you are faced with a difficult situation or a new challenge, remember a similar situation in which you prevailed and review exactly what you did to be successful. Using your past experiences as a roadmap for your present task will give you solid evidence that you can create successful outcomes for yourself. Ultimately, there is no way you can guarantee you'll be prepared for everything. But what rehearsing can do for you is build your confidence and help you develop positive habits on which you can rely, so you will be better prepared for success.

Lea is a personal and business coach who works with clients to develop effective self-presentation skills and to express themselves with confidence and ease in every situation. Visit her at: creatingstrategies.com.

another, equally qualified candidate, they might rattle off words like "chemistry," "gut feeling," "intuition." You can boil this down to one word: "fit." Being a good organizational fit won't save you if you lack the basic qualifications to do the job, but it can go a long way toward compensating for small deficiencies in your experience that make you look less than ideal on paper. That's great news for you as a candidate: you can't manufacture work history out of thin air, but you can convince whoever's interviewing you that you're "their type of person." As you're doing your company research, try to get insight as to what type of people thrive in the organization and think about whether you'll fit in if you're hired. Do you think you'll get the experience you're seeking? Is there room to grow? Will you respect the work of your prospective co-workers? Will you interact well with your manager? These are not trivial questions; they will affect your motivation and success significantly.

Another important variable in the job offer formula is enthusiasm. Quite simply: do you want the job more than the other candidates? This matters to employers! You need to prove that you are more interested and willing to go that extra mile than anyone else. Don't be coy. Put your interest in the job on the table, and go out of your way to prove you want it.

Finally, the wild-card factor can tip the odds for or against you. Here's where alma maters, business contacts, and family friends can give you a "halo effect." Maybe mentioning to your prospective boss that you're a scratch golfer or that you can finish *The New York Times* crossword puzzle in under an hour can put you over the finish line. When it comes down to the wild-card factor, you just can't anticipate the results. When you click, you click. It's sort of like a blind date—you can't control how another person feels about you. No matter how well you think you fit or how enthusiastic you are, sometimes it just doesn't work out. When this happens, suck it up and move on (and take comfort in the knowledge that we've all been there).

I was really looking forward to an interview I had with a major consumer goods company. When I got there, the first thing the interviewer asked me was why I chose to attend Duke's business school. "Well," I said, "I grew up in Florida, went to college in Atlanta, and lived there for two years after graduation. I was born and raised in the South and it's where I plan to spend the rest of my life. I figured I should choose the best school with the strongest alumni network in the region." He looked at me with a furrowed brow and said, "You do realize our company is based in Hackettstown, New Jersey?" "Oh, yes!" I said. "Ever since I came here I made a lot of friends from the New York/New Jersey area and now I'm thinking that may be a good place for me to live." Even though I was very interested in moving, I had totally sold myself as a Southern boy. I never heard from him again.

—JAMES, RECENT MBA GRADUATE

THE GREAT SALARY NEGOTIATION BALANCING ACT

Most people look for a new job to increase their responsibility, to get a promotion, and of course, to get a nice bump in their salary. You'll recall from Chapter 6, "The Lost Art of Correspondence," that it's a bad idea to be too up-front about what *you* want and expect from the job in your cover letter. That's because the cover letter forms that all-important first impression in the mind of the hiring manager or recruiter, and you don't want that impression to be one of greed or arrogance. But as you move along in the process, there will come a point when you and the interviewer need to start discussing your expectations. Don't get caught unprepared; you need to know your own requirements—acceptable salary range, desired title, and expected level of responsibility—before you get to the interview.

It's a fine line we're talking about here. You're not going to slam your fist on the interviewer's desk during the first interview (or any other time, perish the thought) as you lay out what it's going to take to get your precious self on board. But there needs to be a subtle give-and-take between you and the company to make sure your respective expectations are not totally out of sync. Be careful; this is a sensitive mating dance. Sometimes the interviewer will try to get you talking about your salary requirements and other expectations very early in the process. Think twice before giving a direct answer: they may be looking for concrete reasons to ding you ("this guy's way too expensive") or they may be pulling one of those insidious interviewer tricks aimed at exposing the real you ("Is this woman a clever negotiator who knows how to be diplomatic? Is she a good salesperson who knows not to talk price until the prospect is definitely interested?"). Use your spider-sense. If you feel you haven't even established your credentials, personality, and ability to do the job, it's probably too soon to be talking money. It's not easy to avoid answering a direct question like "What kind of money do you expect to earn?" but try a response such as "I'm confident that your company is offering a very competitive package, and it seems like a fantastic place to work. But before we get to that topic, is there anything else you feel you need to know about my experience?" Don't be coy, however. If the manager persists, it's because he or she really needs to know, and will get annoyed if you go all Clintonesque. When you answer, give a salary range, and emphasize that you are willing to be flexible as you gain a growing understanding of the entire package of job responsibilities and benefits.

There's an exception to this rule. When you are talking to a headhunter, answer right away about your salary requirements. They don't have time to beat around the bush, and will dump you if you try. Remember that it's their job to act as a go-between; they will handle the spin control when they pitch you to their client (or they will not pitch you at all if the numbers are totally out of line), but they need to know the facts in order to do their job. And above all else, don't ever make a headhunter look stupid by telling them one thing and then telling the hiring company something different in an interview. You'll never hear from that headhunter again.

Salary Makeover: Simple Steps to a Firmer Longer-Lasting Paycheck

Contributed by Johanna Schlegel

Are you the "before" photo for salary satisfaction? Like your appearance, once in a while your career can benefit from a fresh look, or outlook, as the case may be. If you want to spruce up your physical appearance, you can book some time in a spa or a salon. But where can you turn for a *salary makeover*?

Start by taking a hard look at your values regarding work and pay. How important is your earning power to your sense of self-worth? Would you rather have a career, or a series of jobs? Is work a means of finding professional fulfillment, or just a way to support yourself and perhaps your family? Do you actively manage your career, or just let it happen? Is your pay as rewarding as your job? Is your job as rewarding as your pay? And regardless of your reasons for working, do you actively ensure that you are compensated fairly, or do you assume your employer will do that for you?

Now, let's dispel some of those myths that have been holding you back from getting to the right number and from building a healthy foundation. Myth #1: your employer cares about your bills and mortgage payments. Myth #2: you deserve more money just for showing up. Myth #3: if you counter your employer's salary offer, people won't like you.

Here's a new foundation: your time is of value to you and to employers. Optimizing that value is the goal. The value of your time depends on the contribution you make to the company. That value is negotiable. Employers pay for things you bring to the job. (The Personal Salary Report from Salary.com focuses on the eight things that are most likely to influence your pay: performance, experience, education, certifications, boss, people reporting to you, shift, and hazardous working conditions.) Other factors come into play, too, such as the size of the company, the industry, the importance of your role to that organization, and so on. You put yourself in the best position by emphasizing the factors the company is willing to pay for. Note that your mortgage isn't one of them.

In your salary makeover, focus on the skills needed to get the next promotion. Suppose an entry-level financial analyst has learned photocopying and binding, research, spreadsheet analysis, even presentation skills. At the next level, that analyst should focus on the most valuable skills for that next job—probably analysis and presentation skills *plus* any management experience. The management experience will become a major factor in the future.

Salary markets change, and sometimes salaries even decrease in the aggregate, as we saw in the second half of 2001. If this happens to your job title, you might have to accept a lower salary than the one you received at your last job. Make sure your salary expectations keep pace with the changing market, even if the market rate for your job decreases. If that happens, be sure your enthusiasm for the job comes across to a prospective employer despite the pay cut. If you aren't genuinely enthusiastic, the hiring manager or HR person will be able to tell.

You can do a salary makeover after you've been hired, too. It's called a "salary review." Don't wait for your boss to schedule it—you can take the initiative. Your boss will still like you.

The salary makeover is about minimizing flaws as well. There is a concealer for performance blemishes: it's called discretion. Be honest with yourself. Of course, you can't lie to or deceive an employer, and your current employer already knows the details of your performance, but all hope is not lost. Instead of talking about losing a customer, focus on what you've learned about customer satisfaction. In your resume, downplay those less flattering elements in your background.

Most employers try to correlate pay to performance. If your pay doesn't have the look you want, ask yourself whether it has anything to do with your performance. A performance workout might be a critical step in a full and effective salary makeover. Work on all areas of your performance, beef up your weak spots, and periodically tone your performance strengths. That's how those in shape stay in shape. One final touch to your personal salary makeover is to consider all parts of your pay package. It's not *just* about salary. It's about bonuses, stock options, benefits, and perquisites. All of these components together create your total rewards package. If you've already reached the limit on one component, look to another to get that extra lift you want and deserve.

Johanna is Editor-in-Chief at Salary.com, which analyzes pay trends and data for employees and employers, and is author of the popular "Ask Annette" humor column on office culture. She has appeared in national media outlets including NPR's Talk of the Nation, Cosmopolitan, and Entrepreneur.

REFERENCES FOR LIFE

Professional references are the Great Reality Check of the whole job interviewing process. Employers depend upon them to make sure they're not hiring someone who is just a pretty face and a smooth line.

Creating and maintaining long-term relationships with your references is an ongoing process that requires a significant commitment. Many people let relationships with their references lapse until they get the two-minute warning from a prospective employer that they need them. Bad move. Before you have to produce your references, you need to know where they are and to make sure that they haven't forgotten about you.

A good rule of thumb is to get in touch with your references at least twice a year. Doing so is as simple as making a quick phone call or sending a catch-up email. When you embark on a job search, always put in a phone call to your network of references. This way, you've given them a heads up that you'll need them to come through for you in the near future. In fact, a reference is more likely than a new networking contact to keep their ear to the ground for you about job opportunities.

Having an ample and well-rounded list of references from each position you've held will make you a stronger candidate in the eyes of a potential employer. Ideally, you should have two references from positions that correlate closely to the job for which you're applying. Your references should always include direct managers or supervisors who can talk specifically about the quality of your work. Most hiring managers will understand if you can't use a manager from your current employer, but you need to keep tabs on superiors who have left your firm but can still speak to your work experience. You should also consider enlisting some "lateral references": peers with whom you've worked with on major projects. If you're going for a senior position, you might want to have a few subordinates at the ready that can discuss your management style. Client and vendor references can speak to your performance without putting your current job in jeopardy. Whenever you complete a project, make sure that you get the key contact information for all of the people you might want to engage as references at a later date. While having a few personal references is fine, the bulk of the references that you supply from your network should be related to your professional experiences. After all, the employer wants to know how you'll be as an employee, not a friend. By demonstrating that you have nothing to hide, you will put the hiring manager at ease.

References need to be earned. Just because you worked for or reported to someone doesn't mean that they'll automatically give you a good reference. Think about why a person would be a good reference for you (or why they wouldn't). After you ask someone to be your reference, pay attention to his or her immediate reaction. Are they psyched to do it? Or are they reluctant in any way? If you detect any hesitation, back off. You don't want someone who feels uncomfortable to be a reference for you. That air of hesitation could come through in their voice to a prospective employer, and then you're sunk. When asked about your performance, a bad reference might deliver a long pause or might simply say something like, "He performed the job adequately." The subtext here is, "I'm covering my ass by not disparaging anyone, but if I were you, I wouldn't hire this person." A good reference, on the other hand, would go into great detail as to why you would make an excellent hire. In the end, it's better to offer up a few quality references than a bunch of questionable ones.

THE SKINNY: Never list your references and their contact information on your resume. You want to be in control of who gets in touch with them. When they are requested, put together a detailed document with correct contact information, best times to call, and your relationship to the reference (e.g., boss, personal reference, coworker, HR representative).

GET YOUR BLEEPIN' BLEEPERS UNDER CONTROL

Part of getting primed for the interview process is making sure that you're reachable. In this brave new gadget-centric world, hiring managers can get a hold of you just about any place at any time. Depending on your total geek-itude, a hiring manager might email you, reach you through your Palm or BlackBerry, leave a message on your home voice mail, call your cell, or even page you. The ways and means of communication are endless, which can also prove dangerous to your job hunt if you haven't idiot-proofed the process. Loose lips sink ships. So do uninformed roommates, parents, or kids who pick up the phone when they haven't been briefed about an impending phone call from your future boss. This is exactly why you need to control every point of contact that a hiring manager has with you.

✓ HOME PHONES: When you're not home and a hiring manager or recruiter calls, one of two things can happen. The phone can ring through to your answering machine, or someone can pick it up (if you don't live by yourself). The safest thing is not to use your home phone at all and to direct people related to hiring to call you on your cell. If that isn't an option, the next best thing is to hope that your answering machine picks up before a family member does.

The Myth of References

Contributed by Hanan B. Kolko, Esq.

Many job seekers operate under the misconception that unless a former employer is going to give you a good reference, the only information they can divulge by law is date of hire, last day worked, title, and final rate of pay. This is simply untrue. As a general matter,* your previous employer is free to give you a bad reference without violating the law. There are limited exceptions to this: an employer can't knowingly lie on a reference, and an employer can't give you a false reference out of malice. However, in general, the law allows your former employer to accurately describe your performance, to explain the true reason for your departure, and to give his or her opinion about your quality of work, even if it is negative. While you may want to consult with a lawyer if you think you are being victimized by a bad reference from a vindictive former employer, you shouldn't assume that the law provides some silver bullet against bad references. If you want to make sure that your former employer only says certain things about you, negotiate it before you depart and put it in a severance agreement.

Hanan is a labor and employment lawyer wih the law firm of Meyer, Suozzi, English & Klein, an adjunct professor at Cornell University's College of Industrial and Labor Relations, and the Secretary-Treasurer of Working Today, an advocacy group for the emerging "free agent" workforce.

* This issue is governed by state law and thus will vary from state to state.

Just make sure that there is a professional message on the machine.

When a loved one or roommate picks up the phone, the odds of things going wrong increase exponentially. Long before you start interviewing, you need to establish ground rules. Tell the people who share your home phone that you are about to start interviewing and that you'd appreciate some care in how they answer the phone over the coming weeks. We've all been brainwashed to spew venom at annoying telemarketers. But while you're in the throes of interviewing, you need to make sure that anyone and everyone answering the phone will be polite and upbeat. If you happen to be home and within earshot, it doesn't mean that the person who picks up should scream, "BOB, PHOOO-OOO-OOO-NE'S for you." Instead, they should say, "Just one moment please," and walk over and get you. Don't leave the caller on perma-hold. Instruct the person answering to take a message if you're not within a few steps from reaching the phone. Brief all parties on how to take a message. It usually entails writing details and contact information down on a piece of paper with a pen that has ink. Remind everyone that it's not okay to ask the person to call back and leave a message. Call waiting should always be ignored. If you're now panicked, do what actors do and hire an answering service out of the Yellow Pages.

✓ CELL PHONES: While mobile phones can be priceless on a job hunt (just think about all those times you need to confirm directions), they can also be incredibly annoying. Multitasking is something you do while you're at work, not in the middle of an interview. If you're driving or walking down the street, let the phone ring through to your voice mail or else pick up and ask if you can return their call at a designated time. Then haul ass to a quiet place where you can concentrate and be heard. Nothing is more distracting than horns honking or frappuccino makers grinding during an interview. Not only that, if you're driving while you're on the cell phone, you're more likely to shout instead of speak. (Not to mention the possibility of hitting a telephone pole.) Make sure that the message you leave on your cell phone's voice mail is short and professional.

Dress Rehearsal

In the golden, olden days of "The Organization Man," everybody wore the same gray flannel suit to work. Today's dressed-down style can be problematic for those of us who have to dash out of a casual workplace for a high-powered interview. Here are some quick-change tips to keep the suspicious minds at bay:

- Keep your suit in your car.
- During the winter, take off your suit jacket at the same time you remove your coat, keeping it inside and tucked away from view.
- Wear half the outfit. Put the tie or scarf back on after you leave the office for the interview.
- Change at a friend's office or the office of your headhunter.
- Do a quick change at your gym.

✓ HAND-HELD DEVICES: Palm Pilots, Visors, and BlackBerries are phenomenal gadgets for responding to intra-company emails and the like. But they're not so great for handling job-hunt-related correspondence. Messages sent from these devices tend to be short, filled with slang, and riddled with typos. So don't rush to respond to a hiring manager's inquiry if a hand-held device is the only tool you have at your disposal. Instead, collect your thoughts and get thee to a computer so you can respond appropriately. One thing is for certain, a slight delay in responding won't kill you: it's not as if the overburdened hiring manager is waiting breathlessly for your response.

How to Sneak Out of Work Without Getting Caught

The ugly little truth about interviewing is that unless you want to waste one of your precious few vacation days, you will have to invent excuses to get out of work. Nobody likes to fib, but you don't want to get fired for disloyalty, either. The easy excuses—business lunches and doctor's appointments—wear thin pretty quick, so here are a few diabolical plans that will keep your boss nice and clueless.

Work-imposed conditions. *Sneaking out of my firm was like getting off "The Rock"—damn near impossible. The best excuses to throw at management are work-related conditions you need to check out, like Carpal Tunnel Syndrome. Even if they don't care about you, they understand as "management" that there is little they can do but pretend to be concerned if they want to avoid a potential lawsuit.*

—Wendy, Webmaster

Have a plumbing emergency. *If you have an early morning interview, you can leave a message on your boss's voice mail saying that you have a "plumbing emergency" (i.e., the toilet in the apartment above yours overflowed, so now there's a big leak in your bathroom, and you have to wait for the plumber) so you'll be late to work. (For added effect, call from the bathroom with the sink and tub running in the background.)*

—Beth, Account Manager

Fake a meeting. *Tell your boss that you're taking a client meeting, when in truth you're really on an interview. One time I did this and really lucked out, as my interview happened to be in the same building as one of my clients. After my interview, I popped my head in the door to say hello to my client. Later, my client mentioned to my boss how nice he thought it was that I came by to check on things. Score!*

—Alison, Project Manager

Lie like a rug. *I hated my new job and had to get out! The only problem was that my new boss was super-neurotic and had an unwritten rule: no one on her staff is allowed to take time off during the last two weeks of every month. This made it nearly impossible to get out there and meet new employers. A couple of weeks before I thought my interviews would be in full swing, I started telling everyone at work that I had taken up jogging and was really into the sport. (In reality, I hate to exercise!) At eleven p.m. the night before the interview, I drove to an emergency room and used the pay phone there to call my boss' voice mail. With sirens blasting, I left her a message that I had sprained my wrist while jogging and informed her that I wouldn't be at work the next day. While I was at the interview with my prospective new boss, flowers arrived at my apartment from my worried co-workers. Confession: I felt a bit guilty, but was relieved that the ruse had worked. From that day on, I wore an Ace bandage on my wrist every day to work. This way, if I needed to sneak out for a meeting, people would believe that I had a doctor's appointment. I ended up getting offered a new job almost immediately (although I did spend a small fortune on Ace bandages at the local drug store).*

—Barbara Ann, Financial Analyst

NOW GO WORK IT!

Here's the Takeaway:

- When it comes to interviewing, preparation is essential. Learn all you can about the company and department from web searches, online and offline publications, company web site, investment sites, your network, and the headhunter.

- Anticipate likely interview questions. Be ready to talk about all relevant experience, giving specific examples of what you have done. Practice your responses with a buddy (the best way to avoid rambling).

- Organizational fit, enthusiasm for the job, and wild cards (personal connections, interests, and other intangibles) all have a big impact on landing a job. There's always more to the equation than just your experience.

- Keep your professional references ready at all times.

- Manage all contacts with the interviewing firms carefully and professionally.

- Be ready to discuss your salary requirements when the time comes.

8

Be a Rock Star:

How to Shine in the Interview Arena

The spotlight will soon be upon you. Sure, you worked hard to get in the door, but now is the moment of truth: the interview. You're prepared; now it's your turn to be a rock star. The next time you go on an interview, it should feel like you're taking the stage for the best show of your life. When you treat an interview with this much conviction, you're bound to impress a hiring manager. They'll take note and you'll start to build a strong internal fan base. Everyone will be buzzing about you, the hot ticket.

The Countdown

The day of your big interview has arrived. You've earned the opportunity to be here. You've done your homework: you've gone over the list of anticipated questions, you know what's happening with the company and the industry trends that will impact it, and you know what information you want the interviewer to know about you. You want the job, you can do the job. Just don't get a sudden case of stage fright. Before you walk into the interviewer's office, make sure that you:

✓ **Plan ahead.** Get exact directions, floor numbers, and extensions of people with whom you are meeting. Have your follow-up questions written up and ready to go for referral during the meeting.

✓ **Check the news.** Read the paper or do a sweep of industry web sites to see if there is any timely company information or industry event you can discuss during the interview.

✓ **ARRIVE FIVE MINUTES EARLY (BUT NO MORE THAN THAT).** Few things make you look more disorganized than arriving late, and "it's not my fault" doesn't change that. Allow extra travel time for the unexpected—traffic, construction, delays in public transportation.

✓ **FIND A MIRROR.** The last thing you need is a peppercorn hitchhiker glued to your tooth and distracting the interviewer. Before strolling into the building, run the tooth-breath-nose-armpit-hair drill and make sure everything looks good. While there will be plenty of mirrors around, avoid checking yourself out in the lobby, elevator, or halls. You never know who's watching you do that little hair flip thing that you do.

✓ **GET THE SUPPORT STAFF ON YOUR SIDE.** Always be especially polite and respectful to the administrative staff at a company with which you are interviewing. Receptionists and secretaries are trusted employees, and you can be certain that they'll be watching your every move. If you're rude to the person who answers the phones, that information almost always gets passed along to the hiring manager.

✓ **SIT STILL.** Never make a call from the reception area using your cell phone or the company phone. You're guaranteed that as soon as the call goes through, the interviewer will come out to get you. And never, ever answer your cell phone during an interview. In fact, turn it off *before* you walk into the office.

✓ **BE PATIENT.** Sometimes an employer will schedule interviews back to back, or will be delayed in a meeting. Don't get irritated; just sit there patiently. You're on their turf, so you play by their rules. This is a nice, quiet time to study your resume or read an article about the company.

An interviewer kept me waiting for an hour once. I just pulled out my book, a non-fiction historical tome, and started reading until the interviewer was ready. When he came out, he apologized profusely. I could see that he was stressed. I smiled and said "no sweat." I think the fact that I was so patient made him like me more. As it turned out, the interviewer had just finished the same book I was reading, so it served as a nice icebreaker to get the interview rolling.

—DEB, USABILITY CONSULTANT

Before a big interview, I use a deep-breathing technique for the few quiet minutes while I'm waiting in the reception area. Breathe in deeply from the diaphragm for four counts, hold for eight, then breathe out for four counts and repeat. The great thing is that no one knows you are doing it and it really takes the edge off. It's even good before a telephone interview because it takes the tension out of your voice.

—DIANE, MANAGEMENT CONSULTANT

I was working as a recruiter at a large recruiting firm, and was interviewing a very promising candidate for a high-level marketing position at a prestigious company. He was bright, articulate, well qualified . . . but not perfect. We were about twenty minutes into the interview when his cell phone rang. Instead of apologizing and switching off his phone, he took the call and proceeded to start talking for about five minutes (while I waited). Let's just say, he never got the chance to see the client.

—LORI, EXECUTIVE RECRUITER

The best interviewing advice I ever got was from a random stranger on the subway just before going on my first interview. He said, "Remember that you are just as smart as the interviewers." In every interview since, his advice has been in the back of my mind.

—DAVID, SALES ASSOCIATE

THE TAO OF INTERVIEWING

When the interviewer comes out to meet you, stand up, look them straight in the eye, then greet them with a warm smile and a firm handshake. Keep in mind that the interview setting could be anywhere, from a conference room or a person's office to the cafeteria. (During the Internet boom, for instance, real estate was so rare that some people interviewed right at elevator banks.) When you enter the interview room, don't just plop down in any chair—wait for the interviewer to offer you one. If you happen to be meeting in the interviewer's office, quickly glance around for any clues, like books, diplomas, photos, or awards, that indicate you have something in common. Shared interests can serve as great conversation openers. *Warning: never, ever play with the squeezy balls sitting on the interviewer's desk,* however tempting they may be.

Above all else, relax. You've already made it this far. That means that something about you has impressed the right people. The hiring manager is not out to get you. They rarely have hidden agendas, they just want to make a good hire. They need answers to their questions: Will this person fit? Can they do the job as they claim? Will I like working with them? Hiring managers want to hear about you, why you're interested in working at their firm, and how your previous work experience would make you a good candidate. You know the drill.

✔ CARPE DIEM. After the usual small talk, seize the opportunity to summarize why you're there. Let the interviewer know that you're very *interested* in the job, that you *can do* the job and that you're *the best* person for the job. It's like watching a preview for a coming attraction at the movie theater. The trailer builds excitement for upcoming flicks. In your case, you're getting the hiring manager intrigued and charged up, which can help to set a positive tone and direction for the rest of the interview.

✓ KNOW YOUR STUFF (COLD). The "So . . . tell me about yourself" question is simple to answer, and *still* people choke. Worse still is when a hiring manager asks, "Why don't you take me through your resume," and the candidate responds with: "Uh . . . what does it say down there?" You need to feel confident about discussing every item featured on your resume, or don't bother showing up. This is the sole purpose of an interview.

✓ EVERYBODY HAS A BULLSHIT DETECTOR. A large part of an interviewer's job is to separate people who really have relevant work experience from those who only claim they do. When you put work experience on your resume, you are outlining your previous comparable work. You don't want to make a small role on a project seem larger than life on your resume, because it will come back to haunt you. Once a hiring manager senses that you're embellishing, you're dead. (And they will enjoy making you squirm.) You've got to be honest about your experience. Nobody wants a con artist working for them (would you?).

✓ ASSUME THE POSITION. You need to get the hiring manager to see you as the most suitable person for the job. Before you walk in the door you should have familiarized yourself with the position, the job requirements, and the expectations for the role. If you've done this, then every time you answer a question, you should be able to provide examples as to why you're a good fit for the position. Don't get cocky: if you tell the hiring manager that you're the best thing since sliced bread, you'll be toast. Check your ego at the door; be humble, but not self-deprecating. The only thing worse than an egomaniac is someone who's complacent, so act like you want to be there.

✓ LESS IS MORE. Attention spans are short and getting shorter by the day. Sometimes interviewees deliver more information than an interviewer could possibly digest in one sitting. Edit yourself.

Don't overwhelm the interviewer with minutiae—they don't need to know every detail of every job you've ever held. Articulate your work experience succinctly before the interviewer loses interest. Watch the interviewer's face and reactions for visual cues to wrap up your response, including: losing eye contact, incessant nodding, darting of eyes away from you and toward computer or papers, looking at their watch, or interrupting you.

✓ **CAUTION: TWO-WAY STREET AHEAD.** Focus on what the interviewer is saying and make sure that you're responding to the questions they actually ask, not just the ones you want to answer. Sometimes you can get so caught up in the process of "selling" yourself, you might forget that an interview is also a time to figure out whether you think you'll succeed in the organization. You are there not only to give information about yourself, but to gather more information about the company. Now is a perfect time to learn things about the firm you would never be able to dig up through third-party sources, like management style, team structure, and corporate culture.

✓ **GET GOOD AT PROBING.** It's the interview, and not the job description, that will give you the details and insight you need to figure out what the daily grind would be like (and whether you'd actually enjoy doing the job). Ask probing questions that will allow you to zero in on what the company *really* needs. You'll know you've struck a chord when a hiring manager starts harping on a subject (or a project that has gone untouched for months). If you're perceptive, you'll be able to tailor your message on the spot to what matters most to him or her. It also helps when you ask open-ended questions that will elicit more than a simple yes or no answer. If possible, try to get a handle on the departmental organizational chart. This way you can see who reports to whom and whether or not the group is flat or excessively hierarchical. This could give you a handle on how much room for growth there is in the group. Pay attention to any political underpinnings within the organization.

✓ LISTEN AND DIFFERENTIATE YOURSELF. People enjoy being listened to more than they like being talked at. When it comes to an interview, delivering information is only half the battle. By listening to what's important to the interviewer, you can adapt your answers. Pay attention to the industry buzzwords and listen to what parts of the job are important to the interviewer. Consider each nugget of information as a gift. These are clues you can use to determine what is essential for success in the position.

✓ SILENCE CAN ALSO BE QUITE A POWERFUL TOOL. You can gather critical information by simply keeping your mouth shut and letting the other person talk. The key to being a good listener is to participate in the conversation in subtle ways that do not interrupt. Use visual cues, like nodding, opening your eyes widely, smiling, and using your eyebrows, to demonstrate that you are listening. To keep the interviewer talking and to show them that you are indeed listening, say things like "this is very helpful," "how interesting," "I see," "please go on," "can you elaborate?"

✓ BE PERCEPTIVE. Pay attention to the interviewer's body language. When you deliver a response, look to see how the person is reacting—just be sure to give them a second to absorb what you've told them (especially if they're writing stuff down). Notice their visual cues: is the interviewer leaning in, using facial expressions that denote understanding? This indicates that they're with you. Conversely, are they leaning back in their chair away from you, looking confused, crinkling their nose, crossing their arms? This could mean that you're overloading them with information, leaving them thinking, "Will this guy ever shut up?"

✓ TAKE NOTES. Even if you have a fantastic memory, it's a good idea to jot a few things down because it signals to the interviewer that you too are listening. Plus, as you're wrapping up a point, you can glance down and make sure that you did indeed respond to their initial question. By staying engaged, you make yourself likeable, which is very important in getting hired.

✓ THE DOG AND PONY SHOW. During the interview process, you might unexpectedly get shuffled around to meet "the rest of the team." Basically, when a hiring manager does this, they're having their co-workers do the "sniff test." If you're meeting with people at your level, or even more junior than you, always remember that you're still on an interview and don't treat them as peers (you only get to do that after you're hired). A word of wisdom: if you happen to run into the friend or business contact that got you in the door, do not get super-buddy-buddy with them in front of others. You don't want to appear overly confident by association, as this may imply that you think you already have the job. Be friendly and acknowledge the connection without turning it into a class reunion.

Bring lots of extra resumes with you, and every time you meet a potential co-worker, or any new person for that matter, present them with your resume. It's also a good idea to summarize where you are in the interviewing process and which people you've met so far. When you have to endure several interviews in a row at the same company, it's easy to let your guard down. Companies make you run the gauntlet to see how you do under pressure and/or to try to get you comfortable with those doing the hiring. Always keep in mind that you're still interviewing straight through until the bitter end. Ultimately, you need your potential co-workers to think of you as someone they want to have around fifty hours a week, and as a potential asset to the organization.

PARTING IS SUCH SWEET SORROW

When you're reaching the end of an interview, last words count as much as first impressions. When the person you're interviewing with leans in and asks, "Do you have any additional questions?" don't laugh nervously and look up at the ceiling like you are trying to summon a sentence from the dark recesses of your mind. And don't just sit there like a bump on a log and say, "No, I think you've covered it all." Even if you think you know everything there is to know about the company, dig deep and pull out at least one last question. If you really can't think of anything pertaining to the position, ask about corporate culture. Or, what kinds of people succeed at their company or on your new bosses' team. If you ask intelligent and articulate questions based upon your research, you're going to end on a positive note. If the interviewer seems to be in a hurry, volunteer to email them a few follow-up questions. This will set you up for a nice email dialogue.

Ask for the job! This sounds like it should be a basic tenet of job hunting, but candidates rarely do the obvious. Hiring managers love it when candidates are enthusiastic about the job. If you've aced the interview, why not ask for the job? Or at least clearly indicate that you are interested in it. Before you leave, inquire about the next steps to the interviewing process and ask when you might expect to hear something. Finally thank the interviewer for his or her time, and excuse yourself. If you can keep the interviewer engaged and get them to walk with you out to the elevator bank, even better.

> Never forget: end every interview with the question "I am very interested in this job; do you have any reservations about choosing me to fill the position? If you do, I'd like the chance to clear them up right now."
>
> —LAURA, DATA AND INFORMATION SALESPERSON

A couple of years ago, I showed up for an interview where the headhunter forgot to tell the client that I was coming in. I wound up getting the job, believe it or not, but it was a challenging interview. Because the person I was meeting with wasn't prepared to sit with me and in fact had something else scheduled, I had to work a little harder to ensure that I was able to keep his attention and direct the meeting. I learned that the preparation for an interview completely determines the outcome. In my preparation I had envisioned how I would have liked the interview to progress, including subjects covered and questions asked. I practiced aloud exactly what I wanted to ask and rehearsed precisely what I wanted to highlight about myself. Had I not done these things the meeting would have never gotten off the ground and I certainly wouldn't have landed the job. Chalk one up for being a bit obsessive.

—ANDY, MUSIC MARKETER

I like to run a fun, informal interview. By making the environment extremely comfortable, I can catch someone off guard and learn a lot. When I can get a candidate to sink into a conversation and forget that it's a job interview, that's when the real person comes through, for better or worse. I will often ask someone to walk me through his or her resume as if I haven't seen it. I'll pick little things apart; I'll change the direction of the conversation more frequently just to see how the candidate can handle shifting gears. I also listen intently to the candidate. Silence makes people nervous, which it shouldn't. But the juiciest information comes when I ask a candidate for more information after they've performed their whole rehearsed script. I like to grill candidates when they try to gloss over things.

I tend to spend more time on sociological and psychological questions, rather than resume questions. It lets me know a substantial amount: whether a candidate can carry on intelligent conversations; whether he respects other people's opinions; whether he listens; whether he knows what he's talking about (or can successfully fudge his way through). I want to know what sustains a candidate, and why they are proud of who they are as a person.

—MARIA, TECHNOLOGY RECRUITER

It's a known fact that people love to talk about themselves, and the more you can turn the conversation around and give out warm, energetic vibes, the more someone will want to hire you to join their team. I truly believe that I landed my last job because I asked each interviewer how they got to where they are now. By doing this, I gave

The Interview-After-the-Interview

Contributed by Lena M. Bottos

You did it. You crafted the perfect resume, donned the suit, and answered their questions like a pro. The interview is finally over. Or is it? Don't kid yourself: the interview is *never* over. Not until you're safely in your car with the windows rolled up and headed home. Letting your guard down too soon could chip dollars off your salary, or worse, reduce your chances of landing the job.

Chit-chat can seem harmless when the interviewer is laughing and sharing personal stories. But the interview-after-the-interview can be dangerous if you overshare. *Don't* disclose that you were so nervous you wore two undershirts. *Do* fondly recollect the parts of the interview that went well, or explain which information was helpful in understanding more about the position. The things you say in the interview-after-the-interview may be more important than anything else—and could make you seem more or less valuable in the employer's eyes.

Responses to questions about hobbies and interests can enhance or diminish your perceived value. Keep in mind the risks associated with gushing about your vast comic book collection. A well-documented and indexed collection shows initiative, organization, and drive; but how goth is the corporate culture? Super-introverted couch potato hobbies like multiplayer games are best kept to yourself if you're interviewing for a job that requires, say, cold-calling. Team sports are great—if you actually play them. If you say you love softball, prepare to join the company team when you're hired.

If you are taking a course that will help your career or expand your capabilities, you portray yourself as a self-starter, and the additional skills may be worth premium pay.

Talking about your current job allows you to impress the interviewers with your work ethic and temperament. But say only nice things about your most recent employer. Interviewers know you are leaving your job for a reason, so don't dwell on it. Instead, discuss some fun projects you've had or people you've enjoyed working with. Never disparage.

You too can ask questions in the interview-after-the-interview. What are the work hours? What do people do for lunch? Are there nice, relaxing places to eat outdoors? Is there anywhere nearby to run errands? Is the interviewer satisfied with his or her work/life balance?

Some interviewers break the code and tell all. Be very afraid if an interviewer complains about the work or the company. It means not only is this a tough place to work, but also the company isn't savvy enough to take its disgruntled staff members off interview duty. If it hasn't come up yet, ask the interviewer about the company's benefits and compare them with what you're used to. The company could make up any difference in your base pay.

Lunch is a great time for interviewers to see your true colors. So brush up on your meal etiquette, and order something impossible to spill. Companies know that sharing a meal away from the office puts you more at ease and may loosen your lips. They want to do more than just feed you. They want to know whether you "fit"—whether they would enjoy being your colleague. Show them, by your every maneuver and gesture, that you can command top dollar.

Skip the burger and order something that shows you appreciate quality. Don't get carried away, though, by ordering a meal that's more fabulous than the job, or an expensive entree that comes with a bib. And try to eat the way everyone else does—nibbling ravioli in a spiral pattern is just weird.

The folks who take you to lunch are likely to be your age and in comparable jobs. They will probably ask how your morning interviews went, or even how you liked the interviewers. Hint: they went just great.

Once you're home, it's over—for now. But every contact with the company gives more insight into who you are and how you function in the business environment. A call for a second interview, or even an offer, is a critical point of contact. Your employment is not final until your first day of work.

Lena is a compensation market analyst at Salary.com, which researches pay trends and data for employees and employers. Drawing from her experience on both sides of the negotiating table, she is the author of several career-related articles covering topics from interview etiquette to salary negotiations.

a nod to their accomplishments. Also, it helped me decide whom I
would want to be my mentor, in case I decided to work there.

—MEREDITH, PR ACCOUNT EXECUTIVE

PHONE INTERVIEWS:
THE NEXT BEST THING TO BEING THERE

Wireless technologies, telecommuting, teleconferencing, the Internet: nowadays, you can interview anytime and anywhere. So don't be
surprised if a hiring manager requests a phone interview. Given the
influx of resumes that hiring managers and headhunters receive,
they may have to review hundreds of new candidates for each and
every job. Many firms choose to save precious interview time for "serious" candidates by first doing phone interviews. Think of this as an
evolutionary, yet necessary change that goes along with the Internet
Revolution. Remember, a tremendous amount of business these days
is conducted on the phone, so it's extremely important that your
phone personality be consistent with your face-to-face persona. A
good phone interview will weed out unsuitable candidates sooner
than later because people ease into their comfort zone when they're
on the phone, often forgetting that they're on an interview. This lets a
hiring manager know how the candidate would be with clients or
co-workers. This means that it is important to take a phone interview
seriously.

The importance of good phone skills doesn't end with a phone interview. You'll receive follow-up calls throughout the screening
process. Each time you do, remember to treat each call with the care
you would give to an in-person interview. You don't know the "real"
reason for the call—it might be the interviewer's tool for sizing you up
vs. your competition. Your main goal in the phone interview is to be
one of the people asked back. Don't over-think it. You want to come
across as compelling, engaging, and qualified not only in work experience but also in how well you can fit in with the organization. Here's
how to prepare to give good phone:

✔ **FIND A PRIVATE SPACE.** Make sure that you are in a quiet place where you won't be interrupted by family or roommates while you are on the phone. If your kid or roommate busts in, not only will that be distracting to your train of thought during the interview, but it also makes you look unprofessional. It's a good idea to put a "Do Not Disturb" sign on the door. If you can lock the door, even better.

✔ **CHOOSE YOUR PHONE WISELY.** Use an ordinary phone with a handset and a cord. Portable phones are off-limits—nothing is worse than a battery going dead or a channel going haywire when you're on an interview. Cell phones are even more annoying. You don't want the interviewer to know that you're doing the interview from the street corner, your gym, or the local Starbucks. If you need to use a cell phone, use it in a very quiet place. Pay phones are okay if they are quiet, and if you use a calling card so that you won't be cut off or interrupted to insert more change. Do not attempt to do a phone interview in the middle of a shared office space. Excuse yourself to an available conference room or schedule a meeting "out of the office."

✔ **PLAN ENOUGH TIME.** Don't squeeze in twenty minutes for a phone interview. Phoners have been known to last hours, and you need to be flexible. Always be courteous and ask the hiring manager how much time they have and let them know your time constraints. If you're approaching the max time allotted (typically a sign that the interview is sailing along positively) ask them nicely if they want to continue or if you should schedule a time to come in.

✔ **TREAT A PHONER LIKE AN IN-PERSON INTERVIEW.** Be professional from the time you answer the phone to the moment you hang up. Avoid the urge to answer call waiting. If you're very interested in the position and you feel as if your skill set is a match, as you wrap, be sure to let the interviewer know that you are eager to do a face-to-face and that you would be *very* interested in pursuing the opportunity to work at their firm.

✓ GET YOUR CRIB NOTES OUT. Keep your resume and notes in front of you. A phoner is an open-book exam. Glance down and refer to projects and work experiences specifically as you need them. Just don't let them hear you shuffle papers.

✓ BE EXTRA ENGAGING. A phone interview is not a quick conversation to review your work experience. It's a time to engage the interviewer. One-way phone conversations can be tiresome to both parties. After you've described a particular work experience, try to get the hiring manager talking in order to obtain additional information about the position.

✓ LISTEN INTENTLY. By now, you've already done your research on the company and have compiled a list of questions, so get ready to ask them. First, the interviewer will know you did your homework, which immediately will set you apart as a proactive candidate. But the best part is that you'll be able to take copious notes from the conversation. (Just don't let it distract you from listening.)

✓ DON'T FORGET THAT YOU'RE ON AN INTERVIEW. The interviewer is waiting for you to slip into your relaxed self. Don't attempt to multitask. Don't tempt yourself by having your email open while you're conducting a phone interview. It's downright disrespectful for the person on the receiving end of the phone call to hear that "you've got mail."

I called a candidate at home once, and he picked right up. We were having a great interview, when he suddenly asked me if I could wait for a minute while he climbed out of the tub. I was privy to the whole bath-draining, toweling-off experience. When he finally picked up, which took a while, I had trouble concentrating on what he was saying because all I could do was picture him in the buff.

—Pat, Headhunter

NOW GO WORK IT!

Here's the Takeaway:

- The interview is your time to shine. Be confident, personable, and, above all, prepared.

- Don't let the b.s. get in your way. Check the news for late-breaking events. Allow plenty of travel time, confirm time, and directions. Don't be late.

- Turn off all cell phones and other bleepin' devices before you arrive at the interviewer's offices.

- Don't be humble about your qualifications and experience, but keep your ego in check.

- Relax. You've prepared for this, you've practiced and polished your responses. Just wow them.

- Treat phone interviews with the same level of focus and seriousness as you would an in-person interview.

9

SEAL THE DEAL:

Know When to Hold and When to Fold

Get ready, get set . . . now wait. You've officially entered that loathsome period of time between finishing your round of interviews and finding out whether or not the company will offer you the job. Even though the interviews are behind you, the hard work is far from over. If you think it's time to kick back, relax, and wait for an answer think again. Flake out now, and losing that job offer will be nobody's fault but your own. The waiting game is where jobs are won and lost. You need to step up to the plate—especially when there's "radio silence"—and remind people why you're the right person for the position. Now is the time to be as tenacious as ever and make sure that they don't forget why they *need* to hire you and what problems you'll solve once you get inside. You also need to be using this time wisely by preparing your references, strategizing what you want your offer to look like, and gearing up for your negotiation.

The deck will shuffle many times before an offer letter goes out. That's why this chapter is all about playing your cards right. You'll learn how to win at the waiting game, how to figure out when an offer is coming your way, how to negotiate, and how to accept (or decline) the job you've worked so hard to get. You'll also learn how to say *sayonara* to your current company without burning your bridges, which is the real key to building a long-lasting career no matter what company ends up hiring you.

WIN THE WAITING GAME

You are an investment and a lot will be riding on you. Your potential new boss will be agonizing over whether or not you're the right person for the team, the department, and the company as a whole. You can greatly improve your chances by following up. Now is not the time for some lame-ass, how-are-you-doing check-in call. It's during the quiet period that you have to make sure that the key decision-makers know what you can bring to the table. Prove you can deliver by doing follow-up that makes people take notice. Send along idea-generating memos or presentations that let insiders know that you can actually *do* the job. For example, write up a preliminary analysis on a project that you discussed during one of your interviews (then send it via FedEx, so you're sure it'll get opened). Ask to be invited back during the "quiet period" to present the work you've done so far. It's all about taking the initiative. Don't wait to provide follow-up. Just do it. The element of surprise will bring a smile to your future boss's face.

Every interaction you make with a company insider right now can impact whether or not you get hired. If you've proven yourself like-able and able to get people rooting for you from the inside, you've got a better shot at getting the job. Get company insiders to champion your cause and start talking you up. The more buzz circulating around you, the more confident people will be in their decision. Keep the outreach going by writing follow-up notes and emails to these people so they know that you really, really want the job. (Remember The Seven-Impression Rule from Chapter 3)?

One equalizer to protect against being a victim of poor timing is the thank-you note. A thank-you note should be sent as soon as possible after an interview so that it will have some chance of influencing the interviewer's evaluation of you. I head up the recruiting committee for our law firm's Associates Program. I could interview three or four candidates in a row before I ever get a chance to sit down and write up their evaluation—more if I have a busy week with depositions or hearings. When this occurs, the candidates that I have interviewed more recently have an advantage, because I remember more about them. A strong thank-you note can take me back to the interview, and if I haven't written the evaluation yet, it can also encourage me to write a more favorable review or offer positive comments at the follow-up meetings when we discuss the recruits. There have been multiple times when a candidate moved from a "maybe" to a "yes" simply because of their follow-up.

—Shawn, Trial Lawyer

Circumstances Beyond Your Control

A long, drawn-out waiting period can crush your confidence if you let it. That's why you need to put yourself in the hiring managers' shoes and start thinking about what's important to him or her right now. The people making hiring decisions are under great pressure to choose correctly. When times are good, hiring processes go faster because head-count budgets are bigger and it's easier to push new hires through. When an industry or company is hurting, the process slows down (way down), and hiring managers can become very cautious about each and every person they extend an offer to. Sure, having an unfilled desk can lower a company's productivity. But hiring the wrong person can cost a company even more.

Hiring decisions can also take longer when the person responsible for the selection has had little or no hiring experience. This is usually because they fear making a mistake and need a chance to fully survey the talent pool. And the more senior the position you're going for, the longer the decision-making will take, because the stakes are higher.

Regardless of the reason for the delay, you need to chill. You don't want to put yourself out of favor by doing something stupid. (That means no whining or complaining.) A decision will happen when it happens, and unless you have a brilliant offer on the table from a company you want to work for equally as much, keep your cool. If you get antsy or start nagging, the hiring manager may start to think that's what you'd be like to work with.

IS THIS THE ONE?

It's time to get into a contemplative state. Use the waiting period as a time to truly evaluate whether *you* want the position and whether you'd succeed in it. It's easy to get so wrapped up in closing the deal that you forget to ask yourself if you ever really wanted the job in the first place. Interviewing is like dating: you don't have to get into a long-term relationship with everyone you meet.

Even if you want the job, will it be a fit for you? Think back to the interviews: did you like the working environment and the people? How about your boss—can you work shoulder-to-shoulder with him or her forty to sixty hours a week? Will you fit in? Did you feel like you had to pretend to be someone you're not to get this far? Did you alter your persona so much during your interviews that you feel like you have to change who you are for the job? If you're not a good fit, admit it to yourself before you get in over your head, and bow out gracefully (before you live to regret it).

WATCH FOR WARNING SIGNS

While you may have put a lot of energy into getting to the offer stage, it's the small stuff that counts. Take off the rose-colored glasses and see if you can find any chinks in the armor of that perfect job. You don't want to accept it and find out later that you're a quick fix to a larger, systemic problem. Here are some warning signs to indicate that it might be time to fold.

✓ **DOES THE DEPARTMENT HAVE HIGH TURNOVER?** It could mean that you're getting yourself into a post that involves impossible deadlines and unattainable goals.

✓ **ARE THERE SEVERAL UNFILLED POSITIONS IN THE DEPARTMENT?** You might end up doing not only your job but also somebody else's—and only getting paid one salary.

✓ **HOW MANY POSITIONS ARE OPEN THAT REPORT TO THE BIG CHEESE?** If there are more than one, you might end up reporting to the boss from hell.

✓ **DID THE COMPANY CHECK YOUR REFERENCES?** If not, they might not follow up on other things.

✓ **DOES THE OFFER SOUND TOO GOOD TO BE TRUE?** If could well be. You don't want to walk into a company that is desperate for anyone, just to have them close down months later.

✓ **ARE YOU GETTING PRESSURED TO MAKE A DECISION?** Good things come to those who wait; good companies know this. Try to figure out what's driving this pressure.

Before the offer letter arrives, you'll want to remind yourself of the original reasons that you decided to pursue a new job in the first place. Will your original goals be achieved with this new opportunity? What are you giving up if you take the job? Will you be better off staying where you are until you find the right opportunity? Also, think about your job title, responsibilities, and promotion potential. Then examine quality of life, working hours, corporate culture goals. Finally, review what it is you need to achieve compensation-wise. Specific items you'll want to confirm include: salary, bonus/commission eligibility, vacation/personal days, holidays, maternity/paternity leave, expense accounts, benefits and insurance, 401K, employee stock ownership, and equity.

How Do I Find My Magic Number?

Contributed by Bill Coleman

Long before the negotiation starts, you need to have the right number in your head. The good news is that salary data is everywhere. These days, everyone can negotiate like an executive. So forget about accepting the first offer on the table.

A "win-win" negotiation happens when both parties believe they have done well. The company's "right number" best supports company goals without being too expensive. Your "right number" will feel fair and consistent with the market, given your skills and experience. Before deciding what to pay an employee, companies research the value of the job. They price the "space," the position being filled, before the "face," the person doing the job. In the old salary negotiation, the value of the space was known only to the employer. Online pay data has revolutionized salary negotiations by putting market data into the hands of employees. Today's online sources go a step further by putting a price on those factors known to make the biggest difference in an individual's pay. Here's how the new salary negotiation works:

1. **Find a generic match for your job.** Companies call this a "benchmark" job, a standard against which others can be measured. Take care to choose a benchmark job you can support with evidence. Be honest—if your future boss is going to give you daily task lists, don't match yourself to a job that emphasizes independent judgment. Get a job description before your interview to help with your research.

2. **Find data for the generic job.** Salary sites offer data on jobs in various industries and regions. Test various "What-if?" scenarios to try different locations, industries, or job titles. *Hint:* Finance or human resources managers typically research three or four generic jobs for every job they price. Bring a printout of your data to your negotiation, just in case. Try to get a salary range. Include the job de-

scription and the method the data provider uses to crunch the numbers. Employers trust data originally reported by HR professionals the most. If the employer questions your numbers, ask to see theirs.

3. **Adjust up or down if necessary.** If the job isn't a perfect match, adjust the pay upward or downward. If you've chosen a job that requires similar skills, but you'll have more supervisory responsibility, give yourself a premium.

4. **Figure out whether the job is worth more or less in this company.** Two employers might place a different value on the same job, so look for the employer who values it more. For example, a security guard at a bank may have more salary wiggle room than a security guard at the mall. Pay is also a matter of location, location, location. If you're an assistant buyer for the only major retailer in town, they're more likely to discount your pay than raise their prices. In your negotiation, ask the prospective employer to describe the company's "pay philosophy." They may not tell you, but if they do, you'll get a sense of how the company typically pays relative to the market.

5. **Sell your performance.** With a new employer you've got a clean slate. They don't know about your sixty-seven-minute lunches, your inability to use a spreadsheet, or your idiosyncratic cubicle etiquette. Keep it that way. Instead, make sure they find out about the things you're best at—especially things they're willing to pay for. Ask how the company measures performance, and which skills and performance standards are valued the most. Salary.com's Personal Salary Report looks at eight factors, or "personal variables," that have an impact on how your pay could compare with the market data. Use the following factors to prepare a negotiation checklist: education, number of people who report to you, person to whom you report, years of experience at this level, last performance rating, professional certifications, hazardous working conditions, working hours.

6. **Agree on a salary.** The right number should fall out of this research and discussion. It'll be a range representing what you are worth to this company, given the relevant market for this job and your skills and experience. Finding this range together represents a positive change in salary negotiations. It's also an almost assured path to a win-win negotiation.

7. **Lather, rinse, repeat.** All salary negotiations should end with a discussion of the next steps for career advancement. So set an action plan. What will it take for you to earn more? What are the steps toward promotion? The job may be yours, but the cycle of excellence is starting all over again.

Bill heads the compensation practice at <u>Salary.com</u>, which analyzes pay trends and data for employees and employers. Job hunters and corporations routinely seek his expertise. Bill is also a frequent source for journalists representing all types of outlets, including the Wall Street Journal, CNN, NPR, *and* Rolling Stone.

DON'T COUNT YOUR CHICKENS

Don't fantasize about telling your old boss to take that job and shove it. You don't have the job until you've got the job. That means you can't stop working until after you've resigned! If you're like most people, you still have a never-ending inbox. If you think you're close to receiving an offer, start wrapping up your projects, so that you can add those duties to your resume after you leave. By working especially hard right now, you might even snare a counteroffer—if that's something you want. A million things could happen between now, when you get the offer, and when you actually start your first day at your new job. Negotiations could fall apart or you might decide after much reflection that you like your current job just fine. By working hard now, you won't leave your boss in the lurch, either (remember, you might want to use the guy as a reference someday).

While you're fighting internal freak-outs, you need to keep your poker face on right now. Don't tell anyone at work that you might be looking unless you want your secret to get out. If your boss catches wind of your job hunt, he or she could fire you on the spot. Be sure to remove important personal items that you have stashed in your desk drawers (but nothing that will conflict with your employment agreement and get you sued). Be sure to leave family pictures and knick-knacks out so that everything will seem to be business as usual.

After three months of interviewing, I had landed a job I had worked incredibly hard to get. The paperwork was signed, sealed, and delivered. I felt like a gigantic weight had been lifted off my shoulders. Better still, I was taking a long weekend to attend a friend's wedding and planned to turn in my letter of resignation the following Monday. Life was great! The only loose end was a quick phone call with my new boss on Friday morning before I hit the golf course for the pre-wedding tourney. I called at the designated time and there was no answer. Weird. I called again, and this time my new boss's assistant picked up. She sounded a little flustered and said that my boss would get back to me ASAP and that I shouldn't go anywhere. Now I started to panic. Finally, my new boss called and my sinking feeling proved on target. The entire division had been eliminated, and there would be no job to go to the following week. The thought of going back to work at my current company was beyond comprehension. I had already checked out. But as much as I didn't want to go back, that's exactly what I did on Monday morning as if nothing had changed. I channeled all the fire and brimstone that I was feeling, and one year later got a big promotion. So, you never know.

—SCOTT, OPERATIONS MANAGER

REFERENCE CHECK-IN

Don't underestimate how long it will take to get in touch with your references. People have lives, jobs, commitments, and you are not their top priority. You're in the big leagues; now is not the time for J.V. moves. Just because you have your references locked and loaded doesn't mean you can get them to speak on your behalf at the drop of a hat.

When you feel like you're about to receive a job offer, get it together and call the references that can best represent you for this particular opportunity. You don't need to use every single reference, just the ones that can discuss and evaluate your performance given the requirements of the job you're up for.

Once they've let you know their availability and have agreed to discuss your abilities, you should email or fax them a copy of your resume. This way they can get comfortable with how you are representing yourself. Don't let your references fly blind. You'll want to brief them by giving them an overview of the job, the role, your responsibilities. The more senior the person you're asking to serve as your reference, the less likely they will be to remember the details of your key projects. So it's good to have a blend of people who can talk about your skills from a macro and micro perspective. People do have selective memories, so you may have to remind people about the details of various projects. Ask the reference to touch on key things that will position you better in the hiring manager's eyes. For example, if project management is a key aspect of the position, your reference could say something along these lines: "It sounds as though project management is a big part of this job. I can assure you that when it comes to Jim, you've got no worries there! He took initiative and followed through on all the projects that we worked on together." Bottom line: you want your references to reinforce your strengths based upon what's important to the companies you're interviewing with.

You need to respect the privacy of the people you list as contacts, and only send their name and contact information to the hiring manager *after* you've briefed them and they've agreed to serve as your reference for this particular opportunity. Always show your gratitude by thanking them with a nice note or a small gift.

WHERE THERE'S SMOKE, THERE'S FIRE

A decision about the offer is likely to be headed your way when there is a sudden flurry of activity after an unbearable dry spell. Your headhunter might check on your status. Or, the hiring manager might call to see if you're still interested. You know the signs are especially good when your prospective boss makes a "Hi. How ya doing?" phone call.

If and when you do get the official call about the offer, don't start doing high-fives around the office. You are a long way from the deal being sealed. Yes, the company wants you, but the negotiation process is still ahead of you, your references still need to be checked, and you have yet to decide whether or not you want to accept or decline the offer. Not only that, offers get rescinded all the time. ("You're not hired till you're hired" still applies.) Think about it: you're hemming and hawing about whether or not you want an offer, your competition is waiting in the wings for you to do something stupid so that they can step in and steal your job. Don't give them the chance.

When you do get the offer, ask to see it in writing, via fax or email. Accept nothing over the phone. Before that offer letter lands in your inbox, ask yourself "Knowing what I know about this job and the offer I'm likely to get, am I willing to compromise on anything?" For example, if you're looking at a position with high promotion potential that will make you a very marketable candidate in the next couple of years, think about what you'll be willing to give up for that opportunity. Salary? Vacation time? A dress-down work environment? If you value normal work hours and lots of vacation, you may pick a lower-paying job because the perks and benefits are excellent. Everything is a trade-off, and you need to select what the most important things are versus the least. By making some key decisions before the offer officially comes in, your judgment won't be clouded by passion or pressure.

THE SKINNY: **Let your headhunter do the talking**. An executive recruiter's job is to broker the deal. Take advantage of their negotiating skills and let them be the middle man. Keep in mind that their compensation is tied to yours—the perfect incentive!

THE MOMENT OF NEGOTIATION HAS ARRIVED

You got the offer. When the official offer letter finally arrives, compare it to your original goals and see how it measures up. Wherever you find differences, you will also discover a road map that shows where you can negotiate. If you managed your expectations and communicated throughout the hiring process it should be pretty smooth sailing. If, after comparing the offer to your original goals, you find it fair and equitable, take it. Not every offer needs to be negotiated. In other cases you may not be so lucky, which means to the negotiation table you must go. The most important thing when it comes to a negotiation is to remember that you're not going to offend anyone if you ask for what you feel you deserve—especially if you back up the request with sound reasoning. Just don't expect the company to roll over on every tiny detail. Here's how to master your side of the negotiation:

✓ BE EXTREMELY ORGANIZED. You won't win every negotiation point, so it's better to pre-select those that you're adamant about winning. Prepare only the points you want to focus on. Don't get bogged down in negotiating for stuff you don't really care about. Once you're done, prioritize. Type up your checklist—it makes you look serious and prepared—and refer to it during the negotiation.

✓ BACK IT UP. If you're going to have any shot at winning on a point, you need to back it up with facts. "Just because" isn't going to get you any more moola in your paycheck. You know your worth, so prove it.

✓ BE CONFIDENT. Attempt to be cool. It all starts by knowing your material cold. If you're doing the negotiation face-to-face, look the hiring manager or your new boss (whomever it is) directly in the eye as you deliver your points. Articulate clearly what you want, and don't become so emotionally invested that you become a basket case. You can avoid this by being prepared.

✓ BE HONEST WITH YOURSELF. Face it: a job negotiation isn't a level playing field. Unless you're a hand-picked CEO candidate you have more to lose than the company because you actually want the job, while the company can walk away. If this particular job is important to you, then you need to make trade-offs so you can get in the door and prove yourself. After that, you need to try and get the most beneficial package you can get, without sacrificing more than you can bear.

✓ KNOW YOUR BOTTOM LINE. A negotiation will hinge on knowing what your bottom line is—the point below which you will not go. Don't lose sight of your goals, and know what you're willing to sacrifice to get them. Be flexible on items that are less important to you.

✓ DON'T REVISIT AGREED-UPON POINTS. Approach a point, come to a mutually agreeable conclusion (hopefully one in your favor), and move on. Once a point has been agreed upon, jot it down and move on to the next one.

✓ DON'T FALL VICTIM TO THE "AND ANOTHER THING" SYNDROME. If you feel the need to negotiate every single point on the offer letter, you probably did a terrible job of communicating your needs to the company during the interview process.

✓ **ADAPT TO THE SITUATION AS IT UNFOLDS.** Negotiations are dynamic. You don't know which way the negotiation will go until it begins. Once it starts, go with the flow and pay attention to what is happening at that moment. A lot will depend on the other party's personality. For example, a hard-ass may want to win the first couple of points right out of the gate, and then might relinquish on a point or two later on.

✓ **DON'T CONFUSE SELF-CONFIDENCE WITH ARROGANCE.** Cockiness is the quickest way to eighty-six an offer. If all goes well you'll be showing up for work in a couple of weeks. You don't want your new boss, the guy you've been working so hard to impress, to think you're a jerk and withdraw your offer. Instead, be firm and assertive without being antagonistic (or loud).

✓ **BE READY FOR THE PSYCH-OUT.** Wait for the company to toss out the first number. Instead of balking or replying with a specific number, pause and reply, "Is there a possibility that you can offer a higher number?" Sometimes the company will have some wiggle room to negotiate, other times their number will be final.

✓ **SILENCE FREAKS PEOPLE OUT.** If you happen to get to a stalemate on a point you feel strongly about, resist the urge to speak. Silence is the most powerful tool you have. At the negotiating table, the person who speaks first generally loses.

✓ **TAKE A POWDER.** At the end of the negotiation you'll get a lot of pressure to make a commitment. Tell them that you'd like to think about it, and ask for a day or two to consider your options.

WHAT DO YOU DO IF YOU'RE #2?

An offer is pending. It's down to just you and another candidate. The call comes in but the answer isn't what you were expecting—they decided to go with the other person. That knot in your stomach just turned into a lump in your throat, followed by a wave of shock and disappointment. Your first reaction might be to fly off the handle and start challenging the terrible decision not to hire you (after all, you're the right person for the job). Not so fast; you don't want to be seen as a sore loser. Most managers have learned through bitter experience that giving direct feedback to a rejected applicant often ends up in an argument. So don't put the hiring manager on the defensive by asking why *you* didn't get the job. Instead, ask what particular strengths gave the edge to the candidate who got the offer. If you read between the lines, you'll be able to figure out if it was decided that number one was a better fit, had more work experience, or if there was just a wildcard reason. Before you finish your conversation, let the hiring manager know that you would be very interested in hearing about any future opportunities at the company or that you'd love to get a call if it doesn't work out with number one. Your graciousness just might leave the hiring manager with a bad case of buyer's remorse.

If you play your cards right, you could get wait-listed, which means that you're the wrong person for the available job but the right person for the company. You've already passed the corporate sniff test, so perhaps the right job at the firm is only a department away. Always leave the powers-that-be with the feeling that you're still very interested in working for them.

Most important, there is always the possibility that you could end up landing the job. Any of the following scenarios could happen to number one: he or she could accept a counteroffer, fail a drug test, or get caught lying on the employment application. A lot can happen in the next two to three months. Keep your fingers crossed. As they say in showbiz: it ain't over until the fat lady sings.

This may sound strange, but you still need to send thank-you notes to everyone you went the distance with. These will be the hardest letters to write in your life, but write them you must. By doing this you're demonstrating that you're a first-class candidate and you could well be strengthening the relationship instead of ending it. If you really connected with someone you interviewed with, don't be shy about keeping them informed of what's up with your career. From time to time, send them an email about special projects you've completed, promotions, or changes in responsibility. You never know when this person might be able to help you out down the road.

> If you don't get your dream job, don't give up hope. Twice I have been second runner-up for a job I really wanted and got called back after the gold medalist's reputation got tarnished by bad references.
>
> —JEFF, COMMODITIES TRADER

> If you were in the final running for a position that you didn't get, you might still fit elsewhere in our organization. Ask in a genuine and sincere way if there might be opportunities elsewhere in the company that might match your background. Even ask the hiring manager for referrals to other companies that might be hiring. HR people talk amongst themselves. This is also a good time to get some feedback. It can never hurt to ask the question: why did you choose the other candidate? What attributes did they have that got them the job? By asking the question like this, you're not putting the hiring manager on the defensive and you may learn how to position yourself for the future.
>
> —KATHY, INVESTMENT BANKING RECRUITER

AND YOUR ANSWER IS?

The negotiation is now complete and the final offer is on the table. Now the ball is officially in your court. But will you accept or decline? Are you going to be happy with the job when you combine the com-

The Armchair Millionaire's Guide to Negotiating Your Employment Package

Contributed by Lewis Schiff

Negotiating your employment package with your prospective employer represents the first time they get to see how you handle yourself in difficult circumstances. The phrase "never let them see you sweat" certainly applies here. Don't think of the employment negotiation as the final word on how much value your employer places on you. It's a smell test between two friendly adversaries. Remember that you both want to win but both of you also need to close the deal with dignity. Leaving a little money on the table, or not fighting for the last dollar, can show your potential employer that you're a long-term thinker.

Here's my checklist for keeping your cool during pay negotiations.

1. Ask lots of questions. During an interview, you are judged by the quality of the questions you ask.
2. Never, ever throw out the first number.
3. Never, ever throw out the second number.
4. Discuss the benefits in detail, including health insurance, retirement package, and vacation policy.
5. Find out if a severance package is something you can agree on before being hired and under what circumstances you'd be eligible for severance.
6. Ask to schedule a salary and performance review within at least six months as a condition of accepting the job. This shows ambition and confidence.
7. Ask for the offer in writing.
8. Don't get personal. This is business, so don't share more about your personal life than is asked and even then, be careful about revealing

too much. This includes family health problems, your financial situation, and your future plans (to get married, start a family, whatever).

9. If you've scheduled a vacation that would occur after your starting date, make sure it will be honored as a condition of accepting the position.

10. Never accept the job on the spot. Always tell them you need time to think about it. If they say they are going to offer it to someone else, let them know that it's an important decision and you expect them to respect how seriously you take the decision. Agree on a deadline, even if it's just twenty-four hours. Make sure to get back to them before the deadline.

11. Conduct yourself in a professional manner at all times. If you want to rise in the company, you need to show them that you can handle yourself in a negotiation.

The bottom line: if you can keep your cool while negotiating your own employment package, you may be management material.

Lewis founded the Armchair Millionaire web site in 1997. His first book, The Armchair Millionaire, *was published in 2001. Today, ArmchairMillionaire.com is a fast-growing community of common sense savers and investors.*

pensation with all the other benefits, perks, etc.? Can you live with your decision and be happy about it? Are you willing to make the work/life/pay trade-offs associated with taking this job? Do you think you have a competitive offer sitting in front of you? Finally, did the company do better than your bottom line? Don't get greedy; just answer the question. Regardless of whether the answer is yes or no, get back to people when you say you will. The company has a business to run, whether you take the job or not.

If you agree to accept a job, take a deep breath—it's now time to sign on the dotted line. Before you do, you'll want to think twice about

Negotiating in Tough Times

Contributed by Chris Taylor

First, the bad news: your negotiating power ain't what it used to be. At the height of the late-1990s boom, anyone who could string two words together could negotiate a handsome package for themselves: their own assistants, a few weeks in Aruba, the works. Needless to say, times have changed. But here's the good news: things aren't as bad as you think. After an economy rebounds, unemployment will crest, and the job market will slowly shift back in the job seeker's favor. (Thank God.) But until a recovery is full-blown and companies move back into frenzied hiring mode, you're still going to have to dust off those negotiation skills and get creative.

If you work in a sector that's in a slump, huge pay boosts, for instance, are not likely to be on the table. The fact is, the firm you're interviewing with probably doesn't have much to give you, money-wise. So get what you're after in different ways. Higher commissions or deferred bonuses are things even cash-poor companies can probably handle. Heavy discounts on the firm's own products or services could turn out to be a nice sum, too. A better work-life balance—getting a few more vacation days, or half-days on Fridays to spend more time with the family, for example—won't hit them in the pocketbook.

Another tactic you can try: negotiate the timing of your first salary review—instead of waiting a year, settle on an earlier date. "We're hearing of people who are taking jobs with the agreement of a review in three or six months, when the company may be better able to afford a raise," notes Wayne Cooper, publisher of Kennedy Information's *Directory of Executive Recruiters.*

How about a few high-tech gadgets to help you telecommute? If it means getting more work out of you, firms aren't likely to turn you down. "Laptops, pagers, cell phones, BlackBerries: those are all win-win perks, because then you're available to work 24/7," says executive recruiting guru John Challenger.

There's more. But to find out what's available to you, Ron Shapiro, head of Baltimore's Shapiro Negotiations Institute, says that proper preparation is the key. Many companies have tuition reimbursement programs, for instance, that most employees don't even take advantage of. Getting free training for yourself is just as good as a raise. Or maybe additional health benefits are something the company is flexible about offering.

Don't scoff at things like a better title, either, if execs have nothing else to offer you. It may not be a boost to your paycheck right now, but a more senior position is fantastic leverage for negotiating in future years. And if you're surreptitiously looking elsewhere for work, a gold-plated job title could launch you into an even higher position at a rival firm. "It's a sign of respect, and not an empty thing at all," says Challenger. "It means more money down the road."

Above all, don't undersell yourself. In a down economy, you may be tempted to take whatever the company offers without a squeak of disagreement. But you may have a stronger negotiating position than you realize, says Shapiro: "It astounds me how even the most talented people are not really good at going in to their boss and just saying what they want."

Chris is the careers reporter for SmartMoney, *the* Wall Street Journal's *personal-finance magazine. He's the former assistant editor of* BCBusiness Magazine, *was a judge at this year's National Journalism Awards, and has yet to find the perfect job, which would pay him seven figures to lounge on a Caribbean beach.*

every document you put your John Hancock to. The employment contracts and all other documentation are designed to protect the company, not you. Don't get all caught up in the miracle of winning the job and just sign every document put in front of you. You need an ironclad employment contract covering your behind just as much as the CEO in the corner office does. Companies know that an employment agreement isn't for that warm, fuzzy getting-to-know-you period when everybody plays nice; it's for when something goes wrong.

The employment agreement will cover all the basic details related to your new job (e.g., salary, benefits, vacation days). The company may also ask you to complete a more detailed version of the employment application. There's no statute of limitations on lying, so don't do it when you fill out an employment application, or else you run the risk of getting caught and terminated. (See the sidebar "Employment at Will" on page 204.)

Now for the ugly business of declining an offer. It's uncomfortable and potentially nasty, but you need to turn down jobs that aren't right for you. You don't want to burn any bridges. If you turn a company down on good terms, you should feel comfortable about keeping in touch with them in the future. It's absolutely essential to send thank-you notes to everyone that you interviewed with as a final follow-up. You want to be known as "the one who got away."

> I think compensation negotiation comes down to knowing what you want (both in terms of job content and money), how much you want the particular job you're negotiating for, and, as with any negotiation, remembering you always have the power to walk away. When negotiating compensation with someone, I aim to be straightforward and fair, so there's no real need for someone to freak out. It is true that in this market, an economic recession, the "buyer" (hiring company or headhunter) has a competitive advantage, but we are not out to trick or swindle the candidate. I guess the bottom line is that I aim to foster a win-win deal. The hiring company gets great talent at a market-driven price and the candidate lands a cool job. There are different theories for negotiation protocol, but my own preference is for the candidate to negotiate in good faith—we're not on *Survivor* here—and to be as straightforward and honest as I am being. I know some job experts advise the candidate not to reveal their compensation. Why? I ask. We're not selling used Ford Pintos. We're bringing a deal together, so let's lay our cards on the table.
>
> —NANCY, EXECUTIVE RECRUITER

THE OLD BALL AND CHAIN: NON-COMPETE AGREEMENTS

Along with your employment contract, you'll often receive the dreaded non-compete agreement. You will be expected to promise that, once your employment at your new company ends, you will not join a direct competitor. Usually, such agreements are for a limited period (perhaps one year) and cover a limited geographic area. Either way, signing it is almost always a requirement for taking a job these days. That's why you need to understand how to protect yourself. While you're having a love affair with your new job, your company is much wiser. They know employees come and go, and out the door with them flies intellectual capital, clients, trade secrets, and more. Your company has a right to be paranoid. In 2001 the consulting firm Accenture found that a whopping sixty-nine percent of the employees who left their firm moved to a direct competitor.* Now, just as a company has to protect itself, so should you. Keep in mind, fat-cat lawyers get paid big bucks by corporations to create onerous non-competes that enforce the most protection possible for the employer. If you sign them without questioning them (like most people) they could come back to haunt you for years. Even if your company fires you or lays you off, you still could be barred from working in your chosen field or specialty. Instead of not signing a non-compete (which generally means you won't get hired), you need to try and limit the power that it will have over you if you ever leave your new company. The best way to limit your exposure is by developing a *short* list of companies that you agree *not* to work at for a given period of time (i.e., six months to one year) after you leave the company. You might even include titles and jobs that don't fall under the non-compete. This would allow you to accept a different position at a direct competitor. By being flexible on some of their points while not caving in to all of them, you're en-

* Source: Accenture study, "The High Performing Workforce: Separating the Digital Economy's Winners from Losers," 2001.

suring your ability to earn a living while letting the company protect itself.

SHOULD YOU STAY OR SHOULD YOU GO?

You've received the written offer and reviewed the employment agreements. Now is the time to decide whether you're going to fish for a counteroffer or accept the new job. If you're hoping to receive a counteroffer from your current employer, you don't have much time, because your prospective boss will want you to resign as soon as possible. So you need to stall as best you can, then immediately try to get a one-on-one meeting scheduled with your current boss. Don't dilly-dally about getting on their calendar. Your boss will have no idea how urgent the timing is. When you step into your boss's office, start the conversation by saying something like, "I have a very attractive offer from another company. . . ." Then let your boss respond. See where the discussion goes. Some bosses are so clueless that you might have to come right out and ask for a counteroffer. Even if he or she asks for time to mull over the options, don't be heartbroken if you don't receive a counteroffer. Most companies don't want to set a bad precedent by being pressured into a bidding war.

If you do get a counteroffer, you need to think long and hard before you accept it. Career experts continually point out that most people who accept a counteroffer end up leaving within the first year. "You should revisit your initial motivation to seek another position. Was salary the only deciding factor, or were there other reasons, such as cultural fit or clashing of management styles, that made you originally look for another job?" says Linda Matias, President of Career Strides, a career consulting and outplacement firm. She suggests that you need to ask yourself, "Does the counteroffer satisfy all of your concerns? And most important, does the individual who provided the counteroffer have the ability to deliver on their promises?" Other things you need to watch out for are: your counteroffer might be your next raise in disguise; your loyalty to the firm might forever

What About Those Other Pesky Employment Documents?

Contributed by Arnie Pedowitz

Companies like non-compete agreements because they limit the ability of their competitors to excel. They can prevent a salesman from bringing customers to a competitor, a doctor from opening an office near his former practice, an advertising exec from working in the area where she has developed particular expertise. During the contract signing period, your employer may require you to sign other protective documents like non-disclosure agreements and agreements not to solicit the business of former clients. A non-disclosure agreement is similar to a non-compete. It says that you won't disclose or use your prior employer's secrets after you leave. This means that you can't copy your computer records or forms and use them in your next job—they belong to your employer, not you. You should know that whether you sign a non-disclosure agreement or not the law will punish you if you use or disclose a prior employer's secrets. An agreement not to solicit the business of former clients is a narrower form of non-compete because it limits your client base. While protective documents can seem foreboding, almost all employers will negotiate or at least discuss their non-compete policies. This does not mean that they will change them, but you should at least try before signing anything. Don't forget that big companies are in so many areas of commerce nowadays that a non-compete, non-disclosure, or non-solicit can stop future employers from wanting to hire you *because* of these limitations. If you signed a protective document and are thinking of working for a competitor, or if you have questions about what to do, don't panic. If your new job is not a direct competitor, your employer may just let it slide. If their agreement is potentially unenforceable, your lawyer might be able to talk the company out of proceeding or negotiate which specific competitors you can work for and which you can't. Whatever you do, don't go it alone. There is simply no good substitute for consulting a lawyer knowledgeable in the area of non-competes.

Arnie is an employment lawyer based in New York City. In addition to practicing law, he writes, teaches, and lectures nationally.

be in question; and you're likely to permanently ruin your relationship with the company offering you the new job. If after all your soul-searching you decide to accept the counteroffer, do the right thing and get right back to the company you've been interviewing with ASAP and inform them of your decision to stay with your current firm.

If after you receive the written offer you decide you want to take the new job—regardless of any counteroffer your current firm gives you—verbally accept and then walk in and resign to your boss. It is imperative that you tell no co-workers about your imminent resignation until after you've had a chance to speak with him or her. While it may seem a bit formal, you need to type up a letter of resignation and address it to your soon-to-be-ex-boss. Having a resignation letter will keep you on track in case things get emotional (which they might). Just be sure to write your resignation letter "for the files." This means that you shouldn't put anything personal in the letter (i.e., rants about co-workers, how the company could have made zillions of dollars if they'd only listened to you more, etc., etc.). This file could live on for a long time in the annals of the human resources department and you don't want it coming back to bite you on the behind. You never know, someday you might be working with these people again.

When you put pen to paper, start out with something like, "After careful consideration, I have decided to tender my resignation from (your current employer) to take up the position of (your new title at your new company)." The resignation letter should be short but needs to include the date you give the letter to your boss and the date that you will effectively be leaving the company. In most companies, plan on giving two to three weeks' notice. Just to be safe, refer back to your original employment agreement, as it might include how many weeks' notice you're required to give before you leave the company. If you really liked working for your boss and/or the company, you can add a final paragraph where you can wax nostalgic about how great it was to work at the firm and that you promise to stay in touch. Do not ask for any favors or recommendations in your resignation letter. If you have a good relationship with your boss, ask for a recommendation or reference in person (although you may want to wait until after they cool down and have accepted your news).

When you resign, don't be surprised if you get escorted out of the building that very day. (See "Don't Punch the Rent-a-Cop" section of Chapter 10.) If you're a popular employee, they may want you out sooner than later so that quitting doesn't start becoming contagious. Usually it's simply company policy and is no reflection on your character.

After you've officially resigned from your company, it's a nice touch to call your prospective boss (or your headhunter, if that's the established protocol) to let him or her know that you're signed, sealed, and ready to be delivered. Make sure that you stay as enthusiastic now as you did during the interviewing phase. Be sure to remind them about your official start date, too. Then send a personal hand-written note or email to the people you'll be working most closely with and to the friends, associates, and references who helped you land the job along the way.

SAY GOOD-BYE GRACEFULLY AND START FRESH

If you're allowed to stick around, be sure to touch base and say good-bye to co-workers and mentors that you worked with, but make sure not to rub their faces in the fact that you just landed a great new job. Once you've resigned, however, don't just breeze through your last two weeks doing the minimum amount of work possible. If you work hard in your last days at the company, you could assure yourself of receiving glowing testimonials years down the line. Blow off your work now, and you'll suffer the consequences the next time you need a solid reference from the boss you left in the lurch. You want to be known as the guy or gal who finished their projects and brought everyone up to speed on anything outstanding. And after you settle into your new position, drop a quick note with a business card to all of your contacts so they know how to reach you for future opportunities.

As you embark on an adventure at your newly adopted company, never forget that a new job is a clean slate (no matter how many setbacks you had at your last job). Landing one is the perfect opportunity to start fresh, get rolling, and get what you want. You can change your history by hitting the ground running, engaging new co-workers, forming alliances, and starting on a brand-new career track. You've already proven that you have the courage to go for it; now it's time to prove that you can be who you want to be. Follow these strategies, and you'll see an immediate improvement in your job hunt right out of the gate. Good luck!

NOW GO WORK IT!

Here's the Takeaway:

- You're not hired until you're hired. Be sure not to give any outward signs to your current employer that your affections are straying.

- Be careful how you play the waiting game. After the final interviews, continue to follow up not just by checking in, but in such a way that reinforces your interest and qualifications.

- Be patient. Put yourself in the hiring manager's shoes: in bad business conditions or when hiring for a senior position, things take longer for reasons he or she can't control. Above all, don't nag or make yourself a nuisance.

- While you're waiting for the answer, have a talk with yourself and be sure that *you* want to proceed. If not, bow out.

- Keep your ears open for any signs of trouble at your prospective new employer. You don't want to jump ship, then find out your new job's on the *Titanic*.

- Make sure your references are warmed up and ready to go.

- Getting the offer is not the end of the story. Get it in writing and don't accept over the phone. Take a day or two to consider the terms and plan your negotiating strategy. What trade-offs are you willing to make?

- Negotiating is a tough test. Keep it cordial and professional, and be prepared not to get everything you want. At the same time, be firm in seeking your interests.

- If you're the number two candidate (no jokes, please!) and number one got the job, be gracious. Send thank-you notes to everyone you went the distance with. You never know; things can change, and you could get the nod later.

- Protective agreements (non-compete, severance, non-disclosure) can be negotiable. Don't be so love-struck with your new company that you don't look out for your long-term interests. Consult your attorney if necessary.

- Decide if you will accept or decline the offer—but do it tactfully and with integrity. Think long and hard about the implications if you're given a counteroffer.

Part III:

BREAK OPEN IN

CASE OF EMERGENCY!

10

THE VULTURES ARE CIRCLING:

What to Do Immediately Before and After You Get Downsized

Pink slip-dom awaits you. You've been working insane hours with an ever leaner staff, and business is not improving. Layoffs are imminent. Every week, your co-workers are called in, and one by one they say good-bye and disappear. Your turn is coming: your boss will tell you how badly he feels about having to let you go, and the conversation will seem like an out-of-body experience. After what will seem like an eternity, the finality of the situation will start to sink in. It's your head on the chopping block. But this isn't *Survivor:* this is your life. And you just got the Pink Slip.

You need to be ready for the shock of getting downsized so you won't be ambushed by it. What you do right now will be instrumental to your immediate job hunt success. Rather than wallowing in the harshness of the situation, you need to apply whatever leverage you still have toward getting what you deserve from your soon-to-be ex-company. The advice in this chapter will provide a moment-by-moment game plan of what you need to do just prior to and immediately following your layoff. There are no guarantees, but at least you won't be taken by surprise as the walls come tumbling down.

THIS COULDN'T HAPPEN TO ME?

Yes, Virginia, corporate downsizing can happen to you. You may feel like you're indispensable, but it's at times like these, when you feel you have job security, that you can be blindsided by a layoff. Noted employment expert John Challenger, CEO of Challenger Gray and Christmas, estimates that today's young professionals are likely to get laid off (or be forced out by quitting) at least five times in their career. So from now on, you need to get used to the idea that every employee, including you, is expendable.

No matter how good you are at your job, you need to maintain a state of constant awareness that it *can* happen to you. Then take control of your future prospects should a layoff befall you:

✓ CONSTANTLY STRENGTHEN YOUR NETWORK OF CONTACTS, especially in good times. Pool together references from jobs and projects in which you have performed well. If you've done an exceptional job, ask for a testimonial in writing from your client or manager, to keep for your records. Always ask for a recommendation while projects are fresh in your reference's mind. This way you'll receive the highest marks.

✓ KEEP TRACK OF REFERENCES FROM EVERY PREVIOUS JOB. It's nobody's fault but your own if you lose touch. Keeping tabs on your references as they move from company to company is hard work, but the payoff will be tremendous.

✓ MAINTAIN CONTACT WITH KEY RECRUITERS IN YOUR INDUSTRY. You may love your job right now, but that doesn't mean you shouldn't keep your ear to the ground for future opportunities. Keep your cadre of recruiters current on the requirements of your dream job.

✓ KEEP YOUR RESUME UP-TO-DATE. As you gain more responsibility or complete project milestones, always update your resume and have it ready to go. Don't fall into the trap of cobbling your resume together after you've been let go—it won't be your best work.

✓ **MAKE YOURSELF AWARE OF TRANSFER OPPORTUNITIES WITHIN YOUR FIRM.** If your division is doing poorly and another is performing phenomenally, start positioning yourself for a transfer.

My department, human resources, was responsible for laying off eight hundred people. I had a feeling that when we finished terminating everyone, my area would be next to go. I was low man on the totem pole. Rather than waiting around for the inevitable, I hit the pavement, worked my contacts, and aggressively called recruiters that specialized in my area. I ended up getting a new job before I was officially laid off. Plus, I received a nice severance check, which I spent on vacation before I started my new job.

—KATHLEEN, FACILITIES MANAGEMENT SUPERVISOR

I could tell that our company's end was certain. I thought about re-igniting my freelance consulting practice, so I called a few old clients. Sure enough, they wanted me back. And I happily quit. Six months later the company went belly up.

—PHIL, NETWORK ADMINISTRATOR

I DIDN'T SEE THIS COMING

Oh, really? The excuse "I didn't see this coming" is about as valid as "the dog ate my homework." A layoff shouldn't come as a surprise. The economy will always soar and dip, and companies will expand or lay off in tandem. If you see indications that the economy is starting to weaken, you need to be ready to act.

A souring economy isn't the only source of layoffs. Individual companies can dump employees even during a boom. These days, many companies are building "just-in-time" workforces, designed to grow and shrink rapidly in response to corporate needs. Public companies driven by the whims of Wall Street will often bulk up when times are good and clean house when a slowdown occurs or when their stock takes a nosedive. So be alert. Company loyalty toward employees has become little more than a fairy tale.

"Experts say young workers today spend an average of 3.5 years at a job and many will have bounced to seven different positions by the time they turn thirty," says Marc Drizin, employee loyalty specialist with Walker Information, an Indianapolis-based research company. You can take heed of this new paradigm and manage your career accordingly, or you can ignore it and suffer the consequences. Pay particular attention to the following indicators that might foreshadow head-count cuts:

M A C R O : Examine the trends happening in your industry and how they affect your company.

✓ LISTEN TO EARNINGS REPORTS. Has your company missed earnings lately? How about any of your direct competitors?

✓ FOLLOW WHAT'S GOING ON WITH YOUR COMPANY'S STOCK AND THE OTHER STOCKS IN YOUR SECTOR. Track the ratings for the entire basket.

✓ PAY ATTENTION TO THE HEADLINES. What is the press saying about you and your competitors? (Sure, the media isn't always impartial. But neither is your management!)

✓ KEEP TABS ON REVENUES FOR ALL YOUR COMPANY'S DIVISIONS. Which divisions are doing better or worse than the others? Follow whether the buying patterns of your firm's customers have changed. Is your company profitable or at least on the road to profitability? Are sales strategies realistic and achievable?

✓ WATCH MOVEMENT IN CORPORATE MANAGEMENT. Are senior managers getting fired? Are board members being replaced?

✓ EVALUATE CHANGES IN CORPORATE STRATEGY. Is company direction suddenly erratic? Are you shedding businesses or customers? Are departments merging? Has your job suddenly become redundant?

M I C R O : Pay close attention to subtle happenings at your organization when you get an inkling that all is not well.

✓ STROLL THROUGH YOUR HUMAN RESOURCES DEPARTMENT AFTER HOURS. See if HR folks are working unusually late. Are they hovering obsessively over the fax or copier? This could mean that layoffs are imminent.

✓ BE ON THE ALERT FOR A SUDDEN HIRING FREEZE. Companies looking to constrain costs might freeze head count. This could be a way to preserve jobs, but it could also backfire if mission-critical positions are left open indefinitely.

✓ PAY ATTENTION TO THE PINCH OF CASH FLOW CONSTRAINTS. Are vendors being paid on time? (Are they complaining to you?) Is the sales and marketing budget getting cut? Are expense reimbursements taking forever to get paid?

✓ CONDUCT A FIRESIDE CHAT WITH YOUR BOSS. Is he or she direct or evasive about the company future? Is his/her door open or shut? Is HR wearing a hole in your boss's carpet?

I'd been with my company for almost three years, as director of on-line Marketing. I moved my ass out to Utah for them, only for management to change their minds and drag me back to the New York City area after they realized that Salt Lake City wasn't going to be the interactive entertainment capital of the world. They gobbled up a bunch of smaller companies, produced insane redundancy, and then shed the only biz unit that actually made money last fiscal year: mine. I should have seen it coming.

—GLENN, ONLINE MARKETING DIRECTOR

Employment at Will

Contributed by Hanan B. Kolko, Esq.

In many states, a person can get fired for almost any reason—good reason, bad reason, or no reason. The reason for the firing doesn't have to be true. It doesn't have to be related to your job. It doesn't have to be accurate. It doesn't have to be rational. This is known as the "Employment at Will" doctrine, and it is the law in many states. Under this doctrine, you have no right to continued employment—you are an employee at the "will" of the employer, who can fire you at any time, for any reason. People think it is unfair. It is. Get over it. If you want to avoid being an employee at will, negotiate it before you start your job. If you think you have the leverage to do so, you should press to get an employment contract that provides that you can only be discharged for "good cause," or "just and sufficient cause." A contract provision would protect you from being terminated "at will." There are certain exceptions to the Employment at Will doctrine. Federal anti-discrimination laws—which apply to all fifty states—make it illegal for an employer to fire a person based on age, race, religion, sex, national origin, or disability. Many states and localities have similar laws. The federal laws do not cover sexual orientation. Some state and local laws do. If you think you have been fired or otherwise discriminated against for any of these reasons, you should contact a lawyer. If you have complained about workplace discrimination on the basis of age, race, religion, sex, national origin, or disability, and feel that you have been fired or otherwise discriminated against in retaliation for complaining, you should also contact an attorney. Some states have modified the Employment at Will doctrine. If you need specific advice about this area, you should speak to a local employment lawyer who is familiar with whether and how the doctrine has been modified in your state.

Hanan is a labor and employment lawyer with the law firm of Meyer, Suozzi, English & Klein, an adjunct professor at Cornell University's College of Industrial and Labor Relations, and the Secretary-Treasurer of Working Today, an advocacy group for the emerging "free agent" workforce.

THE SKINNY: The truth hurts. Don't confuse getting fired with being laid off. Getting fired for cause means you weren't performing up to the expectations of your employer (or worse, you committed an infraction of company policy). If there's a bright side to getting fired, it's that you'll almost always know the reason why—most companies document the causes and review them with the employee. If you are actually fired, don't discount or ignore the reasons given for the termination. No matter how unfairly you may feel you were treated, there's always a grain of truth you need to learn from, and it's no one's responsibility but your own to correct any chronic issues in your performance. Otherwise, they'll rear their ugly heads in the next position you take.

There Is Opportunity in Chaos

The rumor mill begins to churn: the scuttlebutt is that ten percent of the company will be laid off this month. Most people will start panicking, thinking that heads are about to roll. If you're smart, you'll stay calm. Remember that it's much easier to be one of the ninety percent who keep their job than one of the ten percent who lose theirs. Some (maybe most) employees will get to stay. Why *not* you? A company cannot run on technology alone (at least not yet, anyway).

If you want to keep your job, now is the time to demonstrate that you're a team player. Let higher-ups know that keeping your job is important to you. By staying positive, management may think twice before cutting you instead of some clock-watcher who's surfing the web and counting the days until he gets axed. To make yourself seem more indispensable, take on challenging or mission-critical assignments that everyone else at your organization is afraid to touch. It's also okay to do a little sucking up right now. While everyone else is hanging their head low, knock down your boss's door and let him or her know just how hard you're working. While you're at it, look back at your past performance reviews. Have you improved based upon management's recommendations? If not, now's the time to get cracking.

When rumors start to fly, madness will ensue. Don't get caught up in the chaos. People will stop doing their jobs, and the vicious cycle of paranoia and backstabbing will begin. Keep your nose to the grindstone and do your job well. When people start to quit, and they always do, go to your boss and make him aware that you want to take on the new responsibilities of the people who are leaving. You can't lose. Your extra efforts during your manager's time of need will make him more willing to go to bat for you. Ultimately, even if you get laid off, you may have earned enough extra brownie points to get yourself a more robust severance package or at least a good reference. And if your boss gets laid off with you, he or she just might bring you to the next venture.

I've had this weird situation of being the "last man standing" whenever there are layoffs at companies where I've worked. My motto: the work doesn't stop because people are getting laid off; it just gets redistributed. When times are tough, I never, ever utter the phrase "that's not my job." When things are shaky, and morale is lousy, it's important to keep smiling and keep offering yourself to other areas of the company. In the end, whether I have kept my job or not, I have acquired many new skills that were above and beyond my job description at the time. I have also developed relationships with executives from all over the company. When a company folds or lays off a lot of people, these people then go and work somewhere else. If they've had a positive experience working with me, it will help me that much more when I'm looking for the next position.

—RACHEL, COMMUNICATIONS MANAGER

The magazine that I was working at was about to fold. I offered to stick it out until the bitter end and close the books. I learned the ins and outs of how to wind down an organization. (A much sought-after qualification these days!) The parent company appreciated my loyalty, and after all was said and done, I was able to negotiate a more senior position in a different division of the company.

—MARC, CONTROLLER

THE SKINNY: What's the big guy thinking about? Not you, buddy. If times are getting tough, your manager (and their bosses) will be preoccupied with trying to keep the company afloat (not to mention hanging onto their own positions). It's your job to remind them of your contribution to the company and to the bottom line—without too much brown-nosing.

RIDIN' OUT THE STORM

When a company lays people off, a melange of circumstances will threaten to overwhelm you; co-workers are likely to be weeping, bitching, or, most likely, both. Anger and disbelief will surround the water-cooler. Don't let it distract you. While your head may indeed be next on the chopping block, it doesn't mean that you have to lose it. You still have leverage up until the moment you leave the building. And you need to use that leverage to your advantage while you're still officially employed. This is your last chance to say your piece because the moment you leave the office you will lose what's left of your negotiation power.

Layoffs can easily rock your confidence. Examine the circumstances of your particular layoff and try not to internalize the event as a personal fault of your own. If you take it personally, you will sap the strength you need for your eventual job hunt.

As you prepare for your termination meeting, it is important to be wise to the agenda of senior management. They've got a set amount of severance funds that they can work with, period. They're hoping that you, like most employees, will be a good little drone and take the package without a peep. They're counting on you to be so freaked out by the humiliating layoff process that you'll just slink away. They're also expecting a small percentage of employees to strategize and challenge them. And in some cases, they'll be willing to negotiate. You need to be one of these employees: the few, the brave, and the prepared—the ones who actually stand up and ask for what they deserve.

THE SKINNY: **Not a time for collective bargaining.** When you go in for your meeting, you must remember it's every man for himself. Because funds are limited and can only be stretched so far, phrases like "I think I speak for all employees" will damage your cause. You don't want management to be fearful that they have to give your package to everyone. This is about you.

BE AT THE READY

As soon as you sense the Grim Reaper lurking around your cube, you need to be ready. Your company is going to want you to sign a binding separation agreement, after which you will be officially terminated. Long before doomsday arrives, you need to anticipate what your company might *not* include on the document. Then, you need to create a list of negotiation points that you want added to your separation agreement. You knew this day was coming, and you should be ready to seize on every opportunity that can improve your situation.

It's a given that the negotiation will be awkward. Keep your list and all supporting documents locked in your desk so that they are available at a moment's notice when you go into your meeting. There's a good chance that you'll get flustered; that's what the other side is counting on. But if the information you need is at your fingertips, you'll be able to cover all of your wants and needs with regard to your severance package.

Keep your ear to the ground. Glean as much information as you can about the current severance packages offered to co-workers who were laid off before you. Visit online bulletin boards that focus on specific companies, like the ones on Vault.com and F***edCompany.com.* Here you can gather piles of insider information, which nevertheless should be taken with a grain of disgruntled salt.

Evaluate your circumstances and determine whether you should

* If you want to pull up this web site, you'll have to spell out the naughty word, people.

volunteer for the package. If you volunteer before a mass layoff, you may be able to negotiate a fatter package and give yourself a better financial cushion to find a new job. You should always have your negotiation points ready to go, whether you volunteer or not. Always keep in mind that the longer you wait, the worse the severance package is likely to be. Take a long, hard look at what is happening at your company. Determine whether or not waiting it out and maybe saving your job is worth the risk of eventually getting less or no severance.

> The last time IBM downsized, I cashed out, voluntarily took their standard severance package, and went to law school. It was the best decision I ever made.
>
> —ROB, CORPORATE LAWYER

THE SKINNY: Next time get an ironclad severance agreement. The best way to get a solid severance package is to have it included in the fine print of your employment agreement before you start to work at your company. Think of it like a pre-nuptial agreement.

DON'T DILLYDALLY

So much to do, so little time: you have to take action! If you sit around now, you have no one to blame but yourself if you're not ready for your impending layoff. Skip these steps and you might be out of more than a job.

✓ HIRE A LAWYER. The best way to ensure that you'll come out on top is to engage counsel that specializes in employment law. Have your paperwork ready to go. You'll want to review your negotiation points and any relevant documents related to your employment with your lawyer before you go into your meeting. The documents that your lawyer most likely will want to review include your employment contract, employee handbook, code of conduct, confidentiality agreement, and non-compete agreement. Having thought through your negotiation points and arguments before you go into your lawyer's office will save you money.

✔ CREATE AN ALUMNI NETWORK OF CO-WORKERS. Is there a directory of everyone's home addresses and telephone numbers? No? Start a list and begin passing it around your office. You should also make sure that everyone includes their non-work email address. Set up a co-worker homepage or create an egroup on Yahoo! in case the lay-off occurs sooner than you expect. Your network doesn't have to cease just because your job was terminated.

✔ GET EVERY REIMBURSABLE EXPENSE IN. If the company owes you money on travel, dinners, or education expenses, fill out the re-ports and get them signed by your supervisor. If you don't get the paperwork in the pipeline you risk not getting reimbursed. (You'll need that money later.)

✔ BACK UP ALL YOUR IMPORTANT DOCUMENTS, ADDRESS BOOKS, AND ROLODEXES AND BRING THEM HOME! Most likely, if you get laid off, you won't be able to access your files. The only one who can cover your ass is you. If you don't save your personal documents and bring them home for safekeeping there are no guarantees that you'll ever get that information back. You should follow any confiden-tiality agreements that you have agreed to. Use your judgment and sense of ethics, which means don't take anything you're not authorized to have. Hopefully you've packed up or backed up your:

- Rolodex and/or Palm Pilot contact list

- Email address book/email paper trail

- Evidence of work that you've performed to use for future inter-views

- Letters/emails of recommendation (that demonstrate strong performance)

- HR and benefit manuals you have received as an employee

- Contracts/letters of employment/important documentation

- Employee reviews

- Important personal information that you keep on your computer at work

- Personal belongings (without being too obvious)

✓ DON'T BE TEMPTED BY THE FIVE-FINGER DISCOUNT. Bring home only materials that belong to you and that will make your job hunt more successful. If you think that no one will miss that five-dollar stapler, think again. Helping yourself to computer equipment and office supplies in lieu of money you think you deserve is theft. Do you really want to risk a grand larceny charge going on your permanent record?

THE SKINNY: **Don't let management know you're on to them. If you think a layoff is imminent, keep your exterior environment looking the same. That means keeping photos, tchotchkes, and other assorted desk accoutrements out and visible as if nothing has changed.**

THE SQUEAKY WHEEL STILL GETS THE GREASE

Speak now, or forever hold your peace. The worst-case scenario is happening to you: you're losing your job. While you can't change the fact that you're about to be laid off, you can ask for what you are entitled to. As you head into joblessness, extra funds and benefits can give you the breathing room to land your next job.

Most employees who've been laid off do not treat the moment of their termination like a business meeting. As such, they can feel inadequate and unprepared. Remember that the person sitting across the table will seize upon any moment of weakness. So approach the ending of your employment the same way you would negotiate a new job. The only difference is that instead of haggling over salary and a bonus, you're instead negotiating for a nest egg and benefits that can get you through your unemployment.

What's the downside to asking for more than the current package? Nothing! You're already being let go, right? After all your tough negotiating, you might still end up receiving exactly the same package as everyone else. But at least you went for it.

Of course, the best-case scenario could also happen to you: management might actually surrender on a point or two. You could end up receiving a much better severance package than you were anticipating, just because you had the courage to ask. "Nothing ventured, nothing gained," never meant so much as at this moment.

> When it became clear that my time at the company might be running out, I started making a list of all the loose ends that might need to be tied up. In doing so, I left nothing to chance and assumed that nothing was too obvious. In my exit interview with my boss, the COO, I discussed these points with him verbally, and then before leaving the office, I handed him a letter that set out my explicit understandings and expectations as to the amount of salary I was owed, options in which I was vested, and vacation pay and expense reimbursement I felt I was entitled to, and a bonus amount that I felt I had earned. I attached a copy of my employment contract to the letter and made specific reference in the letter to my contract whenever possible. My boss was a bit taken aback by the letter and wondered if I didn't trust him. I simply said I wanted to make sure everything was clear and explicit, to avoid any potential oversights or mistakes. The company agreed to everything in the letter, including, to my surprise, the bonus payment.
>
> —EDWARD, PRODUCT MANAGER

No Guts, No Glory

Let's get one thing straight: this is a negotiation. A give and take is naturally implied. Don't be rigid. It is imperative that you decide which points are most important to you before your meeting, as it's highly unlikely that you'll get a favorable reaction to all of them. Manage your expectations by prioritizing each negotiation point and staying focused. Be prepared for a bit of a runaround. The person who actually conducts your termination meeting may not have the authority to agree to any of your negotiation points. This means that items might still need to be run by a higher authority. Don't get discouraged. This is the process.

If you're successful at winning some of your negotiation points, get *everything* in writing. Immediately following the meeting, draft an addendum to the termination agreement. Turn the document around ASAP and get all interested parties to sign and date it before you sign your termination agreement and ideally before you leave the building for the last time. We've put together a list of "No-Brainer" negotiation points where you've got excellent leverage. In fact, many severance plans may already include some or all of these points, depending upon how good they are. You should focus your attention on the "No-Brainers" category, as working through these points represents your best chance at victory. We've also put together a list of "Hail Mary" negotiation points. Use these at your discretion, but know that winning them will be a long shot.

The No-Brainers

✔ GET PAID FOR YOUR UNUSED VACATION AND PERSONAL DAYS. Many times companies will wait for the employee to mention that they are owed this. If you don't, they may not address it, and it'll be your loss.

✓ GET REIMBURSABLE EXPENSES PAID BACK. Many people leave their firms thinking that they can't get compensated for their reimbursable expenses. But you are entitled to them (as long as they were originally authorized)—just make sure you get it in writing.

✓ HAVE YOUR BONUS AND OUTSTANDING COMMISSIONS PRO-RATED. Calculate how far into the year you are, then determine how much of the bonus you would be owed. If you've worked at the firm for more than a year, you can point to historical evidence on what bonus you had been previously paid to establish a track record. Or, if you put a target bonus into your employee contract, point to that as evidence.

✓ ASK FOR A LETTER OF RECOMMENDATION. If the layoff has nothing to do with your performance, you should ask for a letter of recommendation from your direct manager and any senior management with whom you interacted on a regular basis. Make sure the letter is on their letterhead. Just remember that playing hardball on your severance terms could poison the waters on getting a favorable reference, at least until your former boss cools down. You need to decide what you need more: the money or the recommendation.

✓ REQUEST AUTO-REPLY AND EMAIL FORWARDING. If you've listened to our advice so far, you've already backed up your email address book before your termination meeting. But just in case, you may want to ask to have an auto-reply message set up that provides your personal email information for a set period of time, or to have your emails forwarded to your personal address.

✓ WEIGH YOUR OPTIONS. Many companies require you to surrender options or restricted stock upon termination. Take a good look at what you're owed or have to exercise, and remember that there could be tax implications at the end of the year.

THE HAIL MARYS

✓ **REQUEST MORE SEVERANCE PAY.** Severance pay is often tied to how many years you worked at the company. That said, you might have some leverage if you joined the firm under special circumstances (e.g., you were heavily recruited from a competitor where you were on the fast track).

✓ **GET THE NON-COMPETE AGREEMENT WAIVED.** They're releasing you. Now is the time to ask them to waive restrictions on your ability to take a job with a competitor. This will give you a greater ability to find work when you're ready. Management may not entirely waive the non-compete, but they may at least remove a few firms from the direct competitor list or shorten the duration of the non-compete restriction.

✓ **OFFER TO CONSULT.** It is not uncommon for companies to cut head count too deeply. In some cases, management will ask employees to stay on in a consulting capacity. Swallow your pride and fatten your wallet, letting your employer know that you would like to be considered for this type of contract assignment if the opportunity arises. This can be highly lucrative: you get paid as a consultant on an hourly or daily rate on top of your negotiated severance package.

✓ **ASK FOR A HEALTH CARE EXTENSION.** At termination, your medical coverage is normally converted to a COBRA plan. Ask to have your current health care plan extended for a set period of time in the future (say, three-to-six months). Offer to pay the employee contribution part (which you had been paying anyhow as an employee). This does two things: it keeps your current health care provider until you land a new job, and it delays the start date of COBRA, which is more expensive and has a set term of eighteen months.

✓ REQUEST OUTPLACEMENT ASSISTANCE. Outplacement (off-site career counseling services) can be the fast track to keeping you focused on getting your next job. You might get access to an office with computers, fax, and Internet access as well as guidance on resume writing, career management, and financial planning. If your company doesn't offer this, ask to receive a stipend for career coaching or tuition reimbursement.

✓ NEGOTIATE USE OF YOUR OLD OFFICE. In some cases, your company may allow you to use the office computers and fax machines for a few days, after the layoff. This is especially true if the company is going belly-up. See if management will allow you to use their equipment for a set period of time before you have to trudge off to Kinko's and start spending your own money.

✓ ASK FOR ADDITIONAL TRAINING AND EDUCATION. Discuss your individual training needs with the termination team. You might be surprised to find them willing to subsidize a class or two to improve your ability to find another job.

✓ COMPUTER EQUIPMENT. Most likely, your office computer's value has already depreciated significantly. Its value to the company will be a mere fraction of its purchase price. To you, however, a computer for home use during a job search can be very valuable. Try to negotiate your trusty computer into your package. It costs the firm very little and can be a great asset to you.

IT'S THE LITTLE THINGS

Paying attention to subtle nuances at the negotiation table can improve your position. The trick here is to do everything in your power to put yourself on an even playing field with the person handling your termination.

1. **KNOW THE COMPANY'S AGENDA.** If you're going to get anywhere, you need to keep the interests of the company in mind and work toward a common goal. Remind management about what you'll both get if they help you on each important negotiation point.

2. **SILENCE DENOTES STRENGTH.** When you ask for something, wait for the other person to answer. Don't be afraid of silence—wait it out. If you speak again before you get an answer, you'll probably say something that weakens your position.

3. **BE CONFIDENT WITHOUT BEING ANTAGONISTIC.** As you deliver your points, you want to come across as serious without being overbearing. You need to win the person over, and being hyper-aggressive won't help.

4. **LET THEM KNOW YOU HAVE A LAWYER.** Don't be shy about letting them know you've retained legal counsel. Pepper your conversation with phrases that mention this relationship in a non-threatening manner. For example: "When I discussed this with my lawyer," or "My brother-in-law, who's an employment lawyer, says . . ."

5. **DON'T LET THE MEETING GET RUSHED.** Management wants to sail through things as quickly as possible. Don't let them. Ask questions regarding the package and then have your list of requests ready to go. Don't answer anything too quickly. It's okay to get back to them after the meeting (but before you sign anything).

6. **WEAR A POWER SUIT.** This is one of the most important negotiations you can have. If done right, you can give yourself more security and time to find the next job. Take it seriously by looking serious. You may want to keep a suit in the coat closet in case the meeting takes you by surprise.

7. BODY LANGUAGE IS EVERYTHING. Don't shrug or cross your arms. You're at the table as a master negotiator. Act the part.

8. LOOK THEM IN THE EYE. Be highly engaged. If you look down, they've won. Be warned: things will get emotional, but try to hold back those tears until you are out of the meeting.

9. GET ON AN EVEN KEEL WITH THE PERSON HANDLING THE SEVERANCE MEETING. Pay attention to small things like seat height and where the seat is located. Try to get the seat of strength—facing the door, with your back to the wall.

10. DON'T GET INTIMIDATED. You may get pressed to sign the termination agreement then and there. You don't have to. You have the right to take your time. Don't let bully tactics unnerve you.

Take a Bite Out of COBRA

If you were terminated by a company that had more than twenty employees (and is still in business), by federal law you should be eligible for COBRA (Consolidated Omnibus Budget Reconciliation Act of 1985) coverage. Think of COBRA like an eighteen-month extension of your former employer's group health care coverage. The difference is, you pay for the entire monthly bill, which includes not only what you contributed out of each paycheck but also what your employer contributed on your behalf. COBRA coverage can last up to eighteen months (and sometimes longer), but you are allowed to end coverage once you get a new job. After you're terminated, you should get a notice from your benefits administrator that you are indeed eligible for COBRA (make sure you find out who your plan administrator is before you leave your company). If you don't hear from them, you need to contact them. You have sixty days after you get your COBRA notification to accept coverage and forty-five days to make the first payment in full. One thing to note is that if your company goes bust, you won't be eligible for COBRA because your former company will no longer have an administrator to oversee the coverage.

Get ready to be flabbergasted by the cost of the COBRA monthly premiums, especially if your deductions have been automatically sucked out of each paycheck. The cost of COBRA varies depending on your former company's plan, but you can estimate that the coverage will run you at least 250 dollars a month if you're a single person, and double or triple that if you are covering your family.

What are your options other than coverage via COBRA?

- If you're married, see if you can switch to your spouse's health care coverage. It may be cheaper than paying for COBRA.
- Join an industry or professional association that has a health care program. Oftentimes, such organizations provide group plan discounts to their members. Not only will you reap the benefits of coverage, but you'll also gain great networking opportunities, too.
- Check out plans on the web that you can purchase as an individual, i.e., not through work or an association, such as <u>eHealthInsurance.com</u> or <u>WorkingToday.org</u>.
- Stay current: health care advocates are working every day to try to get better coverage for workers. Also check with your state's Department of Insurance for any nuances in the law, as rules can change from state to state.

Unfortunately, health insurance can be a murky area when you are unemployed. It is also one of the most important things to continue while you are out of work. One debilitating illness or accident, and you could quickly end up in financial ruin and set back for life. Try at all costs to keep your coverage going while you're out of work.

Don't Punch the Rent-a-Cop

Your severance meeting is over and you're officially an ex-employee of your company. By the time you reach your computer on this fateful day, you may very well find that you've been locked out of your computer system. In many cases, you may get sent home immediately, with your box of personal items (packed by someone else) to follow. As if getting terminated isn't bad enough, you may even get escorted out of the building by a security guard hired to protect the company from you. Somewhere in the *Evil Boss Handbook,* there is a chapter that encourages managers to treat their loyal employees like criminals on the day of the dirty deed. Of course, they should know better—you would never steal from the company, you just want to escape with a few family snapshots and a little bit of dignity. But the game has officially changed: the company is simply protecting their franchise. Just don't hold it against the poor rent-a-cop.

Been Wronged?

Do you feel you were treated unfairly by your former employer? Are you being denied unemployment benefits that you feel you are eligible for? Is your former employer withholding final wages that you rightfully earned? Legal questions abound after a layoff or a termination, especially when there is money on the table to which you might be entitled. In this and in so many other cases, you must defer to the experts, because your ability to win a settlement completely depends on your individual situation. Employment laws vary from state to state and it will be safest for you to get an expert opinion from an attorney in the state in which you worked. An employment lawyer can guide you safely through the nuances of the law and how it pertains to you and your ability to win the case, and hopefully a judgment in your favor. If in the event that your company goes bankrupt or you get stiffed on your last few paychecks, gather as much evidence as you can to prove that your company owed you this money (i.e., pay stubs, time sheets). Then head straight to your State or Federal Department of Labor and file a "wage and hour" claim. Basically, the DOL will investigate and if they find your claims to be true, they will list you as a creditor of the company. All you can do then is wait. If there is any cash left for claims such as yours after the company has been liquidated or reorganized (a big if), you might see some money—but don't hold your breath.

There are a few additional things to consider when you think you have cause for an employment lawsuit:

✓ **GET AN EXPERT.** Now is not the time to call in a favor from your pal who practices real estate law. Hire an employment lawyer who specializes in employment contracts, discrimination cases, non-competes, severance agreements, etc. You would hire a labor lawyer if you work in a unionized setting or an employment lawyer if you work someplace that is not unionized. In either case, discuss the ins and outs of your situation so that you hire the right kind of lawyer. If you're young and broke, but still think you have a solid case, pitch it to a lawyer anyway and work out a long-term payment plan.

✓ **MAKE SURE IT'S WORTH IT TO YOU.** Many laid-off workers have fantasies about slapping lawsuits on their former employers. Consider whether or not your company has deep pockets. The lawsuit really needs to be worth it to you. Remember the "thirty-three percent rule": after all is said and done, you'll be splitting your winnings into thirds. The feds will take a third, another third will go to the lawyer who handled your case, and then you will keep the final third. So, if you win a hefty $9,000 settlement, your actual take-home will be a paltry $3,000. You need to make sure that the end settlement will be worth all your time and energy. Don't forget that suing is time-consuming and will distract you from pursuing new career opportunities.

✓ **REMEMBER YOUR PAIN.** Eventually, you will get a new job offer. When it comes time to sign on the bottom line, keep in mind what you wish you had put in your previous employment contract, such as a detailed separation agreement or severance package. Here is where an employment lawyer can really pay off!

TIMING IS *ALWAYS* BAD (AND IT'S WORSE WHEN YOU'RE BROKE)

One thing is certain: there is no good time to get laid off. Being financially ready if a layoff happens is absolutely critical. Don't be the chump who lives high on the hog when times are good, only to get slammed when the economy melts down. Be prepared with an emergency war chest of funds so you can live while unemployed. That nest egg will give you the financial independence to make smart career decisions. You don't want to feel pressured into taking the first job you get because you need the paycheck—especially if it's not the right job.

When your job is stable, or times are good, attempt to stash away between four to six months of living expenses so you can pay for things like rent, utilities, food, and (modest) entertainment. Try to hold off on making any big purchases and put the money you would have spent on, say, a new car or TV into your emergency fund. You should keep the money in a highly liquid, interest-bearing account like a savings or money market account (although with interest rates so low these days you almost might as well stuff it in your mattress). Try to get the lowest-rate credit card you can; just beware of low but short-term "introductory" rates that balloon up at just the wrong time. Your best bet is to try to pay down your credit card balances to zero while times are good. Once you are laid off, use plastic as little as possible; you know how easy it is for those balances to pile up! (For more belt-tightening advice, jump to Chapter 12.)

Going forward, get in the habit of saving money. When you land a new job or get a bonus, stick money in your emergency war chest. If you don't trust yourself, see if your company can direct-deposit funds into your account. Just remember to make a vow to yourself that the next time a layoff is in the works, you'll be ready. Take the steps that we've covered in this chapter so that if you ever get laid off again, you'll have the peace of mind and financial wherewithal to get through it.

NOW GO WORK IT!

Here's the Takeaway:

- Layoffs can happen to anybody, especially in a down economy or a troubled industry.

- Know the warning signs that layoffs may be coming, and keep your eyes open for them.

- Take steps to prepare yourself, so you can make your search for a new job as painless and quick as possible. Reconnect with contacts, references, and headhunters. Up the intensity of your networking. Get your resume ready to go with your latest job experience included.

- If you truly want to stay at your company, take steps to be one of the survivors. Volunteer for projects. Make yourself visible and useful. Look for opportunities in other departments that may not be affected.

- If you're looking to change jobs anyway, consider volunteering to "take the package" if that's an option.

- If the ax does fall on you, keep your head. Part of getting laid off is the severance package, and there's room here for you to negotiate. Know ahead of time what you want to ask for. Get everything in writing. Don't sign until you know you've got the best deal you can get.

- Don't take it personally. Keep your composure and your sense of ethics—don't seek revenge by lashing out or stealing company property or information.

11

PINK SLIP TO PAYCHECK:

Avoid Pink Slip Paralysis and Put Your Layoff Behind You

It's official: you've been downsized, pink-slipped, laid off, axed. Whatever word you choose, the reality is the same: you're out of a job and the great unknown awaits you. Like many layoff victims, you will have many questions, the biggest being "How will I survive?" Your initial inclination might be to embark on an intensive job search: Don't Have Job. Must Find Job. Any Job. But don't press the panic button just yet! While the short term won't be a walk in the park, it doesn't have to be unbearable, either, especially if you make good use of your involuntary time off.

These days, with mega-mergers creating mega-redundancy and Wall Street rewarding CEOs for slashing head count, you can expect to get downsized several times before you retire. Prepare yourself for the inevitable. The one thing you should never do after getting the pink slip is embark on a frenetic job hunt. You'll regret it. Your mindset immediately following a layoff is very different from what it will be after you've had a chance to clear your head. You need to step back and lick your wounds so feelings of resentment don't boil up during an important interview. Worse still, if you don't take time off to re-evaluate, you might end up taking the wrong job because you rushed into a situation. Keep in mind, you want to find the *right* job, not *any* job. By jumping at anything that comes your way, you could easily set yourself further back than the day you got laid off. Be discerning. Instead of pounding the pavement, take a deep breath and put this dark period behind you so that you can make intelligent career choices that aren't clouded by the painful experience of being canned.

Be forewarned: the so-called "good intentions" of family and friends will increase the pressure to start your job hunt immediately. Initially, their probing may annoy you. You may even feel suffocated. Instead of lashing out, though, ask loved ones to give you some time to examine your situation and let them know that you'll need their assistance . . . later. If you communicate and keep them in the loop, then they'll be well prepared to help you out when you need it.

DON'T SUCCUMB TO PINK SLIP PARALYSIS

It happens to the best of us. After a layoff, you will have moments of anger, disbelief, and self-doubt. Hold tightly to any one of these emotions and you could easily fall victim to "Pink Slip Paralysis." This dangerous plague can be brought on by a number of frustrating realities: the shock of losing your job, a competitive and ever-changing job market, hiring managers and headhunters who don't return your calls, and a deep-seated paranoia that you've got a gigantic bumper sticker on your forehead that reads: "DOWNSIZED LOOOSER." Combine these factors with the seemingly heroic motivation you need to have a successful job hunt, and a bout of Pink Slip Paralysis will set back even the most motivated individuals.

HOW TO IDENTIFY PINK SLIP PARALYSIS

Self-diagnosing Pink Slip Paralysis isn't easy. But you can count on family and friends to recognize that you're coming down with a bad case—you will be acting completely out of character. Be on the lookout for:

✔ SUDDENLY FEELING UNMOTIVATED. Are you wondering where each day is disappearing to? Are you still in your pajamas when it's time to get back into bed? Are you avoiding simple tasks like talking to friends, working on your resume, or taking out the garbage? (Are you using empty pizza boxes as a coffee table?)

✓ **GETTING FRUSTRATED.** Has your patience dropped drastically? Are you getting into "misunderstandings" with the neighbors? Are you losing your temper with friends, family, and unsuspecting grocery store clerks? (Note: if you're a New Yorker, none of this may seem so abnormal.)

✓ **FEELING EXHAUSTED.** Are you a morning person who has suddenly started sleeping until noon? Are you skipping activities like working out because you're inexplicably tired? Are you experiencing prolonged periods of tiredness or sleeplessness?

✓ **IMPULSE SPENDING.** Are you buying things you can't afford just for that fleeting "shopper's high"? Are you avoiding getting a receipt from the ATM because you're afraid to see the balance?

✓ **TROUBLE CONCENTRATING.** Is your focus impaired? Are you finding that you have a very short attention span?

✓ **WALLOWING IN SELF-PITY.** Are you complaining or griping more often? Do you talk incessantly about your layoff and the dismal state of the job market?

✓ **PLAYING THE BLAME GAME.** Are you pointing the finger at everyone except yourself? Do you find yourself making up excuses for your current situation? Are you embarrassed because you were laid off? Are you turning sarcastic, bitter, and generally no fun to be around?

PREVENT PINK SLIP PARALYSIS

Pink Slip Paralysis occurs because as crummy as recent events have been, they're less scary than the unknown that's ahead. But you'll never move forward if you're always focused on what's behind you.

Like quicksand, Pink Slip Paralysis can suck you in and pull you under. Here are some tips for avoiding its insidious attraction.

✓ **ALLOW YOURSELF TO BE UPSET.** The first few days or weeks after you've been laid off may be the strangest of your life. You'll replay in your mind over and over what you could have done to avoid getting laid off. You may be overcome by a powerful sense of loss— *even if you didn't like your job in the first place.* Recognize that these feelings are normal (start talking to fellow Pink Slippers and you'll see how much so), and don't get alarmed.

✓ **DON'T LET YOURSELF GET BITTER.** You may be completely disgusted with the way your employer treated you, or you may still be in shock. You have a right to be upset, but don't let these feelings of anger stop you from moving forward. It's extremely important for you to be in the right frame of mind before you schedule any interviews. Bitterness is the worst baggage to carry with you into an interview, and employers can spot it a mile away. Recognize when it's creeping into your life, and keep it at bay.

✓ **LET YOURSELF MOURN.** As you work through your grief, you need to define a mourning period that will allow you to balance your mental and physical health with your financial needs. This will help you put some distance between yourself and a painful situation. It's not a time for job hunting; it's a time to come to terms with the trauma of losing your job. Once you've committed yourself to closing the book on your last job, you need to think about how much time you can take off. Depending on your financial situation, you could spend as little as a few days or as much as several weeks or months on putting your layoff behind you. If you must undertake an immediate job hunt, give yourself an hour off before each interview you go on. Select a quiet chill-out spot, like a park, bookstore, or coffee shop near the interview location, then spend that time alone. Put yourself in a "good place" where you can visualize yourself moving beyond the layoff and into a better opportunity.

✓ **Don't overwhelm yourself.** Focus on accomplishing just one goal a day. If that is still too difficult, compartmentalize efforts into mini-goals. For example, if you're having trouble concentrating on your job hunt, work on only one section of your resume a day. Or contact just one reference a day whom you anticipate using for your job hunt. If you can't focus on job-related tasks, take a class or start a project around the house, like sorting through pictures and assembling them in a photo album. Once you're successful at accomplishing small tasks, you'll be more comfortable going for bigger achievements.

✓ **Use the corporate "Aloha Room" (or create your own).** You may get access to outplacement services as part of your separation agreement. If you do, spend as much time as possible there. In some cases, you'll get a certain amount of days you can spend at the center, say sixty days. Ask around; in some cases you don't have to start the clock immediately, and can wait until you feel ready to start your job search. A lot of people blow off this severance perk; you shouldn't. Outplacement firms specialize in helping people undergoing career transitions. That means that they can help you navigate a career change too, not just find a job doing the same old thing. Many outplacement firms have career counselors who can help you get back on track. Be a sponge and soak up the free advice while it's available to you. You can incorporate your visit to the outplacement center into your daily routine, and you'll find that using their office equipment is a lot cheaper than going to Kinko's every day.

✓ **Get a coach.** If outplacement services aren't part of your severance package, consider hiring a career coach to help you through this tough transitional time. There are all kinds of career coaches: ones that specialize in particular industries, others that focus on particular traits (e.g., coaches for introverts or extroverts), and still others who specialize in less common roadblocks

How to Find a Coach

Contributed by Todd Cherches

In my time as a coach, I've been amazed to discover how many people are running around calling themselves "coaches" without any background, credentials, experience, or credibility. While some coaches come from the business world (general management, HR, etc. or from a background as an academic or practitioner in the areas of psychology and social work), still others come out of the fields of aerobics, manicuring, and tarot card reading. I've even met an "Astrological Aesthetician Coach" who makes sure that the color scheme and style of people's wardrobes and offices are in alignment with their position, personality, and horoscope. Yikes!

"Career Coaching" is a specialized area that requires expertise and training. For example, I am an Executive or Management/Leadership Coach with twenty years of firsthand management experience to draw on, along with a master's degree in Organizational and Interpersonal Communication. I specialize in working with managers and leaders to resolve their people-related problems, as well as other organizational issues like team development, motivation, performance management. But I am *not* qualified as a career coach. Why? Because a career coach specializes in helping individuals determine the right career for them, helps them guide themselves in the right direction, and motivates them to achieve their vision. A career coach should be both a thinking partner and experienced guide. When it comes down to achieving your own objectives, you need to find someone who can do all three C's: Coaching, Counseling, and Consulting.

To find a coach you can work with, it's best to stick with word-of-mouth. What's important is the coach's experience, track record, and most important, prior *results*. The only way you really know if they are for real is by getting recommendations or references and setting up an informational interview to get an idea as to whether or not you'll enjoy working with them.

Todd is an executive coach who focuses on managers who want to improve their leadership skills.

(e.g., coaches for MBAs who've lost their way). To find a career coach, ask around and see if any of your friends or co-workers can recommend one, or go to the International Coach Federation or CoachU.com. Coaches range in cost, so you'll want to ask upfront about their hourly fees or whether they offer discount packages. Another way to reduce costs is to participate in a group coaching session (this usually is great for camaraderie and networking to boot). If limited funds are hampering your options, seek advice from friends and co-workers who've survived a layoff or two. By speaking with them, you'll learn that you're not alone.

ROUTINE RULES

Just because you're unemployed, don't let self-discipline fly out the window. The tried-and-true way to get your game face back on is to institute a routine. Right now, you need to establish guidelines that include keeping appointments and setting deadlines. Once you start to let things slip, you'll lose sight of the things that are important to you, and time will start evaporating. Here are a few ways to stick to a routine after you've been laid off.

✓ **FIRST, GET OUT OF BED.** Sleeping half your day away isn't going to get you any closer to landing a job. Step one to getting back on track is literally getting out of bed. Set your alarm and get up (and make your bed so you don't crawl back in).

✓ **GET OUT OF YOUR PAJAMAS.** While wearing your PJs a few days in a row may save on dry cleaning costs, it certainly won't make you feel professional or productive. Throw on regular duds, even if they're ratty old jeans. You don't want to find yourself stinky at midnight, not even having accomplished a shower that day.

✓ **TURN OFF THE TELEVISION.** Put yourself on a TV moratorium. Television is the great time-sucker. Sure, you may feel better about

What Are You Bitter About?

Contributed by Tami Coyne and Karen Weissman

Laid off by an employer that promised you the world? You probably think that you're justified in wallowing in your pain. But let's be honest: bitterness is a form of regret, and we usually regret not what others have done to us, but our own sacrifices that didn't work out as intended. Sure, management could have handled the situation more fairly, but that's their karmic debt to pay, so what good does it do you to take it as a personal affront?

The truth is, we're mad at ourselves, and the first step toward ending bitterness is to forgive ourselves for making some wrong decisions. So what if selling bibles on the web to overseas missionaries wasn't the next eBay. Get over it. You need to look at how those decisions may have actually been right under different circumstances. You took a shot, and you learned something. Perhaps you made good friends and contacts along the way, or at the very least, learned what *not* to do in the future. The fact that the job ended doesn't negate these achievements. It simply means it's time to move on. There are always other opportunities waiting for us once we muster the courage to let go of our pain and get out of bed.

One final thing: whether our goals are lofty or modest, it pays to be true to them. If we compromise ourselves for someone else's ideals, we get lost in bitterness and regret, whether the business venture was a success or not. But if we focus on enjoying the ride and doing our best in the here and now, we become open to all that life has to offer. Things may not always go as planned, but when there's no bitterness to hold us back, things usually turn out even better than we could have imagined.

The Spiritual Chicks, a.k.a. Tami and Karen, are the authors of "The Spiritual Chicks Question Everything" (Red Wheel/Weiser), an outrageous, no-holds-barred quest to know, feel, and apply universal goodness and authenticity to life. Check out articles and more at spiritualchicks.com.

your own situation after watching the *Jerry Springer Show*, but don't get hooked. If you've already got a serious TV habit, select a show or two to watch as a treat for having accomplished a particular goal for the day. And, of course, the best way to cure this disease (and save some money) is to cancel cable while you're unemployed.

✓ KEEP A CALENDAR. Now you're no longer working for The Man, you're working for yourself. And it's your job to fill each and every day with tasks that will make an impact on your future. That's where keeping a calendar comes in. Assemble a master plan of all the goals you want to achieve during unemployment. Be sure to include all those household chores and personal hobbies that you blew off while you were working 24/7. Your calendar will serve as a record of goals set and met, while helping you put your few months out of work into the proper perspective.

✓ GET OUT OF THE HOUSE. Blast yourself from your crib and say, "Hello, Cruel World!" Put together a list of things you've put off over the last year and focus on getting them done: make appointments to meet old friends, get your cavities drilled by the evil dentist, and go see your old college roommate's new kid. Once you start, you'll realize how much of the rest of your life you were neglecting while you were trying to take over the world. You may even begin to wonder how on earth you had time to work.

✓ START A SPECIAL PROJECT. Embark on a side project that you can execute in tandem with your job hunt. Select something that will keep you happy and motivated, like taking a non-career-related class or learning a new sport. Try volunteering for a worthwhile cause: it can really help you get your priorities in order while providing an unbeatable sense of accomplishment and self-worth. Embarking on a little home improvement, like cleaning your closets or painting a room a new color, is great therapy, too. Any productive activity that takes the pressure off your impending job hunt is sure to help keep you in balance.

✓ **PUT THE SMACKDOWN ON YOUR BAD SELF.** All games worth playing reward performance and penalize rule-breaking. Put yourself in the penalty box for blowing off goals that you set for yourself. If you don't make headway on your resume during the week, you're grounded: stay home on a Saturday night and finish it.

✓ **DON'T WITHHOLD.** If you cut the things you absolutely love out of your life, you're unfairly punishing yourself. You won't be happy, and worse still, your dour attitude could hurt your interview process. Instead, reward yourself each time you achieve a goal (and no, we're not talking about replacing the batteries in your remote control). Buy a small gift that you know you'll enjoy, like a CD or tickets to a movie. Just because you've been pink-slipped doesn't mean that you have to give up the little joys in life. (Just put emphasis on "little." Hold off on charging that Rolex or those new Prada boots till you can pay the bill.)

✓ **DO THE GRUNT WORK ON YOUR JOB HUNT.** There's a boatload of crap that you need to take care of before you can really start to interview for a new job. Now is the time to get all that preliminary work done. Rebuild your resume. Do the homework on your target companies. Touch base with your job references. And definitely, definitely start networking. Revisit Chapters 1 through 6.

✓ **TAKE A VACATION (EVEN IF IT'S A MENTAL ONE).** There's nothing like getting out of Dodge for a few days or weeks to put your life in perspective. But be prudent, and take a close look at your finances before you take off on a road trip. If you're short on fun money, play tourist in your own city or take a day trip. Play hooky and check out museums and attractions while everyone else is playing desk jockey from nine to five. If you're really broke, get a library card and take a "video vacation" by checking out movies from the public library (you won't believe the free selection).

THE SKINNY: (This one's literal, folks.) Don't wear loose-fitting clothes when you're unemployed. It's frighteningly easy to pack on the pounds when you're idle (and perhaps a little depressed), and baggy sweats don't give you that early warning pinch as your waistline expands. You don't want your only interview suit fitting you like a sausage skin when you finally hit the pavement.

My company closed on August 11, 2001, and I think I was the only one who was happy to be laid off. I just couldn't write another catchy marketing phrase. Three weeks later the opportunity to join a yoga teacher-training program came from out of the blue—I would have to start the following week. I had my doubts, of course. I knew I could handle the physical poses, but did I have the ability to teach the subtleties of a five-thousand-year-old science? I asked everyone I knew "Can you see me as a yoga teacher?" The standard answer: "Duh—you've only been talking about it for the last five years." I got the picture, so I took a leap of faith. I had one week to get used to the idea of a major life shift—I needed to arrange a work/study exchange (as I couldn't afford to pay in full), reach out and ask friends and family for help and support (that's never been easy for me), and believe that everything was happening as it should.

It's hard to write what the last nine months have been like. Basically, I feel like I just gave birth to the true self inside of me. I feel that the most important steps I took to make this transition a reality were facing emotional risk, redefining my idea of success (not the expectations of my parents or trying to impress friends), going back to my childhood fantasies, and being open and flexible. This may sound like esoteric mumblings, but I needed to surrender to wherever life was leading me. I also had to get familiar with my natural talents and deepest needs in order to recognize the right opportunity when it came along. Once I got over my fear of not making "enough" money or not being successful, or making excuses as to why I couldn't pursue an unconventional work life, I felt like opportunity was all around me. I just went with the flow and let life move me in the right direction. Now I'm making half of what I was earning at my previous job, living a much simpler life, and I've never been happier. The lesson I've learned: never look outside of myself for happiness (whether it's a prestigious job, corner office, or high salary), but to have a sense of who I am, what I need, and how I can be useful to others. Faith in myself has pulled me through, and it always will.

—JEN, YOGA INSTRUCTOR-IN-TRAINING

UNEMPLOYMENT: TO COLLECT OR NOT TO COLLECT

If your apartment burned down, would you hesitate to collect on your renter's insurance? No way! You paid the premiums; you deserve to get the money. The same analogy holds true to applying for unemployment. Whether you realize it or not, out of every paycheck you earn, you make a payment into the state and federal unemployment system. If you don't believe it, take a look at the fine print on your pay stub. Now it's time to stake your claim.

The sooner you apply for unemployment, the better off you'll be financially. So apply immediately after you get the pink slip. Each week you'll be eligible for an amount that is calculated based upon how much you earned at your previous job. It may not be as much income as you're used to, but those checks can tide you over so that you don't take the wrong job out of financial desperation. Just remember that the government is expecting that you are actively seeking employment throughout the time that you collect. In most states you can collect up to twenty-six weeks of unemployment during a fifty-two-week period that starts when you first apply. You must report any freelance or part-time income you earn while you're collecting unemployment. Since every state's rules for collecting unemployment are different, you need to spend time learning the ins and outs of your own state to determine your eligibility.

Your company won't just sign you up for unemployment, you need to do it yourself. In some states you can actually call in to establish your unemployment benefits via telephone or the Internet. If you're not one of the lucky ones, you'll have to visit your city's unemployment office in person, take a number and wait, and wait, and wait. The whole experience is pretty darn close to getting your driver's license. The good news is you get a check each week when you're done. Use the time sitting in the unemployment office to work on your resume or pore over the want ads—it's like having a three-hour study hall. Also, believe it or not, the unemployment office will have job opportunities available, so be sure to ask your administrator to show them to you.

Eligibility depends on a variety of factors. If you quit your job, you're ineligible. So, even if you detest your boss and hate your job, hang in there until they fire you unless you've got something lined up. If you were a temporary or contract worker and have not been paying into unemployment, you are also ineligible. Finally, as unfair as it may sound, if you were employed for only a few months and didn't meet the minimum contribution to unemployment, you won't be eligible to collect. But apply anyhow, just to be sure.

Unemployment checks are considered income. The government giveth and then hits you with a big fat tax at year end. If humanly possible, opt to have your federal taxes withheld before you get your check. Week to week, it won't seem like you're missing out on that much money, and it will be a heck of a lot better than writing out a bigger check to Uncle Sam on April 15.

FREELANCE FOR EXTRA INCOME

If you're already an expert in your chosen field, you may be in a fantastic spot to pick up some side projects as a freelance consultant or independent contractor. The assignments that you can expect to get will generally be short-term in nature and have set delivery or completion dates. Many times, a contract assignment can be an entrée to a full-time job at a company—in a slack economy, they'll be quicker to

The Layoff as Breakup

Contributed by Lynn Harris

On Sunday, I moved my stuff out of my boyfriend's house. On Tuesday, I got laid off. With that, I learned a valuable lesson: if you want to get over your boyfriend, just lose your job! It's true: in a way, a layoff is like a breakup. My company basically said, "It's not you . . . it's the bottom line." I wanted to say, "You're letting me go!? What if I . . . give you more space?"

Actually, in many ways, a layoff is worse than a breakup with a significant other. Arguably, while your boyfriend or girlfriend is your partner, your job is your identity. Sure, your main squeeze is part of your life—part of you, even. But when you lose your job, you're left with that uncomfortable, gaping blank after "I'm a . . . _____."

Also, while you may not be psyched to be single, you can survive; you might feel love-starved, but you're not going to STARVE starve. You can start thinking about looking around for a new partner at your leisure—when you're ready, not when rent is due.

Finally, even though being between jobs and between partners are both exceedingly common—even celebrated (ironically, at least) in these lean, mean times—being un-partnered still carries much less of a stigma than being unemployed. (If you really want to drive your parents over the edge, try being both at once.)

Still, some of the techniques for surviving a breakup do work quite well when applied to a job loss. And actually, it's not about just surviving; handling this nightmare healthily is what will put you in the position to land your dream girl/guy/job.

Run for mayor of Wallow City. Go ahead: Hurt. Hate. Hoover up the Häagen Dazs. For a week. You need this time to purge the layoff toxins. Time does cook raw feelings the way citrus cures red snapper. Don't be a martyr or a tough guy; a stiff upper lip will only crack later. Do whatever it takes to let anger and resentment out now, so that they won't spew forth at the least op-portune moment. In other words, even though you may have every right to be angry and bitter, let's just say that grousing about your old job in an interview is about as attractive as bad-mouthing your ex on a first date.

Then: Get back out there. Remember, you're on a deadline. If you can afford more than a week to chill, fine. But "stop waterworks; start job search" should be red-inked on your calendar in advance, before you take off to Tahiti. Again, no matter how much time you remain career-celibate, well, it's like ro-mance: the longer you remain a wounded single person, the longer you remain a . . . wounded single person. And the longer you nurse those layoff wounds, the more opportunities pass you by, and the worse you feel. While you need to let off all that bitter steam, you do need to go ahead and get back out there when you feel ninety percent better—not 110 percent better (that day may never come). Though job hunting has its own set of grating indignities, you will get rid of the remaining ten percent of bitterness just by virtue of gettin' busy.

A job interview is like a date. I don't need to tell you how to impress an inter-viewer. Remember, the interview is for you, too. When it's going well, it's your chance to find out if a position is right for you. And even if now's not the time to be choosy, an interview serves, at the very least, as practice. You'll hone your skills and each one will feel like less of a huge, scary "This could be *it!*" deal. (For the same reason, I think people should go on as many first or sec-ond dates as possible. It makes each one just a date in the life, not the chance of a lifetime.)

Make this a learning experience. So when do you get to stop *learning from* bad bosses and tough losses and lame lovers, and actually *get to the actual goal* that all this "learning" is somehow supposedly preparing you for?! I really wish I could tell you (not to mention me). But see, if you *don't* learn from this bummer, then it really is a total loss.

So back to the "it's not you" thing. If the economy stinks, it really proba-bly *isn't* you. Still, you may be tormenting yourself thinking, "Yeah, but really.

What could I have done to have made myself totally indispensable?" Well, stop tormenting yourself. The thinking part is actually good as an exercise in self-improvement, not self-flagellation. When you leave a relationship, it's worth considering: what am I now sure I need in a partnership? How could I be a better friend, partner, lover next time? Same goes for your career and for yourself as an employee, colleague, manager. Not because you messed up, but because you really might as well. Get back out there with that newfound— or at least reconfirmed—knowledge on your inner cover letter, and everyone will want your number.

Lynn is an actor, comedian, and author of Breakup Girl to the Rescue! A Superhero's Guide to Love, and Lack Thereof *(Back Bay, 2000).*

hire a known quantity than to pay a headhunter to bring in an outsider.

So how do you find out about freelance gigs? Many employment agencies have listings available in addition to full-time openings, so be sure to mention your interest in taking on this kind of job if you are open to it. In a weird twist of fate, you may be able to get your former company to hire you back on a contract basis, sometimes at a higher hourly rate than your previous salary.

When you work as an independent contractor, you are considered self-employed. That means your clients will pay you one hundred percent of your billable income. They will not withhold taxes and you won't get a W-2. Instead, at year end each of your clients will send you a Form 1099 showing the amount of self-employment income you earned from your assignments. Because you're a freelancer, it's now your responsibility to report to Uncle Sam how much income you earned, and to pay the full amount of tax that you owe. To avoid a brutal lump sum payment, get in the habit of putting at least a third of your self-employment income away in a savings account. And find out from your accountant whether you need to make estimated tax pay-

ments during the year; you may get hit with penalties if you don't follow the rules.

Just remember that finding a full-time job is a full-time job. If you
take on a freelance gig, it could cut into your job-hunting time. So be
sure you've thought through things like time commitments and deadlines before you accept any assignment.

GET YOUR GAMEFACE BACK ON

People talk about their jobs all the time. For some it's fundamental to
their very identity. If you were laid off, you probably feel like you've
lost a big part of yourself, which can lead to an understandable fear
of getting back out there. First thing you know, you're avoiding networking opportunities because you simply can't face the dreaded, and
inevitable, Big Question: *"So, what do you do?"* But self-imposed
isolation isn't going to help you overcome your fear. Your task is to
learn how to answer the Big Question whether you're employed or
not. If you practice your response ahead of time until you're comfortable delivering it, you'll quickly conquer your fear and be ready to
engage new acquaintances. Here are a few tips for handling the Big
Question:

✓ DEVELOP A BRIEF ANSWER. When asked about what you do,
briefly mention your circumstance and then move on by re-
directing a probing question back. Sample response: "I was the
sales manager at a start-up that just went belly-up. It was the experience of a lifetime. It was tough shutting down and I have to
admit I took a bit of a break. I'm now back on the market and am
ready to start looking for a new job. What line of work are you in?"
The important thing is to be brief and to the point, and then to
move on.

✓ ALWAYS TURN THE CONVERSATION BACK. Many laid-off workers respond to the Big Question with *"Oh, I just got laid off."* End of

story. Not only will this curt response elicit the non-ego-building response "Oh, I'm sorry," but it will also almost certainly cause an awkward pause. Besides ruining a good conversation, it doesn't provide a correct response to the question. If you're a programmer, say, "I'm a programmer." If you decide you want to share that you've been laid off, go ahead, but ask a probing question at the end of your response, so as not to end on a down note. For example: "I'm a programmer. My company downsized recently and I decided to take the package. I'm taking some time off to rethink what I want to do next. What is it that you do?" First, it puts the person back into their comfort zone, especially if they don't know how to respond to your laid-off status. Second, you're leading the conversation to a positive place so that it can continue on a pleasant note.

✓ FOCUS ON PERSONAL PURSUITS AND STAY POSITIVE. No one sounds boring if they talk about what they love to do. Take a moment to let them know what you do, then quickly mention an activity that you're pursuing with your time off, such as traveling or training a new puppy. You can then move on to asking them a pertinent question that relates to your conversation. Example: "I'm a management consultant, on 'sabbatical.' Our whole industry is taking a hit right now after that Enron debacle. Anyhow, I've decided to take the next six months off and travel. Southeast Asia is first, ever been there?" This takes the person out of the delicate area of dealing with your layoff and allows you to build a rapport by discussing something other than work.

✓ PRACTICE YOUR RESPONSE *BEFORE* YOU'RE ON THE SPOT. Discussing your unemployment may initially make you feel uncomfortable. Grab a friend and practice what you want to say before you're in a social setting. Still feeling embarrassed? Being prepared to answer the Big Question will put you at ease whether you're discussing your situation in a small group or in a room full of people. The more comfortable you feel discussing your situation with others, the more open people will be to talking to you about it and more important, about how they can help you out.

✓ **FINALLY, DON'T MAKE STUFF UP.** Don't make a bad situation worse by embellishing the truth. Piling up a bunch of fibs can have two results: 1) You might not get caught, but you will feel stupid and have nothing to show for it. 2) You might get busted (it's a small, small world out there), and the consequences are just too embarrassing to contemplate. Almost everyone will survive a layoff in his or her career. When you discuss your situation with grace and dignity, people will be enthralled by your confidence.

I was devastated. I was given notice that I would be out of a job in exactly one month. After a weekend of tears, I simply put my pride aside and shamelessly networked every single person and angle, hoping that my resume would get forwarded all over the place. Within a month of my layoff, I had met with dozens of prospective employers; some who just wanted to meet me for "exploratory" interviews, others sizing up my credentials (and me sizing up theirs!). Even when I got the occasional "thanks, but we're not interested" note, I'd send a follow-up email asking the person to forward my resume to anyone else s/he knew. I know this will sound crazy, but I had so many people talking about me that one day, two friends of mine were talking in an elevator about my plight, when the guy who is now my boss asked them who on earth they were talking about. When they told him my name, he said it sounded familiar, that he'd just heard my name somewhere else. The coincidence was uncanny. My friend gave him my resume and I got called in to interview for the job of my dreams. I wanted it, and I got it. Bottom line: let everyone know that you're looking for a job. You need to have your network out there working for you while you're out networking with others.

—TONI, MARKETING MANAGER

SPEND MORE TIME WITH THE PEOPLE WHO COUNT

You've been downsized. So what! It happens to everyone at one time or another. That you lost your job is a fact. Don't isolate yourself from others because you're afraid that people won't know how to react. In your time of need (and getting laid off certainly counts as one of those times), friends and family want to be there for you. Don't shut them out. Your loved ones usually know you better than you know yourself. They can help you identify which new opportunities could be a good fit for you. Don't lash out if they are brutally honest with you, because that's exactly what you need right now. And don't make it all about you; you're probably not the only one who deserves a pity party, so be sure to give back when those who love you need you. This might also be a great time to reconnect with old friends you haven't seen in a while. You have the time, so use it. You might be surprised at what you've been missing.

Commiseration is yet another way to get past the post-downsizing dark period. Establish a network with former co-workers. Have your own Pink Slip Party at a local watering hole or coffee shop. If you can't get everyone to meet in person, set up an email group on a portal like Yahoo! (it's free) and have a weekly bonding session where you can discuss your experiences. Compare notes; if a number of you are experiencing similar issues on the job hunt, try to develop solutions together. By doing this you'll gain a sense of solidarity, and realize you're not alone.

I started working for Pseudo.com, an interactive Internet television company, in December 1999. It was my first job in New York City and I was psyched to get it. To my chagrin, the company died a quick and painful death on September 18, 2001. After the bad news was delivered, the whole company went down to our local watering hole and got drunk—really drunk, sentimental, and sad. I thought that it would be the last time we would all be together, and that the Pseudo community we had built would disband forever.

But that never happened. We created an egroup called Pseudo-Lives where we post messages. We call. We email. We Instant Message one another. We forward job listings. We refer friends for positions. We call in favors. Our egroup is a members-only site for former employees. No spam. No breach of trust. It's a secure forum where people who shared a once-in-a-lifetime experience can stay in touch. You can post as often or infrequently as you like. You can check the site on your own, get every message sent, or request a daily summary of the site's activity.

Just because we don't work together anymore doesn't mean we're not still working together. I miss Pseudo madly. What I don't miss is the sense of community. It still exists. And it's anchored on-line, where it belongs, among the people who created it.

—Jacki, Interactive TV Producer and On-Air Anchor

NOW GO WORK IT!

Here's the Takeaway:

- When you've been pink-slipped, resist the urge to grab a job, any job, just to be employed. Have a game plan first.

- Don't succumb to Pink Slip Paralysis. Avoid bitterness, don't blame yourself. Keep a routine in your life and seek opportunities to accomplish tangible objectives.

- Find out if you qualify for unemployment insurance. If you do, then collect. It's your money!

- This might be the perfect time to strike out on your own. Consider becoming an independent contractor.

- Keep your confidence and maintain a positive outlook. Get back into the networking game (if you ever stopped playing). Be ready for The Big Question: "So, what do you do?"

- Don't carry the burden alone. Commiserate with friends, reconnect with ex-co-workers. Just don't let it turn into a sobfest; keep positive.

12

SUCCESSFUL UNEMPLOYMENT:

Belt Tightening and Budgeting
When You're Looking for Work

Being broke sucks. Being broke and jobless, well, that really sucks. As hard as it is to do, you've got to face the reality of your money situation if you want to stay out of a financial hell that will linger long after you find a new job. But there is a bright side: with careful financial self-management, "Successful Unemployment" can be yours. The key to achieving Successful Unemployment—whether it lasts a few months or even longer—is to pay strict attention to your spending habits and personal finances. If you plan ahead, you'll be prepared to make the financial and lifestyle adjustments that will give you the flexibility to hold out for a new job that you really want instead of grabbing the first paycheck that comes your way.

TIGHTEN THAT BELT, THEN SQUEEZE

There is no time like the present to get frugal. To achieve Successful Unemployment, you need to start now. Even if you have a small nest egg socked away that you're planning on using to finance your unemployed state, you need to be careful. Look first at how you're spending your Benjamins. But be brutally honest about which expenses are "must have" vs. "nice to have" vs. "can't have until I'm gainfully employed." Each of us is different, so only you can decide where you can save money. Here are some belt-tightening tips that will keep you on track and out of debt. (Before embarking on any major financial change, it's a good idea to consult your tax accountant or financial advisor.)

✓ **USE CASH WHENEVER POSSIBLE.** Somehow, forking over cold hard cash is a lot more painful than slapping down a credit card. If you leave the plastic at home, it's certain that you'll spend less on impulse items. Instead, go to the bank and take real cash money out. When you literally see and feel the money leaving your pocket, you'll soon start paying more attention to where it's going. If you're really low on self-control, put the money you can spend for the week into an envelope. When it's gone, it's gone!

✓ **KEEP A BALANCED CHECKBOOK.** Keep track of every dollar down to the last penny. Start by keeping your checkbook or online checking account up to date. Then, as bills come in during the month, write out the checks (just don't send them in until they are due). This will provide you a true picture of your cash flow, and you won't be tempted to spend money that you don't really have.

✓ **PAY BILLS AT THE LAST MINUTE.** Do what successful entrepreneurs do when they launch start-up companies—stall paying bills to conserve cash. (Don't do what unsuccessful entrepreneurs do—blow your money on thousand-dollar chairs and foosball tables.) You need to hold onto every dime as long as you possibly can. Don't pay bills before they're due. And pay the important ones just before they are due. Also, try to determine ahead of time which monthly bills can be paid a bit late without having your service interrupted or your credit affected.

✓ **NEGOTIATE LEVEL BILLING.** It's tough to get a grip on your expenses if your bills are fluctuating wildly from month to month. Nowadays, service providers and utility companies offer many billing options. See if you can set up a level bill payment structure for as many accounts as possible.

✓ SCRUTINIZE EVERY BILL. You've got the time; use it. Examine every bill you get for unexpected charges and random fees that you might have overlooked when you were too busy bringing home the bacon. If you find an error, call customer service. By following up, you might receive credits to your account or free services to which you didn't even know you were entitled.

✓ GET THE PHONE COMPANIES TO COMPETE FOR YOUR BUSINESS. Calling plans are moving targets. As soon as you sign up for one, a better deal comes down the pike. Call your current service providers (long distance and mobile) and negotiate to get on the best plan currently available based upon your calling habits. You won't believe the money you'll save.

✓ TRY TO CUT YOUR RENT. Most people's biggest expense is keeping a roof over their head. The rent or mortgage check can be a brutal one to write each month, even if you're gainfully employed. Now might be the time to get a roommate to share rent and other expenses. Alternatively, you can always consider subletting your space and opt for a couch-surfing adventure. If you're in plush digs that are suddenly out of your league, you might want to think about trading down to save money (just do the math and make sure you include the cost of moving before you do anything). Your last option (gulp) might be to move back home with your parents. This will certainly motivate you to get that job as fast as you can.

✓ LIVE LOW ON THE HOG. Who hasn't been here: you go out at night with five crisp twenty-dollar bills. The next morning you awake to find only a couple of crumpled one-dollar bills and a pack of matches in your pocket. Dude, you've just spent your gas and electric bill for the month on a bad hangover. While you're living in the land of unemployment, go out with a set amount of money for the night that you can afford to spend. When it's gone, mooch off your friends or go home.

✓ **PUT OFF LAVISH PURCHASES.** Put off budget-busting expenditures until you get your new job. If you couldn't afford it when you were employed, now is definitely *not* the time to buy. Don't justify purchases with the handy excuse "I owe this to myself." You'll just spend money you shouldn't be spending in the first place. Rather than buying something on a whim, do the research on a big-ticket item you've been eyeing and reward yourself with it after you land a new job.

✓ **SPREAD OUT BIG UNEXPECTED BILLS.** Say your car breaks down, your pipes burst, or Uncle Sam informs you that you owe more on your taxes than you originally thought. Before you cut a check, discuss payment options upfront with the plumber, the mechanic, or the friendly IRS man. Explain your situation and tell them you'd be willing to pay a little more to have the bill stretched out in installments instead of paying a large lump sum. Generally, if your credit is good, service providers will work out a special payment plan.

✓ **FIND HIDDEN RESERVES.** If you have a brokerage or mutual fund account, consider cashing in the dividends you earn instead of automatically reinvesting them to buy more shares. Even if your brokerage account is minuscule, it might be worth it. Just do the math and you might find an extra hundred dollars a month for the time you're unemployed. Think of this as a temporary solution that will give you a fixed income stream during the time you are unemployed. Just remember that you cannot do this with your qualified retirement accounts. And set the account back to reinvest after you land the job.

✓ **DO *NOT* BORROW FROM YOUR QUALIFIED RETIREMENT PLANS (I.E., 401K/IRA).** When you get your monthly statements, don't salivate. The funds you've saved in these accounts are officially off-limits: they are for your retirement, not your unemployment. You'll incur

Down-to-Earth Tips for the Down-and-Out

Contributed by Galia Gichon

Pull the plug on premium cable TV. Do you need your weekly fix of HBO for *Sex and the City* and *The Sopranos*? Think again. Now you can rent them at the local video store. The rental fees will come to far less than your premium cable subscription. Hint: you can keep your Internet access and cut the premium channels.

Don't get rid of your cell phone. And the next time you pick up the phone to make a call, think for a second whether you really need to call that person *now,* or whether you can wait until your unlimited rate kicks in (especially if it's long distance). By doing this, you will save thirty to a hundred dollars per month.

Buy and wear clothing that does not need to be dry cleaned. Enough said.

Avoid shopping as entertainment. Before you buy anything that costs more than a hundred dollars, wait twenty-four hours. Chances are you will not end up buying the item. And before you head off to the grocery store, make a shopping list and don't veer from it.

Consolidate accounts at one bank to qualify for free checking. See if your bank charges for using a debit card. Most banks are starting to charge for the use of debit cards and those uses can rack up an extra twenty to forty dollars per month. Definitely apply for overdraft checking to maintain good credit.

Galia is the founder and President of Down-to-Earth Finance. She has an MBA in finance and has more than a decade of financial services experience. For more financial advice, visit: downtoearthfinance.com.

hefty penalties for early withdrawal that will make the exercise hardly worthwhile. For example, if you have $100K socked away, you could lose fifty percent or more to taxes if you withdraw it before reaching age fifty-nine and a half. If you take it out, you'll regret it for the rest of your life.

✓ **Get a loan before you lose your job.** Think about applying for a home equity or personal loan as a financial cushion. This is a great means of tiding yourself over until you land a full-time job. Before you commit, make sure that you have the wherewithal to pay it back. Keep in mind that it will be almost impossible to get a loan like this once you're unemployed.

THE SKINNY: Don't get caught deep in debt doo-doo. If you took out a loan against your 401K when (you thought) your job was secure, and have since been laid off, you may have to pay back the entire principal immediately. *Yow!!!* It all depends on what bylaws are established by your company. Check in with your plan administrator and see if they might be willing to negotiate an extension at least until you land on your feet with a new job.

Declare Martial Law on Credit Cards

Credit cards may seem like salvation when you're out of work. Think again! If you use them while you're unemployed, and continue to pay only the minimum each month, your balances will grow to the size of the Stay-Puft Marshmallow Man. Here's how to defeat the revolving debt demons by beating them at their own game:

✓ **Shop around for low interest credit cards.** Comparison-shop to find credit cards that reward you by offering a low interest rate both on balances transferred to them and on new purchases. Also make sure that the interest rate stays put for at least six months from the time that you move your funds to it.

Absolutely Fabulously Broke

If you can't cut out the Starbucks (and really, who has that much willpower?), then here's a valuable discovery: refills at Starbucks are fifty cents, provided you bring your cup back to the counter for the refill. People really do take advantage of this. I once saw a well-dressed woman surreptitiously pull out an old, many-times-used cup from a Ziploc bag, proceed into the store, stand in line, and order a fifty-cent "refill." Not exactly honest, but I guess if you're hurtin' . . .

—Valerie, Art Director

Get friends who travel a lot on business to scavenge free mini-shampoo, soap, etc., from hotels for you.

—Elena, Management Consultant

Cancel your membership at the gym. Then, starting in your own neighborhood, visit every gym in town and tell them you are interested in joining. Most gyms will let you in free for a few days or a week so you can "try before you buy." The monthly membership fee you save will probably pay your phone bill.

—Anastasia, Marketing Manager

Cook in bulk, then eat the same thing for dinner every night until it's gone. Suggestions for bulk cooking: meatballs and sauce, lasagne, chili. All of these can be divided into meal-size portions and thrown in the freezer. With a week's worth of ready-to-nuke dishes, you eliminate waste, rot, and impulse take-out.

—Eva, Special Projects and Event Manager

When it comes to cosmetics, go from class to mass. Maybelline, L'Oréal, and Lancôme are all owned by the same company, which uses identical ingredients and formulas (right down to the pigments) for all three brands. The cost difference comes from the packaging and the perceived image. Why spend sixteen dollars on lipstick when you can spend four-fifty?

—Valentina, former Cosmetics Marketer

Forget the fancy hair salons, and go to a good old-fashioned barber. You get a great cut and a close shave for a third of the cost of going to a salon. I even know a lot of women who do the same thing—except for the shaving part.

—**Stanley, Interior Designer**

Change your shopping habits and become a loyal thrift-shop patron. Just be sure to draw the line at underwear. Ick.

—**Linda, Web Mistress**

Find out which night of the week is "special pick-up night" (when the trash collectors take couches, appliances, and stuff)—it's the ultimate Dumpster-diving extravaganza. On one good night, I got a sofa and matching chair, a lamp, and a boogie board. My whole apartment was furnished without spending a cent! For a little extra spending cash, sell the stuff you don't want on eBay!

—**William, Chemical Engineer**

If you are a little short at the end of the month, "accidentally" send in your bills with the checks in the wrong envelopes. Thus, the gas company gets the check for the phone bill, the phone company gets the cable check, etc. If you're in a real pinch, it might buy you some time and help you avoid the late payment charges.

—**Bill, Credit Manager**

Buy an iron, and iron your own shirts instead of taking them to the cleaners. It's cheaper, no missing buttons, doesn't take three days, and you always get your own shirt back.

Katia, Production Assistant

Dating on a budget can be brutal. Get creative. Make a pasta bracelet for your girlfriend (just add food coloring to some dry pieces of any pasta with a hole in it and string it along a piece of thread) and tell her that you made it in second grade and were saving it for the right girl.

—**Donald, Tax Accountant**

✔ **CONSOLIDATE YOUR DEBT ONTO ONE CREDIT CARD.** You should move all of your outstanding credit card balances to only one credit card. By doing this, you'll have one level payment a month, which will make managing your finances much easier. In fact it will seem more like you're paying off a student or personal loan. If you absolutely must put additional purchases on this card, you'll have everything itemized in one place, which will make it easier to see where the money is going.

✔ **ALWAYS PAY THE MINIMUM (AND MORE IF YOU CAN AFFORD IT).** Now that you have consolidated your credit card debt onto one credit card, you need to treat it like a loan. Determine what monthly payments you can afford, and try to pay more than the monthly minimum if at all possible. If you can't manage to pay more than the minimum, you'd better cut way back on your spending and commit yourself to paying the rest down as soon as you land a new job. If you use your credit card during the months you're unemployed, try to pay back the exact amount you used each month, so at least your balance won't balloon as quickly.

✔ **NEVER BE LATE ON YOUR CREDIT CARD PAYMENTS.** You don't want to let a few months of joblessness hurt your ability to get credit later on. Pay off the minimum due on your credit card before your other expenses.

✔ **NEGOTIATE TO LOWER YOUR CREDIT CARD INTEREST RATES.** Once you've moved balances away from your current credit card accounts, your phone will start ringing. The credit card companies that didn't get your money will start begging you to transfer your balances back. Don't be tempted, as too many transfers in a short period of time can affect your credit rating. Instead, tell them that you would consider moving your money back if they agree to lower their interest rates on purchases and balance transfers. This way, if you ever do need to use those cards, you've got low, competitive rates already established. Once the companies agree to your terms, put the credit cards away for safekeeping.

BUILD A SIX-MONTH SURVIVAL BUDGET

Keeping an eagle eye on every dime coming in and going out can be a depressing, anal-retentive way of life. Fun, spontaneity, impulse purchases—they all come to a screeching halt when you don't have a steady paycheck. But if you plan ahead, that doesn't have to be the case. Now is the time to buck up and put your personal finances in order so that you can make educated choices about how to survive if you don't get a job immediately. Your financial management skills will be tested to a new extreme once you're forced to live on a budget made up of dwindling savings, limited unemployment insurance, and fixed expenses. Now more than ever, what you don't know will hurt you.

In order to achieve Successful Unemployment, you need to become the Chief Financial Officer of your own life. That means biting the bullet and creating a budget. Skip the back-of-the-envelope scribbling and take the time to create a budget that will ensure that your money can last for at least the next six months. You may initially feel stressed out about sitting down and doing this, but once your budget is complete, you will feel a lot less anxious and a lot more in control.

To help you manage your finances, we've created an idiot-proof, do-it-yourself Six-Month Survival Budget designed for someone who is out of work. To get started, copy the template we've set up into a format that you are comfortable working in. Type it into a spreadsheet program like Microsoft Excel or use a personal finance package like Quicken. (Or you could always go old school and photocopy the budget and fill in by hand.) If you know how to set up a spreadsheet, by all means do your budget that way. A spreadsheet will allow you to try different scenarios, where you can cut back on several expenses while leaving other expenses the same.

Your Six-Month Survival Budget will be a valuable tool for managing your personal finances while you're unemployed. Because it will show you how long your funds will hold out, you will have a good idea of how much time you really have to find the right job.

✓ **ESTIMATE YOUR MONTHLY INCOME.** How much money do you have coming in? You no longer draw a salary, so you have to look at every possible source of income that can get you through your unemployment for the next six months, without tapping into your savings or retirement. Estimate the amounts that you'll be receiving on a recurring basis, like that bi-weekly unemployment check and any regular freelance gigs that you get.

✓ **ADD IN SEVERANCE AND OTHER ONE-TIME LUMP SUMS.** On the income side of your budget, you also need to include any one-time payments, such as your severance check or final paycheck. (Remember, count only the after-tax amount.) Now, divide each lump sum by 6—the number of months you want your money to last—to get your effective "monthly income" from that payment. As an example, suppose you get severance equivalent to eight weeks' salary, and your bi-weekly salary after taxes was $2,000. First, calculate the total lump sum that you have coming to you. Your total severance after taxes will be $8,000 ($2,000 times four bi-weekly checks). Next, divide that amount by the number of months you expect to be unemployed (six). That means $8,000 divided by 6 months, giving you an effective monthly severance "income" of $1,333.33.

✓ **INCLUDE SAVINGS AND LOANS.** Do you have any savings? Do you qualify for a loan? Can you borrow money from a family member? For survival budgeting purposes, this all counts as income. If you do tap into your savings or take out a loan, decide whether you want to burn through all of the money during your unemployed time, or whether you want to have some of it left by the time you are working again. For example, if you have $10,000 worth of savings, you might decide that you only want to use up half of it. That

Six-Month Survival Budget

	Lump sum payments received	Estimated Monthly Income (if lump sum item, divide total by 6 mos.)	Actual Monthly Income
MONTHLY INCOME			
Severance-Related Income:			
Final Paycheck(s) (enter in lump sum column)		÷ 6 =	
Final Expense Reimbursements (enter in lump sum column)		÷ 6 =	
Expected Severance (enter in lump sum column)		÷ 6 =	
Expected Bonus/Commission (enter in lump sum column)		÷ 6 =	
Vacation Pay Owed (enter in lump sum column)		÷ 6 =	
Loans:			
Loan from Family/Friends (enter in lump sum column)		÷ 6 =	
Home Equity Loan (enter in lump sum column)		÷ 6 =	
Personal Loan (enter in lump sum column)		÷ 6 =	
Dipping into Savings and Other Funds You Have Put Away:			
Savings (enter in lump sum column)		÷ 6 =	
Cash from your brokerage account (enter in lump sum column)		÷ 6 =	
Emergency Fund (enter in lump sum column)		÷ 6 =	
Additional Household Income:			
Salary of Spouse/Significant Other			
Unemployment Insurance			
Other Sources of Income:			
Brokerage/Fund Account Dividends*			
Rental Income (from Roommate/ Sublet)			

Other Sources of Income *(cont.)*

Interest Earned on Bank Accounts _____ _____

Self-employment/temp job income _____ _____

Other _____ _____

Total Monthly Income:

MONTHLY EXPENSES ** Mandatory Expenses Household:	Estimated Monthly Expenses	Actual Monthly Expenses
Mortgage/Rent/Maintenance	_____	_____
Utilities (Heat & Electric)	_____	_____
Groceries	_____	_____
Telephone	_____	_____
Local	_____	_____
Long Distance	_____	_____
Internet Service	_____	_____
Travel:		
Car Payment(s)	_____	_____
Car Insurance	_____	_____
Commuting/Parking/Mass Transit	_____	_____
Gas	_____	_____
Insurance/Medical:		
Health Insurance (COBRA)	_____	_____
Life Insurance	_____	_____
Disability Insurance	_____	_____
Required Prescriptions	_____	_____

	Estimated Monthly Expenses	Actual Monthly Expenses
Financial Expenses:		
Credit Card Payments	_____	_____
Student Loans/Other Loans or Debt	_____	_____
Bank Charges	_____	_____
Education:		
Tuition	_____	_____
Child Care/School/ Activities	_____	_____
Pet-Related (Food/Vet/Dog-Walking):	_____	_____
Job Hunt Related:		
Computer Equipment	_____	_____
Paper Supplies (Resumes/ Business Cards)	_____	_____
Kinko's	_____	_____
Coaching/Consulting	_____	_____
Networking (Lunches/Dinners/ Drinks)	_____	_____
New Business attire (suit/ Briefcase/Palm Pilot)	_____	_____
New Memberships (Business Associations)	_____	_____
Conferences/Seminars	_____	_____
Discretionary Expenses		
Cable	_____	_____
Cell Phone	_____	_____

	Estimated Monthly Expenses	Actual Monthly Expenses
Discretionary Expenses (_cont._)		
Entertainment (Movies/Dating/ Dinners)	_____	_____
Health Club/Hobby-Related Activities	_____	_____
Travel/Vacation	_____	_____
Books/Magazines	_____	_____
Newspaper Deliveries/ Subscriptions	_____	_____
Fashion:		
Hair Care/Personal Hygiene	_____	_____
Additional Pharmacy	_____	_____
Clothing/Shoes	_____	_____
Dry Cleaning	_____	_____
Other:		
Household Emergencies (Plumber, Roofer)	_____	_____
Cleaning (Service/Supplies)	_____	_____
Monthly Total Expenses:	_____	_____
Total Budget Surplus (Deficit if Negative) (Monthly Income − Monthly Expenses)	_____	_____

* Remember to tell your broker/fund company to send you a monthly check for dividends, instead of reinvesting them.
** Notice there's no "Miscellaneous" under "Expenses." The whole point of a budget is knowing exactly where the money goes. If you have other expenses, add in specific lines for them.

means allocating $5,000 to the income side of your budget and keeping the rest in a savings account. Using the same approach we used with your severance, you would divide that $5,000 by 6 months, which gives you a monthly "income" of $833.33 from your savings. Make a promise to yourself to pay back any savings withdrawals when you land a job.

✓ **NOW ESTIMATE YOUR MONTHLY EXPENSES.** Now it's time for the reality check: how much money is going out each month? You need to get a handle on how much you're actually spending. How much does it cost to maintain your standard of living? What are the expenses you have to pay each month to run your household? Again, take a look at our sample budget, which lists a whole series of expense categories—some will apply while others won't. As you go through each category, write down what you've been spending. Look back at your checkbook, credit card receipts, ATM receipts, and bank statements and try to piece together a history of your past expenditures, then use that to determine average monthly bills for each expense category. If you're not sure about how much you've spent for a particular category, make an educated guess. When you start plugging in the figures, you may be overwhelmed by the amount you're really spending to finance your lifestyle. Don't freak out. It's important to learn where the "fat" is in your budget so that you know where to cut back.

✓ **ORGANIZE YOUR EXPENSES INTO TWO CATEGORIES.** On our sample survival budget, you'll notice that there are two kinds of expenses: mandatory and discretionary. Mandatory expenses include such necessities as rent or mortgage, health insurance, food, and financial obligations, such as credit card and student loan payments. Notice that we've kept items such as Internet service and car payments in the mandatory section, because they're likely to be essential on your job search. While you must pay your mandatory expenses each month, you should still always be looking for creative ways to cut down on these costs. For example, to bring down your long-distance costs, find a cheaper provider. To reduce your mortage payments, consider refinancing if interest rates are low. As for discretionary expenses, it's here that you'll find the real opportunities to cut back. Discretionary expense categories include entertainment, hobbies, travel, and clothing. Be honest: if you absolutely cannot live without something, move it back up to the mandatory section. But be tough on yourself, too: buying a new pair of shoes every two weeks doesn't belong in the same category as the rent or mortgage.

✓ RUN THE NUMBERS. Add up the numbers in the income section to arrive at your Total Income per Month. Then go down the expense section and total that column to get your Total Expenses per Month. Finally, subtract your total expenses from total income. Now for the moment of truth—are you covering your monthly expenses? If you find that you're in the black (positive) or are at zero, it means that you're a personal finance whiz and that you should be just fine maintaining your current standard of living.

If you're like everyone else and are in the red (negative), you're perfectly normal. But it means that you've got to start shedding costs (for example, by finding a roommate) or finding some additional income (like getting a freelance or temping job).

✓ LIVE WITHIN YOUR MEANS. Once you've made your budget cuts, you now have to commit yourself to living within these means for the next six months. Make a promise to evaluate your budgeting skills in one month's time by keeping track of your actual expenditures for the next thirty days. Starting now, keep receipts for every purchase. Do this especially for small cash purchases (you'll be surprised at how much money disappears on the little things like those four-dollar Frappuccinos). At the end of each day, stuff all of your receipts into a cookie jar. If you're religious about this process, every dime should be accounted for.

✓ DO SPOT CHECKS. At the end of your first month, review the receipts you've saved as well as bank and credit card statements. Then plug the actual expenditures for each relevant category back into your Six-Month Survival Budget. Compare your original estimates against your actual expenditures. If your actual expenditures are less than your budgeted expenditures, you just scored yourself some extra spending (or saving!) money. You should go through this exercise of comparing your budget against actual for each month going forward until you land a new job. It may seem a bit obsessive, but it's better than going broke.

After getting laid off, I decided to take a month off to regroup. During that month, I found a little house that needed some TLC. Realizing the rental income potential, I bought the house, along with gallons of white paint, and got to work. To most people, the notion of buying a house while unemployed would seem like a crazy idea. However, I ran the numbers, and financially it made sense to me. Fortunately, I found a great mortgage broker who ignored the word "severance" on my pay stubs and pushed through my mortgage application.

In the midst of my project, my fiancé asked me to marry him. I was painting on weekends, freelancing from home part-time, and planning a wedding in between. It was the most exciting and exhausting time of my life. It's four years later now, and I run a small business from my home. I also freelance on-site for a few select clients. My little house looks brand new and has doubled in value. I couldn't be happier with the way things worked out.

—CHRISTINE, GRAPHIC DESIGNER

I was laid off in November of 2000 at the beginning of the dot-com bust. My employed contacts were disappearing from the job market fast and joining me in the unemployment line. Luckily, I had a backup plan.

I contacted a friend of mine who had started his own painting and

contracting company and was always looking for some good workers. It wasn't the most glamorous work, but it paid decently and I
would still be able to apply for jobs and go for interviews.

I also did some freelance web work. Not much, but every little bit
helped. Keeping my skills sharp and having some sort of contact with
the web world were important. I also started a small business with
my girlfriend that would bring us some income twice a year. While
many of my peers decided to apply to business or graduate school
to ride out the downturn, I opted to take a class to further my design
skills and make some new contacts. The class also helped me keep
up a constant weekly routine, doing homework and attending classes
as well as socializing with a group of people I would otherwise never
have met.

In a stale economy with many, many candidates applying for few
positions, you have to do whatever it takes to make some money
and keep moving forward. It's important not to isolate yourself. Take
a class, start a small business, or take a job that's totally different
from what you're used to doing. Get out and keep meeting new people and applying for jobs. The economy will eventually recover, and
companies will start hiring again.

—ART, ONLINE PRODUCER

The best thing I ever did was invest in Quicken so I could budget and
figure out where the hell all my money was going. By doing this I figured out what I could spend each week and that was the amount
that I withdrew from the ATM—nothing more. (If there was any
money left over, I treated myself to a pedicure, a music CD, or even
a latte if I was really running low.) Doing this really helped me save a
lot of money, so much so that I recently purchased my very own
apartment!

—EILEEN, TEACHER

When I'm broke, I offer to babysit or provide some other service I
know my friends and family need in lieu of buying gifts.

—MICHELLE, PROGRAMMER

NOW GO WORK IT!

Here's the Takeaway:

- Successful Unemployment means you have the financial where-withal to hold out until you get the job you *want*.

- Start an emergency fund while you're still employed—sock away at least three or four months' worth of expenses.

- When you're unemployed, use cash whenever possible and be very conservative in using credit cards. Trying to maintain your "employed" lifestyle using credit is a sure-fire recipe for long-term financial pain.

- Create a Six-Month Survival Budget: track all of your expenses and estimate all income and other sources of funds.

- Cut back, waaaayyyy back, if your budget doesn't balance: reduce your discretionary, non-essential expenses to the absolute minimum. Look for creative ways to cut back even further. Consider the unspeakable: getting a roommate or moving back with your parents.

13

Welcome to the Real World:

From Higher Learning to Higher Earning
(for soon-to-be and recent college grads)

The best four years of your life are ending, and now you stare into the deep, dark, post-grad abyss. College will soon be a distant memory, and looming large before you is the unavoidable reality: *"I have to get a job!"*

Facing that reality can be pretty daunting. After all, we're talking adulthood here: punching the clock, paying the rent. It's enough to make you want to move home after graduation, back into a safe, peaceful little cocoon where you can sleep till noon, watch cartoons, and make weighty decisions like whether to have Cheerios or Cocoa Puffs for breakfast. But let's be honest here: the "slacker" lifestyle is so 1992. You've got dreams, you've got brains, you've got to get out there and make things happen! But how do you start?

There's No Course Called Job Hunting 101

If colleges were smart, they'd offer Job Hunting 101 as a mandatory course. After all, graduates who land great jobs become successful alumni, who in turn donate beaucoup bucks to the old alma mater. But, sadly, there's no such course, and that goes a long way toward explaining the strange sense of complacency about finding a job that afflicts many college seniors.

If you're like many new grads, four long years of higher learning haven't really prepared you to be anything but a student. You've sat in lectures and regurgitated information the way your profs want to see it. You've memorized facts and theories and analyzed the thoughts and ideas of other people. Maybe you've tallied up a stellar GPA; that might open some doors, but it won't help you create a dynamite resume or ace an interview.

So where will you learn all you need to know to land the job you want? And how will you figure out what kind of job it is that you want? Whether you're an A-student or are just squeaking by, you've got to take it upon yourself to construct a personal course of study that will earn you a J.O.B. degree.

THE J.O.B. DEGREE PROGRAM

Your J.O.B. program has a lot of prerequisites: there's the "figuring out what kind of job you want" track, with courses like Introspection, Self-Assessment, and Industry Research. Then there's the "getting out and finding a job" track: Networking, Resume Building, and Interviewing. If you've been reading the other chapters in this book, a lot of these course titles will sound suspiciously familiar; in fact, this whole book is a crash course. But as a college senior or recent graduate, you've probably found yourself saying, "I'm only twenty-one. I don't have any experience. I don't have a network. These things don't apply to me." *Wrong!* All these elements are critical to finding a job, whether you're twenty-one or ninety-one. It's just that as a recent or soon-to-be graduate, you face some special challenges.

Right now, you're probably putting a lot of pressure on yourself to figure out exactly what you want to do for (shudder) "the rest of your life." And, no doubt, your parents are adding some pressure of their own. Don't blame them; they're products of their era. When they were young, they *had* to figure out what they wanted to do for the rest of their life, because that first job was going to last forty years. Today, however, it's a different story. If you're graduating right now, you need to take into account that you could have at least ten jobs in your career. That means you should think of your first job out of college as simply the launch pad for your career. Since it's only the first step on a long voyage, you can let yourself experiment, discover, and make mistakes.

So, now that some of the existential pressure is off you, it's time to get moving. Whether you've already graduated, are soon to face commencement, or have months (or years) of college bliss ahead of you, it's not too late. But the sooner you start, the better. You may have no idea where to begin, but in fact, you are surrounded by valuable resources: the career services center, a circle of faculty and other contacts at your school, alumni, and the wonderful whirl of on-campus recruiting. The trick is to take maximum advantage of them while you can. If you leave things till the last minute, you'll kick yourself for all the opportunities you'll have missed. But if you lay the groundwork starting *now,* you'll have the time to build quality relationships with people who can help you, and you'll find yourself chilling out and counting your job offers while everybody else sweats.

My dad was the consummate company man: thirty years with IBM, good old "Big Blue." I grew up thinking that work was, well, work, and I resolved to go my own way. Being a creative person, I began a masters' program in design after college, but soon realized I didn't have enough raw talent to make it as a designer. So I dropped out and got a "real job" at an advertising firm, certain that I'd never find a job I truly loved. A couple of years later, I landed a position as director of marketing for a flight school. I was working there for three years before it occurred to me to step into the cockpit myself. The moment I did, that was it. I had found my true calling. Sometimes what you want to do is sitting right in front of you, but you just can't see it. I immediately enrolled at my own flight school to become a commercial pilot, working part-time in the marketing department and flying every chance I got. I gave up my fat salary to join a competitive industry where something like only eight percent of all pilots are women.

Do I regret taking a left turn and becoming a pilot? Not on your life. I still get goosebumps when I put on my uniform. Every day that I fly, I look down at the clouds and think to myself, "I can't believe that I get to love my job as much as I do." My advice for making your own soft landing in a new career:

- If you've got a gut feeling about a path, commit to it. Every step forward that you take makes it that much harder to turn back. Change, while scary, is a wonderful thing when you know it's right.
- Passion alone isn't enough. Change requires hard work.
- Positive reinforcement is essential in making big decisions, so build yourself a support network (family, friends, whomever).
- Try a few things out. Decide whether you like them. It's okay to change your mind.
- Figure out your tolerance for risk, weigh it against the responsibilities you have, and act accordingly. If I had had different responsibilities, I may not have been able to make the choices that I did.

—Kristine, Commercial Pilot

Are You Experienced?

First, let's dispose of one of the misconceptions that is adding to your stress level: "I don't have any experience." Listen: if you've lived to the ripe old age of twenty-one, it's guaranteed that you have *some* experience doing *something.* Think about your last four years, and start writing down all that you've accomplished:

- Academics: group and individual projects, special achievements, heavy course loads, unique minors/concentrations, courses in which you excelled, grades.

- Employment History: internships, co-ops, on- or off-campus jobs, summer jobs.

- Extracurricular Activities: clubs, organizations, athletics (varsity, intramural, whatever), fraternity/sorority. Emphasize any officer roles and the experience you gained.

Chances are you'll be surprised at how much you've done. The key is not so much showing that you've done incredibly unique and impressive things, but rather showing your ability to get things accomplished and demonstrate attributes that would be desirable to an employer: leadership, organization, attention to detail, and so on.

There now, don't you feel better? Good. It's time to take the next step: hitting the career center.

GET THEE TO THE CAREER SERVICES CENTER

You may not believe this, but just by walking through the front door of your college's career services center at least once before you graduate, you'll get a leg up on eighty percent of your clueless classmates. That's right: according to a recent independent survey by Drake Beam Morin (DBM), a leading provider of career transition services, fewer than twenty percent of college students ever set foot in their career centers.

If you've never visited your career services center, here's a quick tutorial about what you're missing out on. Most career centers offer one-on-one career coaching, career strategy sessions, resume makeovers, practice interviews, proprietary database access, introductions to alumni, internships, co-ops (semester-long full-time internships for credit), and access to on-campus recruiters. Career services centers can also provide valuable guidance, in the form of aptitude testing and counseling, to help you decide the kinds of jobs that might be a good fit for you. Set up an appointment: the staff will be thrilled to show you what they have to offer.

When you go in for your initial consultation, let the career center staff know you're a bit green and that you want to learn about everything they offer, soup to nuts. Thereafter, visit the center regularly and work at perfecting your skills. Remember, you're working on your J.O.B., so treat it like it's an additional class. Block out at least three or four hours a week to work on your job hunt. Most career center directors would agree that the students who stay underfoot get the most attention.

It's to your advantage to start visiting the career center as soon as you can (your junior year is *not* too early). This way you can start to build valuable relationships with the people that work there. Don't just drop in; call ahead and make appointments to meet with the counselors. Try to avoid peak times of day and crazy times during the calendar year, and you'll get a lot more attention. Most people stroll into their career center on campus during the second half of the second semester of senior year, when competition is at its fiercest and time is running out. So go early and go often.

If you've already graduated, fear not: alumni of most institutions are still entitled to use their career services centers. Some schools even provide special online career research resources that alumni can access free or for a reasonable fee. Private outplacement firms are also getting into the act: Drake Beam Morin recently launched DBM Real World 101, a program to help recent grads launch their careers.

THE SKINNY: But my career center sucks! Quit whining! If you've had a bad experience at your career services center, it may be your fault not theirs. Think back: was there anything that you could have done to make the experience more productive? Did you go at a peak time, when the staff did not have as much time to spend with you? Did you do a quick fly-by, without an appointment, and scope the place out without asking any questions? Did you look through the on-campus interview logs and decide that none of the jobs floated your boat? Career centers aren't panaceas, but when used intelligently, they're an invaluable resource. Give it another go, and you might be pleasantly surprised.

STRATEGIZE ON-CAMPUS RECRUITING

Your career services center is the starting point for the on-campus recruiting process. Think about it: this is probably the only time in your life when companies will come to you with jobs in hand for the express purpose of interviewing you (okay, and three or four hundred of your classmates). Don't blow it. If you wait until the interview sign-up books are laid out, you might already have missed your best opportunities to get selected. There's so much more that you can do before a company arrives on campus to conduct a round of interviews. Here's how to get noticed:

✓ DO YOUR HOMEWORK. Talk to the career office, and again, plan ahead. Find out which companies come year after year. Hop on the web and see which ones you think you want to work for long before they announce their arrival. Try to get a line on when the interview sign-up will be posted, so that you can be one of the early birds.

✓ ATTEND COMPANY PRESENTATIONS. Many companies have recruiting events a few weeks or months before they come in to do the interviews. Basically, this is so they can do their dog-and-pony show and get students interested in interviewing with their company. Don't blow these off! They're a great way to meet people and make an impression (and a lot of times they have free food to boot).

✓ TRY TO GET A SOLID INTERVIEW SLOT. If you're selected to interview, try to get an early time slot. Be the candidate all others are compared to. Try to avoid the ever-brutal just-after-lunch interview. If you have to go at the end of the day, try not to be the very last time slot. It's not your fault, but the interviewer may be watching the clock because they have a plane to catch.

✓ DON'T WAIT AROUND. After your interview, follow up with each of the company representatives you met by sending a handwritten thank-you note. This ensures that you're already on the campus recruiter's mind when the inevitable stack of resumes arrives from your college for further screening. (If your classmates even bother at all, they'll probably send lame thank-you *emails*.)

✓ **JUST ASK.** If a company you're hot for is not visiting your campus, your career services center might still be able to make inroads for you with them. But you'll never know unless you make the first move and ask.

NETWORKING: YOU GOTTA START SOMEWHERE

You probably don't realize it, but you've already got the beginnings of a network, right there on your campus. Do you have a favorite professor? A faculty advisor? How about a teaching assistant with whom you've worked closely? Academic leaders like these can be a fantastic source of career guidance and job leads. Take them out to dinner or buy them a cup of coffee, and ask them about career directions that might be appropriate for you. Do they have any former students that you could speak with? By keeping your feelers out there, you might just tap into opportunities no one else gets to hear about. Just remember, faculty face time isn't something that you can turn on at the end of your senior year. If you're going to build the trust of these valued resources, you need to put genuine time in.

Alumni of your college or university are another great source of networking opportunities. These folks are well established in their careers, and they're on your side because you share a common heritage—the dear old alma mater. The old school tie is alive and well: alums love to see their younger compatriots succeed. Isn't it nice to know that someone's got your back?

Here's how to build your very own alumni network:

✓ **VISIT THE ALUMNI OFFICE.** Each year, happy alums pour millions of dollars into your school's endowment. Your alumni office can put you in touch with alumni in your industry or profession who would be delighted to work with an up-and-comer like yourself.

✓ **CHECK OUT YOUR ALUMNI WEB SITE.** Even though you're not quite an alum yet, it's okay to do research on your own and determine who might be able to guide you in your job hunt. Email the head of the alumni chapters in the cities that you're thinking about moving to, and ask if they know anyone in the industries you are considering. If there is an alumni email group, add yourself in each city so that you can hear about alumni-only opportunities.

✓ **GO BACK TO THE CAREER CENTER.** The companies that recruit on campus sometimes will send employees who are also alumni of your school to represent them. These people are extremely passionate about hiring fellow alumni. Find out from the career center which alums are coming, and get in touch with them proactively before they arrive. Take advantage of their enthusiasm.

✓ **CREATE YOUR OWN ALUMNI DATABASE.** Once you've identified a few areas you think you'd like to work in, get to work. Start to develop your very own alumni contact list. Highlight the people on the list with whom you'd most like to do exploratory interviews and contact them first.

✓ **BE PLEASANTLY PERSISTENT.** Don't be put off if the alumni you contact don't get back to you right away, and don't get upset if they can only do a phone interview. They are busy people, after all, and information in any form is helpful to your job hunt. If they can't even find time for a phone call, see if you can conduct a Q&A with them via email. Just don't overwhelm them with a marathon email. That will only alienate the very people you're trying to impress.

✓ **GET A LIFELONG EMAIL ADDRESS.** A lot of colleges and universities are starting to give graduating students an alumni email address (e.g., jcollege@alum.stateu.edu). This is great for two reasons: first, you'll have an email address on your resume that never has to change, and second, it gives other alums that you contact a heads-up that you attended the same school!

THE SKINNY: Alumni Salutations. When contacting an alum via email always put your alma mater in the subject line ("B.U. Communications Grad would love a few moments of your time"). It'll get your email opened a lot faster, and better yet, read! When you write an introductory letter to an alum, try to share something with them about what's going on at school or look for a common experience that will seal a bond between the two of you. Instead of asking for a job outright, ask for help in how best to network your resume around to other alums and new networking contacts.

FIND A MENTOR

The great thing about building your network is that over time, you'll start to identify people you feel particularly comfortable with and whom you will start to view as mentors. A mentor is like a co-pilot helping you navigate your career. Knowing people like this—those whom you can consult as you encounter a range of career decisions—is really essential, particularly when you're a new graduate. Mentors can be recent grads, or they can be venerable old-timers. There is no limit to the number of mentors you can have, and you can take them with you from school to job after job after job. You're shooting for a lifetime relationship.

YOU *CAN* GET THERE FROM HERE

The only thing scarier than living with your parents is relocating to a city where you don't know a soul. But if your heart is set on an industry that tends to be centered in one or two specific cities (like Washington, D.C., for the federal government, New York or Los Angeles for entertainment, or the San Francisco Bay Area for technology), you

Expand Your Referral Network

Everybody knows how terrifying graduating into the real world can be, so milk it for all it's worth. Tell everyone you know that you're looking for a job, and they'll all empathize and want to help. In addition to those we've already mentioned, here are some stones you can turn:

- Managers from summer jobs and on-campus jobs
- People you reported to and worked with on internships and co-ops
- Parents' friends
- College roommates' and friends' parents
- High school friends' parents
- Local high school teachers
- Aunts, uncles, cousins, grandparents
- Fellow members of clubs, activities, fraternities, sororities
- Alumni and their friends, co-workers, or associates

Meeting with as many people from as many companies as possible is the best way to educate yourself on what's out there. As a recent college grad, it's your job to be a sponge, and people expect that.

could be looking at pulling up stakes. So how exactly do you conduct a long-distance job search while you're still at college or stuck in your hometown living with your parents? Do you move to the city right off the bat, or do you wait until you land a job and then go? Quite simply, it depends.

The biggest consideration is that four-letter word: c-a-s-h. Moving costs money, so before you fly the coop, do a budget (yes, that's right, go back to the Survival Budget section of Chapter 12). Figure out how much money you need in order to survive until you get a job in your new city. Not only do you have to schlep your stuff from point A to point B, but you also have to slap down your first and last month's

Follow the Good News

Contributed by Bill Lessard

When you're first out there job hunting and you're having trouble finding prospects, it's extremely easy to get caught up in all the bad news. Maybe you feel like a loser, the only college graduate in the world who can't get a job! It's only natural to look for evidence that explains your predicament and proves that none of it is in your control. Getting caught up in the bad news isn't going to get you anywhere, except maybe the lunatic asylum. I know how all this feels, because I used to indulge my negative nature, rolling around in the warm bath of Negativity, screaming at the Unfair Universe, drunk on Doom. Those of you who have been there know how paradoxically reassuring this state of mind can be. So what to do? Simple. Avoid the Bad News, and Follow the Good News. Not only will this approach save your sanity, but it will also make your job search instantaneously more productive. How does it work? Here are a few scenarios, ranging from the obvious to the not-so-obvious:

Scenario 1: *Your friend Joe/Jane gleefully informs you that he/she has just gotten a job, to which you reply, "Congratulations! Are they looking for any other bright, young recent grads over there? Let me send you my resume."*

Scenario 2: *Even though you're a liberal arts major, you start reading the* Wall Street Journal. *You see an article in the paper about how a company in your desired industry just posted positive earnings. Instead of muttering, "Capitalist pigs! Those bastards deserve to go out of business," you fire up your web browser and head straight for the company's "Careers" section. If there are no positions available that fit your credentials, you send one of the hiring managers a friendly note, saying what a great job you think she/he is doing. With any luck, you'll get a mail back, and your virtual butt-kissing will turn into a job opportunity.*

Scenario 3: *While researching a particular industry segment, you discover that all the companies except one have gone through major layoffs. You employ the same technique described in Scenario 2 to wangle yourself an interview at that one company. After all, the absence of Bad News is Good News.*

There are probably thousands of other ways to unearth Good News. But I think what I've said so far is enough to get you thinking in a positive, and therefore productive, direction. Hey, I'm not saying it's easy, especially after hearing nothing back on your resume time and time again. But I can tell you for a fact that once you start looking for the Good, you'll feel a hell of a lot better about your chances, you'll be looking in the right places for work, and Good Things will eventually happen for you, too.

Bill is co-author of NetSlaves: True Tales of Working the Web *and the co-founder of* NetSlaves.com, *the Web's premier independent community for tech workers.*

rent and a security deposit for an apartment. Then you have to think about buying clothes for your new job as well as spending your ever-dwindling cash on all the usual living expenses. Be sure to use a relocation calculator, which you can find on most financial web sites, to determine what you'll need to make when you get to that city. Cost of living differentials will play a big part in figuring out how much you need to earn so that you can live. Once you have all that information down, estimate what it would cost you to travel back and forth to that city to do speculative interviewing while continuing to live at home.

While you're running your budget numbers for the big move, assume that it will take at least four to six months to find a job. And also make allowances for the time of year when you're planning to move. Summers are extremely slow for hiring entry-level positions: most companies have just finished bagging all of their new recruits. Summer vacations tend to slow everything down, too. So if you want to start working by September, you'll need to start your job hunt in March, because July and August are likely to be pretty worthless. The same logic holds true for extremely busy times in your target industry, like tax time for accountants, and at year-end holiday time for just about every industry. Instead of living by *your* calendar, you need to get in tune with the timing of the companies you want to work for. So think ahead: from the time you want to start working, count backward at least four to six months.

To Move or Not to Move. That's the million-dollar question. If you can swing it financially and you're sure of where you want to go, it probably makes sense to just do it, even if there's no job waiting for you in your new city. Interviewers will feel more confident that you're for real if you have a local address than if you're just in town to check things out. Besides, having no money and no job will motivate you in ways you can't imagine.

WHERE THE JOBS ARE

There are three things every college student is qualified to do: use the computer, answer phones, and make copies. If you do decide to pack up and hit town without a job in your new city, your first stop should be the temp agencies. Check your ego at the door when you arrive. Nobody likes a too-big-for-your-own-britches temp. Don't take the point of view that your degree is going to waste either; you're simply financing your ability to find a real job in the city of your choice. The other great thing about taking a temp job while you search for "the real thing" is that you've got built-in flexibility. If you need to take a day off to go on an interview, you can call in to the agency.

When you go to the temp office, ask about the types of companies that they recruit for and tell them about the ones where you would be most eager to work. A temp job can be a great foot in the door for someone who is smart and hardworking, so don't follow the example of all the other temps who are taping their eyelids open and sucking up oxygen. If you go in and hit the ground running, you might just get a full-time offer. Use your temp assignment as a chance to network with the full-timers. Ask people if they need more help. If you're performing well and getting praise for it, don't be afraid to drop hints about your interest in working there. And even if you don't want to work at that particular company, network anyway; you might find that some of the employees and managers have other connections that they can hook you up with.

Taking a temp job is not selling yourself short. You're gaining work experience, you're seeing how companies work, and you're figuring out which types of organizations you work best in. If you really hate your temp job, cool your jets, collect your checks, and take solace that it's only temporary.

GIVE YOURSELF A FAIR CHANCE

When you don't have contacts in a new city, a career fair can be a great way to meet local employers. A lot of people hate the cattle-call aspect of career fairs, with thousands of attendees milling about, sucking up to the few recruiters in the room. Hey, nobody said this would be all fun. Career fairs exist because recruiters like them: it's like "speed dating" for employees and employers, allowing companies to look at a huge number of candidates in a short time. Unlike speed dating, however, you might not even get three or five minutes to impress. "Corporate recruiters will often use career fairs as a way to make first cuts, so that first ten seconds you spend with someone really counts a lot. Many recruiters pride themselves in being able to size up a candidate in no time flat," says Bradford Rand, President of TechExpo USA.

The moment of truth is so short, in fact, that looking good really makes a difference. If you dress like you just rolled out of bed, don't bother showing up. Shine your shoes, wear a crisp suit, and pop a breath mint before you go in (people tend to get really cozy at these things because they're so noisy).

Not all fairs are created equal. It's important to search out the ones that are relevant to your expertise and that include the types of companies that you want to work with. In particular, choose fairs that recruit for entry-level employees. Many local papers hold career fairs to support their Help Wanted listings. And there's always the web: www.JobWeb.com has great college career fair search tools that allow you to slice and dice by city, state, and keyword.

Whatever you do, don't just show up at the career fair cold. Do your homework. Before the fair, check the web site of the company hosting the career fair regularly. Most career fairs will provide a list of the hiring companies that will be present. Scour this list and select the companies in which you are most interested. Check back at the web site as the event approaches for any last minute additions to the list of attendees.

Arrive at least thirty minutes before the official start of the career fair, so that you spend your time making first impressions with recruiters rather than standing on a never-ending line. If you arrive at a booth while the company is still setting up, don't hang around like a lost puppy. Tell the recruiter that you'll be back later and that you're looking forward to speaking with them then. If you're stuck in a line, don't waste time: study the program to see which companies are where. Decide which companies you want to see first. Whatever you do, wait your turn. There is nothing ruder than someone who cuts in on someone else's time. And if someone does this to you, be patient and smile at the recruiter. You'll gain a lot more brownie points than if you try to re-interrupt.

When you do finally get to meet a recruiter, don't overwhelm them. Shake their hand firmly, look them in the eye, hand them your resume (which should already be out) and dive into your pitch. A career fair isn't a schmoozy cocktail party; time is of the essence here. The dynamic of the event is such that the recruiter is expecting you to present yourself to them. You want to leave them with one "nugget" of information about yourself that they can remember and perhaps even relay to another person (see Chapter 3). If you're succinct and position yourself quickly, you will separate yourself from the rabble of underwhelming job seekers. Don't be a time-sucker. If you respect the recruiter's time (especially if a long line has formed behind you) they will respect you, and hopefully put you in the Interview ASAP file. After the career fair, follow up with all the companies that you met with and re-send your resume to them.

THE SKINNY: **Get time on your side.** If you can't get to the show early, try to stay until the bitter end. While you may miss out on the company literature, the recruiters may be able to spend more time with you if they're not trying to whittle down a line.

MUNICIPAL MADNESS: CHAMBER OF COMMERCE

If you grew up in a small town, you probably think of the local chamber of commerce as those guys who ride in big Cadillacs throwing bubble gum to the crowd at your local parade. But the local chamber of commerce can be a great resource for finding jobs. Their mission is to support the interests of the businesses within their community. Many of these businesses are small and medium-sized non-public companies that you may not have heard of, but that may offer great employment opportunities. Chambers host networking and social functions as well as career fairs. Many of them are starting to put member directories and even job boards on their web sites. Be warned: some chamber web sites are exceptional (especially those of smaller cities that have to work a little harder), while others look as if they got stuck in a mid-1990s time warp.

In some cities, economic development councils and other city agencies may also be good information resources, so be open and start digging for information.

THE SKINNY: Sneak onto State U. You will eventually be a taxpayer in the state of your choice. Why not pay a little visit to the state colleges in your new city and see if you can get access to the job boards and resources located there? You might just stumble onto an entry-level job that never made it to your on-campus career center.

THE BIG MOVE

Brace yourself: even if you're the most outgoing person in the world, those first few months in a new city can be traumatic. And if you don't have a job, you can feel even more isolated. That means that you really need to put your networking skills to work, not only to find a new job, but also to make friends. You've already been schooled on how to make the most of alumni and academic references, but think about your extracurricular activities. Do you play softball? Have a passion for politics? Or thrive on open mike poetry readings? Every city has a wealth of clubs for particular sports or recreational activities. Before you move to a city contact the club organizers and get to know them, even if you're not in the city yet. Show your interest, ability, and knowledge. Become an asset and make immediate allies. Chances are, you'll be able to find someone who's looking for a roommate, someone who's looking for a new assistant, someone who's looking to sell a car, and someone who bartends at the bar you've been bookmarking on Citysearch.com.

The job hunt landscape is constantly shifting, so quickly in fact, that the only person who could possibly know what's good for you is you. You've got to prove that you want a job and that you'll do what it takes to land one. So, commit yourself to earning that J.O.B. degree and graduate into the work world with honors.

Shortcuts to Feeling at Home in a New City

Contributed by Syl Tang

1. **Get active in young alumni networks.** This is a great place to start because you already have something in common with the organization's members. Before you move, call or email some of the club leaders. Introduce yourself by simply saying you're graduating and coming to their city and would love to be involved. If there is no organized club, say in a smaller city, chances are your career office might have information on some people who graduated from your school. Rally support for a new club and you've got an instant network. Not only that, a lot of young alumni clubs put together joint events so classmates can socialize. Some great alumni sites are <u>reunion.com</u>; <u>classmates.com</u>; <u>alumni.net</u>; <u>thesquare.com</u>.

2. **Move in with someone.** Whether your roommate becomes your best friend or remains just the "roomie," at least you will have someone who knows which places deliver great subs at midnight! Great sites to find an apartment share are: <u>apartmentshare.com</u>; and <u>roommateservice.com.</u> I also recommend using community-oriented sites, such as <u>craigslist.org</u>, which can get you a roommate, as well as a bed, a bike, and a date!

3. **Subscribe to the local newspaper or magazine.** For example, in New York City, *New York* magazine, in Los Angeles, the *Los Angeles Times*. Make it a point to scour the weekly alternative press. This will instantly give you a sense of what's happening in your new hometown: the restaurants, the people, the gossip! But most important, the listings section will have activities where you will be likely not only to learn about the new world you're inhabiting but also to meet some people.

4. **Go out no matter what and accept all invitations.** When I first moved back to New York, it took about a year to "find" the kind of friends I wanted to have and the right events and parties for me. The life I wanted to have was not with the people I spent time with in the first year, but the people I met through them. So speed up the process for yourself by accepting all invitations. Even if you don't want to go see live music, go anyway. You never know who you might meet or what you might learn. Maybe you're a big salsa fan and that club has salsa nights later in the week.

5. **Connecting with people is not as hard as you think.** You only need two phrases: "hi" and "isn't it interesting about [insert common thread]." The instant you say hi, someone is no longer a stranger. And once you've said hi, now the ball is in their court to say something back. People feel the need to fill silence, so be quiet for a minute and let them say the next phrase. If that person is not responsive, don't let it deter you from trying to meet the next person. Remember that s/he may just be preoccupied or having a bad day. The second phrase you need is to mention the one thing you have in common with someone. And there is always something. If you're standing on a street corner, that something can be as simple as "Isn't it interesting how long this light takes to change?" or "Isn't it interesting how it changed from winter to summer overnight?" If you're at an event, there are many elements to use. "So how do you know [the host's name]?" "What do you think of the hors d'oeuvres?" "Wow, they ran out of wine already?!"

HipGuide founder Syl knows the scoop on hot spots in cities all over the world and she herself has lived on three different continents. Who better to ask about how to descend on a new city than the HipChick herself?

NOW GO WORK IT!

Here's the Takeaway:

- Start *now*. Whether you've already graduated or are still a senior or even a junior, get going right away on your job search.

- Remember, this first job isn't forever. If it doesn't work out, there's plenty of time in your life to make changes.

- Take stock of your experience—jobs, academics, and extracurriculars—and emphasize how you've demonstrated traits desirable to employers.

- Use your school's career services center to the fullest. Get in good with the staff there; they can be great sources of information as well as advice.

- Take advantage of on-campus recruiting. Through the career center, learn about the procedures so you get the interviews you want.

- Start building your network—professors, alumni, advisors, family friends, old bosses—all could be valuable sources of contacts and advice. Get into the lifelong habit of networking by building mutually valuable long-term relationships.

- If you're relocating to a new city, be ready for big changes, financially and personally. Budget carefully, allow ample time (four to six months) to find a job.

- Consider temp work while you look for a full-time gig. It'll pay the rent and provide a great source of contacts, and may even lead to a real job.

- Work career fairs, contact your local chamber of commerce, and get involved in the life of your new city.

FINAL WORDS

If you've made it this far, way to go! You now have the ammo you need to land a job in any economy. Just remember that when the going gets tough or you feel the need for a refresher, go back and re-read the chapters that correspond to your immediate needs. Don't forget the basics:

- Even when you get the new position, job hunting never stops.

- Apply several job-hunting strategies to increase your success—especially networking.

- Always think about what motivates the hiring manager.

- You do not have the job until you have the job.

Good luck! Now go work it.

THE SKINNY: Still craving more job-hunting advice? If you're hankering for more war stories and anecdotes or tips and resources, then head to AllisonHemming.com or WorkItBook. com

ACKNOWLEDGMENTS

The following is a list of the many people who assisted in the creation of this book. If I left anyone out, blame my editors (they said I could say that).

To all of the pink slippers, job seekers, recruiters, and hiring managers: Thank you for sharing your experiences with me and making this a much better book. To Uncle Charlie for your sharp pencil. To Cioci Benay, Barbara, and Doll, because you deserve a special thank you. To my grandparents: Marty & Marcella and Nana & Fred and George. To the Codd Clan: Bart, Dorrie, Ned, Kathryn, Jackson, Graham, Mary, Rich, Richie, Michael, Katherine. To Tara Lynch for your insight and endless ideas. To Jude Sanjek for helping me keep my sanity (and the books).

To the good folks at Simon & Schuster, especially to Matt Walker, philosopher-at-large, who plucked me from obscurity and to Cherise Grant, who carried me home. To Daniel Greenberg, who continually watches my back (I hope). To Aaron Stoker-Ring for your sense of humor. To Ellen Ullman for your eleventh-hour support. To Mike Daisey (and Jean Michele), for finishing your book before mine so I could witness the torture that would soon befall me. To advertising maven Karen Smith. To my mentor and good friend Heather Evans. To Sara Horowitz, who simply rocks. To the boys at Angel Networks.

To my soul-sisters: Chrissy, Rita, Eileen, Tara, Nancy, Laura, Ilze, Robin, Cornelia, Susan, Lauren, Megan, Barbara, Elena, Amy, and Kathy. To the Castle Girls: Michelle, Tracey, Anne, Barbara, and Reem.

To my sidebar contributors: Steve Baldwin, Lena M. Bottos, Lea Brandenburg, Alexandria K. Brown, Bill Coleman, Tami Coyne, Al DiGuido, Sam Travis Ewen, Galia Gichon, Anthony Giglio, Lynn Harris, Hanan B. Kolko, Bill Lessard, Adrian Miller, Karen Page, Arnie Pedowitz, Louis Schiff, Johanna Schlegel, Melissa Sexter, Eileen Shulock, Syl Tang, Chris Taylor, Karen Weissman, Stan Williams. Thank you. Thank you. Thank you.

To the following people for sharing your stories and advice: Debra

Albert, Mark Ameres, Kristine Anderson, Jeanella Baldwin, Melina Barker, Quint Barker, Patty Beron, Anastasia Bizzari, Jayson Blair, Margaret Bowani, Zak Brocchini, Glenn Broderick, Arlene Camacho, David Cantina, Chris Casaburi, Linda Castellitto, Todd Cherches, Amy Cole, Mark Cowan, Wil Cox, Danielle Cyr, Fedah Dahdul, Eddie Dean, Michael Doctor, Sherie Dolinoy, John Dorian, Allison Dorsey, Susan Erlich, John Federico, Scott and Tracy Fedonchik, Marc Feifer, Donna Fisher, Bob Gartland, Michael Gibson, Leisa Goins, Jessica Goldfarb, Leslie Gottlieb, Stephen Granados, Janelle Grisby, Valentina Guazzoni, Darrell W. Gurney, Kelly Harris, Ken Hein, Bernardo Joselvich, Ben Kaplan, Phil Kaplan, Jade Kim, Patricia Kitchen, Diane Kroll, Randall Lane, Michael LeForte, Scott Lehmann, Nancy Levine, Michael Liss, Andy Lipshultz, Toni LoPresti, Steve Lundin, Denise Lynch, Liz Lynch, Dr. Barbara Marchilonis, Michele Marrinan, Rob Mathews, Linda Matias, Jeanne McIntyre, Bonnie Mincu, Alison Moran, Darlene Newman, Karen Nicolini, Matt Noah, Maureen O'Brien, James O'Neill, Frances O'Shea, Nicole Paolo, Eva Pfaff, Rachel Pine, Kathi Pontarelli, Eileen Quirk, Bradford Rand, Boaz Raviv, Lisa Rayman, Jen Reingold, Chip Rewey, Amanda Richman, Yael Roshwelb, Arthur Rotberg, Jacki Schechner, Lori Schwab, Jim Scott, Sandy Severino, David Sexter, Dave Sherman, Jessica Shevitz, Keith Siebert, Neil Siegel (you won the bet), Ellen Singer, Bill Staniecki, Steve Stidham, Avi Subu, Lisa Sulgit, Wendy Tarzian, Ed Tomasi, J. Travis, Andreas Turanski, Meredith Vellines, David Wade, Jason Wagenheim, Phil Warton, Larry Webman, Kelly Ann White, Chris Wile, Kim Willis, Shawn Woods, Jen Yellin, Dan Yu.

To the many companies and organizations that have helped me out: Big Foot Interactive, Challenger, Gray and Christmas, the old gang from P.O.V., Webgrrls, NYC-WIT, Team Tympanum, Salary.com, Big Frontier, Silicon Alley Station (Bob & Dolly), Alley Event, Free Agent Forum, NYNMA, The Pink Slip Party organizers from around the world, WWWAC, Silicon Alley Cares, NY Cares, Working Today, WAAAC, and to The Hired Guns.

In Memory of Marty Grimm, Tim Badger, and Gus Economos.

INDEX

ABOUT THE AUTHOR

Allison Hemming is an established career authority and the brains behind the world-famous Pink Slip Party, a networking event that benefits the recently downsized. Her commentary about career and workplace issues has been featured in *The New York Times, The Wall Street Journal,* and *USA Today,* and on CNN, CNBC, ABC *Good Morning America,* CBS *Marketwatch,* and many other news outlets.

After beginning her career on Wall Street and then moving into magazine publishing, Hemming became the founder and "Top Gun" of The Hired Guns, a leading interim workforce company based in Manhattan. Her firm creates flexible workforces by tapping into the more than twenty-five million "free agents" or independent professionals working in the United States.

Hemming graduated from the University of Dayton, and lives with her fiancé in New York City.

For more information about Allison, see AllisonHemming.com and The Hired Guns, see thehiredguns.com.